•Something borrowed, something *you*•

VI KEELAND

The Invitation
Edited by: Jessica Royer Ocken
Proofreading by: Elaine York, www.allusionpublishing.com, Julia Griffis
Cover Model: Nick Bateman
Photographer: Tamer Yilmaz
Cover designer: Sommer Stein, Perfect Pear Creative
Formatting: Elaine York, Allusion Publishing, www.allusionpublishing.com

The
INVITATION

•Something borrowed, something *you*•

Stella

"I can't do this..." I stopped halfway up the marble staircase.

Fisher paused a few steps ahead of me. He walked back down to where I stood. "Sure you can. Remember the time we were in sixth grade and you had to make that presentation about your favorite president? You were a nervous wreck. You thought you were going to forget everything you'd memorized and be standing there with everyone staring at you."

"Yes, what about it?"

"Well, this is no different. You got through that, didn't you?"

Fisher had lost his mind. "My fears *all came true* that day. I got up in front of the blackboard and started to sweat. I couldn't remember a single word I'd written. Everyone in the class stared, and then *you* heckled me."

Fisher nodded. "Exactly. Your worst fear came true, and yet you lived to see another day. In fact, that day turned out to be the best day of your life."

I shook my head, bewildered. "How so?"

"That was the first time we'd ever been in the same class. I thought you were just another annoying girl like the rest of them. But after school that day, you ripped into me for teasing you while you were trying to do your presentation. That made me realize you *weren't* like the other girls. And that very day I decided we were going to be best friends."

I shook my head. "I didn't speak to you for the rest of the school year."

Fisher shrugged. "Yeah, but I won you over the next year, didn't I? And right now you feel a little calmer than you did two minutes ago, don't you?"

I sighed. "I guess I do."

He held out his tuxedo-clad elbow. "Shall we go in?"

I swallowed. As terrified as I was of what we were about to do, I also couldn't wait to see what the inside of the library looked like all done up for a wedding. I'd spent countless hours sitting on these steps, wondering about the people walking by.

Fisher waited patiently with his elbow out while I debated another minute. Finally, with another loud sigh, I took his arm. "If we wind up in jail, you're going to have to come up with the bail money for both of us. I'm way too broke."

He flashed his movie-star smile. "Deal."

As we climbed the remaining steps to the doors of the New York Public Library, I went over all of the details we'd discussed in the Uber on the way here. Our names for the evening were Evelyn Whitley and

Maximilian Reynard. Max was in real estate—his family owned Reynard Properties—and I'd gotten my MBA at Wharton and recently moved back to the City. We both lived on the Upper East Side—at least that part was true.

Two uniformed waiters wearing white gloves stood at the towering entrance doors. One held a tray of champagne flutes, and the other a clipboard. Though my legs somehow kept going, my heart felt like it was trying to escape from my chest and take off in the opposite direction.

"Good evening." The waiter with the clipboard nodded. "May I have your names, please?"

Fisher didn't flinch as he doled out the first of what would be a night full of lies.

The man, who I noticed had an earpiece in, scanned his list and nodded. He held a hand out for us to enter, and his partner handed us each bubbly. "Welcome. The ceremony will take place in the rotunda. Seating for the bride is on your left."

"Thank you," Fisher said. As soon as we were out of earshot, he leaned close. "See? Easy peasy." He sipped his champagne. *"Oooh, this is good."*

I had no idea how he was so calm. Then again, I also had no idea how he'd managed to talk me into this insanity. Two months ago, I'd come home from work to find Fisher, who was also my neighbor, raiding my refrigerator for leftovers—a common occurrence. As he ate two-day-old chicken Milanese, I'd sat at the kitchen table sorting through my mail and having a glass of wine. While we talked, I'd sliced open the back of an oversized envelope without checking the address on the front. The most stunning wedding invitation had been inside—black and white with raised gold leaf. It was like a gilded work of art. And the wedding was at the *New York Public Library,* of all places—right near my old office and where I'd often sat and had my lunch on the iconic stairs. I hadn't visited in at least a year, so I was seriously pumped to get to go to a wedding there.

Though I'd had no idea whose wedding it was—a distant relative I'd forgotten, maybe? The names weren't even vaguely familiar. When I turned the envelope over, I quickly realized why. I'd opened my ex-roommate's mail. *Ugh.* That figured. It wasn't me who was invited to a fairytale wedding at one of my favorite places in the world.

But after a couple of glasses of wine, Fisher had convinced me it *should* be me going, and not Evelyn. It was the least my deadbeat ex-roommate could do for me, he'd said. After all, she'd snuck out in the middle of the night, taken some of my favorite shoes with her, and the check she'd left behind for the two months of back rent she owed had bounced. At a minimum, I ought to get to attend a ritzy, thousand-dollars-a-plate wedding, rather than her. Lord knew none of my friends were ever getting married at a venue like that. By the time we'd polished off the second bottle of merlot, Fisher had decided we would go in Evelyn's place—crash the wedding for a fun night out, compliments of my no-good former roomie. Fisher had even filled out the response card, writing that two guests would attend, and slipped it into his back pocket to mail the next day.

I'd honestly forgotten all about our drunken plans until two weeks ago when Fisher came home with a tuxedo he'd borrowed from a friend for the upcoming nuptials. I'd balked and told him I wasn't going to crash some expensive wedding for people I didn't know, and he'd done what he always did: gotten me to think his bad idea wasn't really that bad.

Until now. I stood in the middle of the sprawling lobby of what was probably a two-hundred-thousand-dollar wedding and felt like I might literally pee my pants.

"Drink your champagne," Fisher said. "It'll help you relax a bit and put some color back in your cheeks. You look like you're about to attempt to tell the class why you like John Quincy Adams so much."

I squinted at Fisher, though he smiled back, undeterred. I was certain nothing was going to help me loosen up. But nevertheless, I gulped back the contents of my glass.

Fisher tucked one hand casually into his trouser pocket and looked around with his head held high, like he didn't have a fear in the world. "I haven't seen my old friend *party animal Stella* in a long time," he said. "Might she come out to play tonight?"

I handed him my empty champagne flute. "Shut up and go find me another glass before I bolt."

He chuckled. "No problem, *Evelyn*. You just sit tight and try not to blow our cover before we even get to see the beautiful bride."

"Beautiful? You don't even know what she looks like."

"All brides look beautiful. That's why they wear a veil—so you can't see the ugly ones, and everything is magical on their special day."

"That's so romantic."

Fisher winked. "Not everyone can be as pretty as me."

Three glasses of champagne helped calm me enough to sit through the wedding ceremony. And the bride definitely didn't need a veil. Olivia Rothschild—or Olivia Royce, as she would be now—was gorgeous. I got a little teary eyed watching the groom say his vows. It was a shame the happy couple weren't really my friends, because one of their groomsmen was insanely attractive. I might've daydreamed that Livi—that's what I called her in my head—would fix me up with her new hubby's buddy. But alas, tonight was a ruse, and I was no Cinderella story.

The cocktail hour took place in a beautiful room I'd never been in. I studied the artwork on the ceiling as I waited at the bar for my drink. Fisher had told me he needed to use the restroom, but I had a feeling he'd really snuck off to talk to the handsome waiter who had been eyeing him since we'd walked in.

"Here you go, miss." The bartender slid a drink over to me.

"Thank you." I took a quick look around to see if anyone was paying attention before dipping my nose inside the glass and taking a deep sniff. *Definitely not what I ordered.*

"Ummm, excuse me. Is it possible you made this with Beefeater gin and not Hendricks?"

The bartender frowned. "I don't think so."

I sniffed a second time, now certain he'd made it wrong.

A man's voice to my left caught me off guard. "You didn't even taste it, yet you think he poured the wrong gin?"

I smiled politely. "Beefeater is made with juniper, orange peels, bitter almond, and blended teas, which produces a licorice taste. Hendricks is made of juniper, rose, and cucumber. There's a different smell to each."

"Are you drinking it straight or on the rocks?"

"Neither. It's a gin martini, so it has vermouth."

"But you think you can smell that he used the wrong gin, without even tasting it?" The guy's voice made it clear he didn't think I could.

"I have a very good sense of smell."

The man looked over my shoulder. "Hey, Hudson, I got a hundred bucks that says she can't tell the difference between the two gins if we line them up."

A second man's voice came from my right, this one behind my shoulder a bit. The sound was deep, yet velvety and smooth—sort of like the gin the bartender *should've* used to make my drink.

"Make it two hundred, and you're on."

Turning to get a look at the man willing to wager on my abilities, I felt my eyes widen.

Oh. Wow. The gorgeous guy from the bridal party. I'd stared at him during most of the wedding. He was handsome from afar, but up close he was breathtaking in a way that made my belly flutter—dark hair, tanned skin, a chiseled jawline, and luscious, full lips. The way his hair was styled—slicked back and parted to the side— reminded me of an old-time movie star. What I hadn't been able to see from the back row during the ceremony was the intensity of his ocean blue eyes. Those were currently scanning my face like I was a book.

I cleared my throat. "You're going to bet two-hundred dollars that I can identify gin?"

The gorgeous man stepped forward, and my olfactory sense perked up. *Now* that *smells better than any gin.* I wasn't sure if it was his cologne or some sort of a body wash, but whatever it was, it took everything in my power to not lean toward him and take a deep whiff. The sinfully sexy man smelled as good as he looked. That pairing was my kryptonite.

There was a hint of amusement in his voice. "Are you telling me it's a bad bet?"

I shook my head and turned back to speak to his friend. "I'll play along with your little bet, but I'm in for two hundred, too."

When my eyes returned to the handsome man on my right, the corner of his lip twitched just slightly. "*Nice.*" He lifted his chin to his friend. "Tell the bartender to pour a shot of Beefeater and a shot of Hendricks. Line 'em up in front of her, and don't let us know which is which."

A minute later, I lifted the first shot glass and sniffed. It honestly wasn't even necessary for me to smell the other, though I did it anyway, just to be safe. *Damn...* I should've bet more. This was too easy, like taking candy from a baby. I slid one shot glass forward and spoke to the waiting bartender. "This one is the Hendricks."

The bartender looked impressed. "She's right."

"Damn it," the guy who had started this game huffed. He dug into his front pocket, pulled out an

8

impressive billfold, and peeled off four hundred-dollar bills. Tossing them in our direction on top of the bar, he shook his head. "I'll win it back by Monday."

Gorgeous Guy smiled at me as he collected his cash. Once I took mine, he lowered his head to whisper in my ear.

"Nice job."

Oh my. His hot breath sent a shiver down my spine. It had been way too long since I'd had contact with a man. Sadly, my knees felt a little weak. But I forced myself to ignore it. "Thank you."

He reached around me to the bar and lifted one of the shots. Bringing it to his nose, he sniffed before setting it back down and smelling the other.

"I don't smell anything different."

"That just means you have a normal sense of smell."

"Ah, I see. And yours is...extraordinary?"

I smiled. "Why yes, it is."

He looked amused as he passed me one of the shots and held the other up in toast. "To being extraordinary," he said.

I wasn't generally a shot drinker, but what the hell? I clinked my glass with his before knocking it back. Maybe the alcohol would help settle the nerves this man seemed to have jolted awake.

I set my empty shot glass on the bar next to his. "I take it this is something the two of you do on a regular basis, since your friend plans to win it back by Monday?"

"Jack's family and mine have been friends since we were kids. But the betting started when we went to the same college. I'm a Notre Dame fan, and he's a USC fan.

We were broke back then, so we used to bet a Taser zap on games."

"A Taser zap?"

"His father was a cop. He gave him a Taser to keep under his car seat just in case. But I don't think he envisioned his son taking hits of fifty-thousand volts when a last-minute interception made his team lose."

I shook my head. "That's a little crazy."

"Definitely not our wisest decision. At least I won a lot more than he did. A little brain damage might help explain some of his choices in college."

I laughed. "So today was just a continuation of that pattern, then?"

"Pretty much." He smiled and extended his hand. "I'm Hudson, by the way."

"Nice to meet you. I'm St—" I caught myself in the nick of time. "I'm Evelyn."

"So are you a gin aficionado, Evelyn? Is that why I didn't smell anything different between the two?"

I smiled. "I wouldn't consider myself an aficionado of gin, no. To be honest, I mostly drink wine. But did I mention my occupation? I'm a fragrance chemist—a perfumist."

"You make perfume?"

I nodded. "Among other things. I developed scents for a cosmetics and fragrance company for six years. Sometimes it was a new perfume, other times it was the scent for a wipe that removes makeup, or maybe a cosmetic that needs a more pleasant smell."

"Pretty sure I never met a perfumist before."

I smiled. "Is it as exciting as you'd hoped?"

He chuckled. "What exactly is the training for a job like that?"

"Well, I have a chemistry degree. But you can have all the education you want, and you still won't be able to do the job unless you also have hyperosmia."

"And that is..."

"An enhanced ability to smell odors, an increased olfactory acuity."

"So you're good at smelling shit?"

I laughed. "Exactly."

A lot of people think they have a good sense of smell, but they don't really understand how heightened the sense is for someone with hyperosmia. Demonstrating always worked best. Plus, I really wanted to know what cologne he was wearing. So, I leaned in and took a deep inhale of Hudson.

Exhaling, I said, "Dove soap."

He didn't look completely sold. "Yes, but that's a pretty common soap choice."

I smiled. "You didn't let me finish. Dove Cool Moisture. It's got cucumber and green tea in it—also a common ingredient in gins, by the way. And you use L'Oreal Elvive shampoo, same as me. I can smell gardenia tahitensis flower extract, rosa canina flower extract, and a slight hint of coconut oil. Oh, and you use Irish Spring deodorant. I don't think you're wearing any cologne, actually."

Hudson's brows rose. "Now that's impressive. The wedding party stayed in a hotel last night, and I forgot to pack my cologne."

"Which one do you normally wear?"

"Ah... I can't tell you that. What will we do on our second date for entertainment if we don't play the sniff test?"

"Our second date? I didn't realize we were going to have a first."

Hudson smiled and held out his hand. "The night's young, Evelyn. Dance with me?"

A knot in the pit of my stomach warned me it was a bad idea. Fisher and I were supposed to stick together and limit contact with other people to minimize our chances of getting caught. But glancing around, my date was nowhere in sight. Plus, this man was seriously magnetic. Somehow, before my brain even finished debating the pros and cons, I found myself putting my hand in his. He led me to the dance floor and wrapped one arm around my waist, leading with the other. Not surprisingly, he knew how to dance.

"So, Evelyn with the extraordinary sense of smell, I've never seen you before. Are you a guest or a plus one?" He looked around the room. "Is some guy giving me the evil eye behind my back right now? Am I going to need to get Jack's Taser from the car to ward off a jealous boyfriend?"

I laughed. "I am here with someone, but he's just a friend."

"The poor guy..."

I smiled. Hudson's flirting was over the top, yet I gobbled it up. "Fisher is more interested in the guy who was passing out champagne than me."

Hudson held me a little closer. "I like your date much better than I did thirty seconds ago."

Goose bumps prickled my arms as he lowered his head, and his nose briefly brushed against my neck.

"You smell incredible. Are you wearing one of the perfumes you make?"

"I am. But it's not one that can be ordered. I like the idea of having a true signature scent that someone can remember me by."

"I don't think you need the perfume to be remembered."

He led me around the dance floor with such grace, I wondered if he had taken professional lessons. Most men his age thought slow dancing meant rocking back and forth and grinding an erection against you.

"You're a good dancer," I said.

Hudson responded by twirling us around. "My mother was a professional ballroom dancer. Learning wasn't an option; it was a requirement if I wanted to be fed."

I laughed. "That's really cool. Did you ever consider following in her footsteps?"

"Absolutely not. I grew up watching her suffer with hip bursitis, stress fractures, torn ligaments—it's definitely not the glamorous profession they make it out to be on all those dance-contest TV shows. You gotta love what you do for a job like that."

"I think you have to love what you do for any job."

"That's a very good point."

The song came to an end, and the emcee told everyone to take their seats.

"Where are you sitting?" Hudson asked.

I pointed to the side of the room where Fisher and I had been seated. "Somewhere over there. Table Sixteen."

He nodded. "I'll walk you."

We approached the table at the same moment as Fisher, who was coming from the other direction. He looked between Hudson and me, and his face asked the question he didn't say aloud.

"Umm...this is my friend Fisher. Fisher, this is Hudson."

Hudson extended his hand. "Nice to meet you."

After shaking with a silent Fisher, who seemed to have forgotten how to speak, he turned to me and took my hand once again. "I should get back to my table with the rest of the wedding party."

"Okay."

"Save a dance for me later?"

I smiled. "I'd love to."

Hudson turned to walk away and then turned back. As he walked backwards, he called, "In case you pull a Cinderella on me and disappear, what's your last name, Evelyn?"

Thankfully, him using my fake name reminded me not to give him my real one as I'd almost done the first time. "It's Whitley."

"Whitley?"

Oh God. Did he know Evelyn?

His eyes swept over my face. "Beautiful name. I'll see you later."

"Uhh...okay, sure."

When Hudson was barely out of earshot, Fisher leaned close to me. "My name's supposed to be Maximilian, sweetheart."

"Oh my God, Fisher. We have to leave."

"Nah." He shrugged. "It's no big deal. We made up Maximilian anyway. I'm your plus one. No one knows the name of the person Evelyn brought. Though I still want to play a real estate tycoon."

"No, it's not that."

"Then what is it?"

"We have to leave because he knows..."

Stella

Fisher sucked back a pull of his beer. "You're just paranoid. The guy has no idea. I watched his face when you said Evelyn's last name, and the only thing he noticed was how beautiful you are."

I shook my head. "No, he made a weird face. I saw it."

"How long were you talking to the guy?"

"I don't know. Maybe fifteen minutes? I met him at the bar and then he asked me to dance."

"Did he seem like the type of guy who would be shy about asking a question if he had a concern?"

I thought about it. He actually didn't. Hudson came off more bold than bashful. "No, but..."

Fisher rested one of his hands on each of my shoulders. "Take a deep breath."

"Fisher, we should go."

The emcee came on again and asked everyone to please take their seats, as dinner was about to be served.

Fisher pulled out my chair. "Let's at least eat. If you still want to ditch after we're done, we can. But I'm telling you, you're just being paranoid. The guy hasn't got a clue."

My gut told me to leave now, but when I scanned the room, I noticed we were the last of a few stragglers standing, and people were looking at us.

I sighed. "Fine. Dinner and then we're out of here."

Fisher smiled.

I spoke softly, aware of the other guests seated at our table that we'd been rudely ignoring. "Where have you been, by the way?"

"Talking to Noah."

"Who's Noah?"

"A cute waiter. He's going to be an actor."

I rolled my eyes. "Sure he is. We were supposed to stick together, you know."

"It didn't look like you were too lonely. Who was that Adonis, anyway? You know I don't like it when you have men in your life better-looking than me."

I sighed. "He was gorgeous, wasn't he?"

Fisher drank his beer. "I'd do him."

We both laughed. "Are you sure you don't think he noticed anything? You're not just saying that because you want to stay, are you?"

"No, we're absolutely fine."

Somehow, I relaxed a little over dinner. Although that might've had more to do with the waiter who kept refreshing my drink without being asked than deciding Fisher was right. It wasn't that I no longer thought Hudson knew we were imposters, but rather that the buzz from my gin martinis left me unable to care if he did.

After they cleared our plates, Fisher asked me to dance, and I figured why not? A girl could have a worse evening than one spent dancing with two handsome men. So we hit the dance floor for a catchy pop song, and when the music slowed, Fisher took me in his arms.

Halfway through, we were laughing in our own little bubble when a man tapped my partner on the shoulder.

"Mind if I cut in?"

Hudson.

My heart started to pound in my chest. I wasn't sure if it was the prospect of being back in the gorgeous man's arms, or the prospect of being found out.

Fisher smiled and stepped back. "Take good care of my girl."

"Oh, I intend to."

Something about the way he said it made me feel uneasy. Though Hudson took me in his arms and started to move us to the music, just as he'd done earlier.

"Having fun?" he asked.

"Ummm... Yes. This is a very nice place for a wedding. I've never been here before."

"Who did you say you were a guest of? The bride or the groom?"

I didn't say. "The bride."

"And you know each other how?"

Shit. I looked up, and Hudson's mouth curved into what resembled a smile, but it definitely wasn't a funny-*ha-ha* type of smile. It was more cynical than jovial.

"I, uh, we used to work together."

"Oh? Was it at Rothschild Investments?"

I wanted to run for it. Maybe Hudson sensed I might do just that, because unless I was imagining it, his grip on me tightened. I swallowed. "Yes. I worked for Rothschild Investments."

The only thing I knew about Evelyn's short-lived job there was that she had worked as a receptionist and couldn't stand her boss. She used to refer to him as *GQ Prick*.

"In what capacity might that be?"

This was starting to feel like an interrogation. "As a receptionist."

"A receptionist? But I thought you were a perfumist?"

Shit. Right. I hadn't been thinking earlier when I'd been honest about my profession. "I, uhh, I'm starting my own business, and things got delayed, so I needed an income."

"And what type of business is it you're starting?"

At least this part wasn't a lie. "It's called Signature Scent. It's a mail-order, custom perfume line."

"How does that work?"

"We send twenty small scent samples for the person to rate from one to ten, along with a detailed questionnaire. Based on the types of smells they like and their answers to our survey, we create a scent just for them. I created an algorithm that builds the formula based on the input we collect."

Hudson scanned my face. It looked like he was trying to figure out some sort of puzzle. When he spoke again, his tone was softer. "That's actually a good idea."

Maybe it was the alcohol fueling my nerve, but I was suddenly offended that he seemed surprised. "Did you think because I'm blond I wouldn't have any?"

Hudson flashed what I suspected might've been a real smile, but it quickly faded back to his stoic face. He stared down at me for a long time as I held my breath, waiting for him to call me out as a fraud.

Finally, he said, "Will you come with me for a moment?"

"Where?"

"I have to make a speech, and I was hoping you could stand nearby. Your beautiful face will give me just the encouragement I need."

"Umm...sure."

Hudson smiled, but again, something about it felt off. What he'd asked seemed harmless enough, though, so as he took my hand and led me to the front of the room, I tried to convince myself that all the weirdness was in my head, stemming from my guilty conscience.

He spoke to the emcee, and then we walked to the side of the dance floor to wait. We stood next to each other as the song ended and the emcee asked guests to take their seats again.

"Ladies and gentlemen, I'd like to introduce a very important person to the newlyweds. He's the brother of our beautiful bride and a good friend to our dashing groom. Let's give a great big round of applause to our groomsman, Hudson!"

Oh fuck. He's the bride's brother!

GQ Prick!

Hudson leaned down to me. "Stay right here where I can see your gorgeous face, Evelyn."

I nodded and smiled, though I felt like throwing up.

Over the next ten minutes, Hudson gave an eloquent speech. He talked about what a pain in the ass his little sister had been, and how proud he was of the woman she'd become. When he explained that their father and mother had both passed away, I got a little choked up. His admiration for his sister was evident, and his speech was an equal mix of serious and funny. As he spoke, I let out a heavy sigh of relief that he hadn't had anything unusual up his sleeve. It was a shame that I'd met him under the current conditions, and that I'd introduced myself with a fake name, because Hudson seemed like a great catch.

At the end of his speech, he held up his glass. "To Mason and Olivia. May you have love, health, and wealth, but most importantly, may you have a long life together to enjoy it all."

A murmur of *salud* went around the room before everyone drank, and I thought that was the end of the speech. But it wasn't. Instead of handing the emcee back the microphone, Hudson turned and looked directly at me. The wicked smile that slid across his face gave me the chills, and *not* in a good way.

"Up next," he said, "I have a special treat for you all. My sister's dear friend *Evelyn* would like to say a few words."

My eyes widened.

He continued. "She has such a great story about how the two of them met. It's really entertaining, and she can't wait to share it with you this evening."

Hudson walked toward me with the microphone in his hand. His eyes sparkled with amusement, but I worried his shiny shoes were about to be decorated with vomit.

I waved him off and shook my head, but that only egged him on.

He spoke into the microphone as he took my hand. "Evelyn seems to be having a case of the jitters. She's a bit on the shy side." He tugged me, and I took two unwilling steps toward the middle of the room before digging my heels in and refusing to move any farther.

Hudson laughed and raised the microphone once again. "It looks like she needs a little encouragement. What do you say, ladies and gentlemen? Can we have a round of applause to help *Evelyn* come up and say a few words?"

The crowd started to clap. I wanted the floor to open up and my rigid body to fall into a bottomless pit. But it was becoming clearer by the second that the only way out of this was trudging straight through. All eyes were on me, and there was no getting out unscathed. I debated making a run for it, but decided it was better to have only a few people chasing me than the entire place.

So I took a deep breath, walked over to the closest table of guests, and asked a random old man if his drink contained alcohol. When he said it was vodka on the rocks, I helped myself, downing the entire contents. Then I smoothed my dress, pulled my shoulders back, lifted my chin, and marched over to Hudson, grabbing the microphone with my shaky hand.

He smirked and leaned down to whisper in my ear, "Good luck, *Evelyn*."

The room quieted, and I could feel beads of sweat forming on my forehead and upper lip. A lump the size of a golf ball was stuck in the middle of my throat, and my fingers and toes tingled. All eyes were on me, and I wracked my brain to come up with a story—*any story*. Eventually I thought of one, though I'd have to improvise a little. But that was par for this evening, anyway, wasn't it?

I cleared my throat. "Hi..."

I'd been holding the microphone with my right hand. Noticing it shaking, I raised my left and clamped it over the other to help keep it steady. Then I took a deep breath. "Hi. I'm Evelyn. Olivia and I met in kindergarten."

I made the mistake of looking over at the table where the newlyweds were sitting. The bride's face was wrinkled in confusion, and she stared at me while whispering to her husband.

I better make this quick... "As Hudson mentioned, I wanted to share how Livi and I met. I'd just moved to the City in the middle of the school year and didn't have many friends. I was really shy back then. My pale skin would turn bright red whenever too much attention was focused on me, so I avoided speaking in class at all costs. One day, I drank an entire bottle of water during recess outside. I really needed to use the ladies' room when we got back inside, but Mr. Neu, our teacher, had already started a lesson, and I didn't want to interrupt him. He was, like, seven-feet tall and scary to begin with, and the thought of raising my hand and having all the kids turn and stare at me when he called my name completely freaked me out. So I held it during his entire lesson, and boy, could that man talk."

I looked over at the bride. "Remember how Mr. Neu would just drone on and tell all those really bad corny jokes? And then he'd be the only one to laugh at them?"

The bride looked at me like I was absolutely crazy. I was pretty sure she was right.

For the next five minutes, I blabbered on and on—standing in front of a room full of people telling them how I ran to the bathroom when the teacher finally stopped talking. But all of the stalls were taken, and I just couldn't hold it anymore. I detailed how I'd come back to the classroom with wet pants and tried to hide it, but one boy had spotted it and yelled "*Look! The new girl peed her pants.*" I'd been absolutely mortified, with tears brimming in my eyes, until my friend came to my rescue. In an act of courage that would become an unbreakable bond for the two of us, Olivia peed her own pants and then stood up and told everyone the grass was wet outside at recess, and we'd been sitting together.

I closed my story by telling a room full of smiling faces how my utmost wish for the happy couple was that they'd have the same love and laughter I'd shared with the bride for many years. Raising one hand, I held up an imaginary glass. "A toast to the bride and groom."

People started to applaud, and I knew I needed to use the time to get the hell out of there. Hudson was still standing off to the side, and if I wasn't mistaken, I thought he might be a little proud of me for not crumbling. His eyes gleamed, and he watched me intently as I walked over and pressed the microphone to his chest.

He covered the top of the mic and smiled. "Entertaining."

I showed him my pearly whites through an exaggerated smile and crooked my finger for him to lean in closer.

When he did, I whispered in his ear, *"You're an asshole."*

Hudson let out a deep laugh as I stormed away, never looking back to see if he was following. Luckily, Fisher was already walking toward me, so I didn't have to search for him before we hightailed it out of here.

His eyes were as wide as Frisbees. "Are you wasted? What the hell just happened up there?"

I grabbed his arm and kept walking. "We need to get the hell out of here *quick*. Do you have my purse?"

"No."

Shit. I debated just leaving it, but my license and credit card were inside. So I veered left and made a beeline for our table. Out of the corner of my eye, I saw Hudson and the groom talking to the maître d' and pointing in our direction.

"Shit! We need to hurry." I rushed the rest of the way to our table, grabbed my purse, and turned back around. After two steps I pivoted.

"What are you doing?" Fisher said.

I plucked an unopened bottle of Dom Pérignon from our table. "I'm taking this with me."

Fisher shook his head and laughed as we headed for the door. Along the way, we swiped bottles of champagne from every table we passed. Confused guests had no idea what to make of the scene, but we were moving too quickly for them to comment. By the time we got to the exit, our arms were full, and we had at least a grand worth of bubbly.

Out front, we got lucky that a few yellow cabs were stopped, waiting at the light. Jumping into the first empty one, Fisher slammed the door shut, and we both got up on our knees to look out the back window. The maître d' and the two security guys who had been checking IDs earlier were halfway down the marble staircase. Hudson stood at the top, casually leaning against a marble pillar and drinking a glass of champagne as he watched the insanity of our departure. Blood rushed through my ears as I looked back and forth between the traffic light and the men closing in on us. Just as they reached the curb and stepped off, the red switched to green.

"*Go! Go!*" I yelled to the cabbie.

He hit the gas, and Fisher and I stayed on our knees, watching out the back window as the men grew more distant. Once we made the right at the corner, I turned around and slumped into the seat. I couldn't seem to catch my breath.

"What the hell happened, Stella? One minute I saw you dancing with a gorgeous man who looked completely into you, and the next you were telling some crazy story to a room full of people. Are you drunk?"

"Even if I had been, I'd be scared sober right now."

"What came over you?"

"It's not what came over me, it's *who*."

"I'm not following."

"You know the gorgeous man I was talking to?"

"Yeah?"

"Well, turns out he knew all—" A sense of panic washed over me as I realized I wasn't sure where my cell phone was. Frenzied, I opened my purse and started to pull things out. Clearly, it wasn't inside, but it just *had* to be. Refusing to accept what I'd done, I turned the purse over and emptied the contents onto my lap.

No phone.

No freaking phone!

"What are you looking for?" Fisher said.

"Please tell me you have my cell."

He shook his head. "Why would I have it?"

"Because if you don't, that means I left it on the table at the wedding..."

Hudson

"**M**r. Rothschild, you have a phone call."

I huffed and pressed the intercom. "Who is it?"

"It's Evelyn Whitley."

Tossing my pen onto my desk, I picked up the phone and leaned back in my chair. "Evelyn, thank you for calling me back."

"Of course. How are you, Hudson?"

Frustrated enough to call my little sister's annoying friend who I hadn't wanted to give a job to, but did anyway, only to have said annoying friend stop showing up to work two months ago and quit without any notice.

"I'm well. And you?"

"Pretty good. Although Louisiana is really humid compared to New York."

Is that where she'd run off to? I didn't care, and small talk with Evelyn wasn't on my packed agenda for today.

"So the reason I had my assistant track you down—a woman came to Olivia's wedding pretending to be you."

"Me? Really? Who would do that?"

"I was hoping you could tell me."

"Jeez, I have no idea. I didn't even think Liv had invited me to her wedding. I definitely didn't get an invitation."

"My sister said she mailed it right around the time you left town. It went to your old address here in the City. Was your mail being forwarded, or was someone picking it up for you?"

"I get almost all my mail electronically—phone bill, credit cards, and stuff. So I didn't do a mail forward. My old roommate still lives in the apartment, so she could have received it."

"You had a roommate?"

"Yeah, Stella."

"Maybe it was Stella?"

Evelyn laughed. "I don't think so. She's definitely not the type to crash a wedding."

"Humor me. What does your old roommate look like?"

"I don't know. Blond hair, maybe five foot five, pale skin, nice curves...glasses. Size seven shoe."

The hair color, nice curves, and skin description were a match, and I supposed the woman could've had contacts in. But who the hell gives shoe size as part of a physical description? "By any chance would your roommate have a habit of smelling things?"

"Yes! Stella's some sort of perfume developer for Estée Lauder. Or at least she was before she quit. We were only roommates for a year or so, but she was always sniffing things—a little odd, if you ask me. She also had a habit of telling long stories when all I asked was a simple question, and giving chocolate bars out to people. But how did you know she sniff—*oh my God*. Was it Stella who went to the wedding posing as me?"

"Sounds like it may have been, yes."

Evelyn laughed. "I didn't think she had it in her."

From the little time I'd spent with Stella, I could tell she had it in her to surprise a lot of people. Most would have bolted out the door when I'd called them to take the microphone. But not Stella. She'd been a shaky mess, yet she'd pulled herself together and taken what I'd dished out. I wasn't sure what was sexier—the way she looked, the way she didn't back down from a challenge, or the way she'd defiantly told me I was an asshole before taking off.

It had been eight days since my sister's wedding, and I still couldn't get the damn woman out of my head.

"What's Stella's last name?" I asked.

"Bardot. Like the old-time movie actress."

"Do you happen to have a home phone number for her?"

"I do. It's in my cell. I can forward you her contact information after we hang up, if you want."

"Yes. That would be helpful."

"Okay."

"Thank you for the information, Evelyn."

"Do you want me to call her? Tell her she needs to pay for the cost of attending or something?"

"No, that's not necessary. I'd actually prefer you didn't mention this conversation, if you happen to speak to her."

"Okay...sure. Whatever you say."

"Goodbye, Evelyn."

After I hung up, I rubbed my chin and stared out the window at the city.

Stella Bardot...what to do, what to do with you...

Opening my desk drawer, I pulled out the iPhone the catering company had sent over the other day. They said they'd found it at Table Sixteen. I'd had my assistant call everyone seated at the table except for the mystery woman. No one had lost a phone. So I was pretty certain who it belonged to. The only question was, what was I going to do with it?

Helena, my assistant, peeked her head into the conference room.

"Mr. Rothschild, I'm sorry to interrupt, but there's someone here to see you. There's no appointment on your calendar, but she claims you invited her."

I held out my hands, motioning to the people seated around the table. "I'm in the middle of a meeting. I don't have anything else scheduled right now."

She shrugged. "That's what I thought. I'll let her know you're busy."

"Who is it?"

"Her name is Stella Bardot."

Well, well, well... Cinderella finally came to collect her glass slipper, did she? It had been six days now since I'd messaged her over a note, so I'd assumed Ms. Bardot didn't have the balls to show up. I had Evelyn's old address in our company records, so I could've been nice and just returned the phone to her. But what fun would that have been? Instead, I'd sent over my business card with a note scribbled on the back.

If you want what you left behind, come and get it.

"Can you please tell Ms. Bardot I'm busy, but if she can wait, I'll see her when I'm done here?"

"Sure, of course. I'll let her know." Helena closed the door to the conference room.

My meeting lasted another forty minutes, but I probably should've ended it after two, since knowing what waited for me in the lobby had me completely distracted. Finally I returned to my office, carrying the files from the conference room.

"Would you like me to bring Ms. Bardot back?" Helena asked as I passed her desk.

"Give me five minutes and then show her in, please."

I had no idea what I was going to say when Little Miss Party Crasher walked in. Then again, I wasn't the one who needed to explain anything. So I decided to play it by ear and see where the conversation went.

Which was a good thing, because the minute she stepped into my office doorway, I could barely remember my own name.

Evelyn—or rather *Stella*—was even more beautiful than I remembered. At the wedding, her hair had been pinned up, but now it was down, and wavy, blond locks framed her porcelain skin. She wore oversized, thick-rimmed glasses that gave her a sexy-librarian look, and the simple navy blue sundress and flats she had on made her look tinier than she had at the wedding.

Keeping my face as impassive as possible, I stood and gestured to the guest chairs on the other side of my desk.

"Please, have a seat."

She bit down on her bottom lip, but nevertheless, walked into my office.

"Will you please shut the door behind you, Helena?" I asked my assistant.

She nodded. "Of course."

Stella and I had a bit of a staring contest before she planted her ass in a seat on the other side of my desk.

"I didn't think you were going to collect your glass slipper, Cinderella."

She crossed her legs and folded her hands on top of her knee. "Trust me, if I had any other choice, I wouldn't be here."

I arched a brow. "Should I be offended? I was actually looking forward to you coming for a visit."

She pursed her lips. "I bet you were. What kind of humiliation should I expect today? Will you be calling in all the employees to laugh and point?"

My lip twitched. "I wasn't planning on it. But if that's your thing..."

She sighed. "Look, I'm sorry for what I did. I already wrote the bride an apology letter and sent a little gift to the return address on the invitation. I didn't mean any harm. When the invitation came, I accidentally opened it, and a few glasses of wine later, my friend Fisher and I concocted the idea that we should crash. I was pissed at my roommate—the person the invitation was actually sent to. She'd moved out in the middle of the night on me, and a bunch of my clothes and shoes went missing when she did. And just that day, the check she'd left me for the two months of back rent she owed had bounced. And to top it all off, it had been my last day at my job, so I really needed her half of the rent." She paused a moment, seeming to catch her breath. "I know none of that excuses what I did. A wedding is supposed to be a sacred and intimate event for families and friends to share, but I want you to know it's the first time I've ever done anything like that." She shook her head. "Plus, I might not have gone through with it if it were anywhere else, but I love that library. I worked a block away for the last six years and had lunch on the steps more times than I could count. I've been dying to go to an event there."

I scratched my chin and examined her face. She seemed sincere. "What took you so long to come collect your phone?"

"Truth?"

"No, I prefer you make up a story like you did at the wedding. Because that ended so well..."

She rolled her eyes and let out a big sigh. "I wasn't planning on coming at all. I even went out and bought a new iPhone. But my rent is due in a few days, and I'm broke because I've sunk every penny I have into my business launch, which has now been delayed. I have fourteen days to return the overpriced phone—and the last one is today. I can't afford a thousand dollars for a new cell, especially now that I don't have a roommate. I need to return the phone, or call my father and ask him to borrow money. Faced with the choice of coming here and taking my lumps for doing something stupid, or calling my father... Well, here I am."

My sister hadn't really even been upset over what had happened at her wedding. Of course she'd been confused about who the woman telling a story about their childhood was, but when I'd explained that I'd caught her pretending to be a guest, Olivia had laid into me for putting the woman on the spot, rather than quietly escorting her to the door. To be honest, even I'd felt a little bad once Stella started to sweat and turn pale with the microphone in her hand. But I'd been pissed that she lied to me. Deep down, I knew it was partly because a woman lying to my face brought back some shitty reminders. It also didn't help that my little sister had chosen to get married at the same place my own wedding had been just seven years before. So perhaps my anger at Stella could have been slightly misplaced.

Opening my desk drawer, I took out the cell phone and slid it over to the other side of my desk.

"Thank you," Stella said. She picked it up and swiped at the screen. The phone illuminated, and I watched her forehead wrinkle. "It's still fully charged. Did you charge it?"

I nodded. "It was dead when the caterer sent it over the day after the wedding."

She nodded, but I could see I hadn't answered whatever question was on her mind.

"Did you...try to guess my code?"

I managed to keep my face straight, even though that was exactly what I'd done. She didn't need to know I'd spent an hour trying different combinations to unlock the damn thing because I was so curious about the woman who'd run out of the wedding. So I sidestepped her question and tented my fingers, speaking in a stern tone. "I needed to turn it on to see if you even had a code, didn't I?"

Stella shook her head and slipped the phone into her purse. "Oh. Yeah. Of course. That's right."

We stared at each other for a few seconds, until the silence became awkward.

"Okay, well..." She stood. "I should be going."

As fucked up as it was, I wasn't ready for her to leave. I had a hundred questions I wanted her to answer—like what her father had done that made her not want to call him, or why her business launch had been delayed. But instead, I followed her lead and stood.

She extended her hand across my desk. "Thank you for safekeeping my phone, and again, I apologize for what I did."

I took her little hand in mine and held it for a tad too long. But if she noticed, she didn't say anything.

After I let go, Stella turned to leave, but then turned back. She unzipped her purse and rummaged through it. Pulling something out, she offered it to me.

"Do you like chocolate?"

I was confused as hell, but nodded. "I do."

"I keep a Hershey bar in my bag at all times for emergencies. It has anandamide, which is a neurotransmitter and helps you feel happier." She shrugged. "Sometimes I give them out to people who look like they need it, but most of the time I wind up eating it myself. I love chocolate. I sent your sister an apology gift, but I didn't send you anything. It's all I have for a peace offering."

This woman was handing me a candy bar to call it even for crashing a seven-hundred-dollar-a-plate event? I had to give it to her; she was unique.

I held up my hands. "It's fine. We're good. You keep it."

She kept her arm extended. "It'll make me feel better if you have it."

I managed to keep in my chuckle as I took it from her hand. "Okay. Thank you."

Stella lifted her purse back onto her shoulder and headed to the door. I followed to open it, but she again stopped abruptly. This time, instead of a chocolate-bar offering, she leaned in to me and inhaled deeply.

"Retrouvailles," she said.

I spoke a little French and knew that translated to *reunion* or something along those lines.

Seeing the confusion on my face, she smiled. "It's the cologne you're wearing, isn't it? It's called Retrouvailles."

"Oh... Yes, I think it is."

"You have good taste. *Expensive* taste. But good. I created it."

"Really?"

She nodded, and her smile broadened. "You wear it well. Colognes smell different on everyone."

Damn, she had some smile. Taking it in, my eyes fell to her lips.

Fuck. I had the urge to bite them.

"Do you spray the cologne on your pulse point?" She pointed to the hollow at the bottom of her throat. "Around here?"

I practically salivated, staring at her delicate neck. "I guess so."

"That's why it lasts so long. Perfumes and colognes reactivate from body heat. A lot of men spray on the sides of their neck, but the bottom of your throat is one of the warmest areas because the blood pumps near the surface of the skin. It's why most women also spray on their wrists and behind their ears."

"Are you wearing any?" I asked.

Her brows furrowed. "Perfume?"

I nodded.

"Yes, it's one I developed also."

I kept my eyes trained on hers as I slowly leaned forward. She didn't budge as I came to within an inch of our noses touching, then dipped my head to the side, placed my nose near her ear, and inhaled deeply.

She smelled fucking incredible.

Reluctantly, I pulled my head back. "You wear your creations well, too."

She smiled once again, but the slight glaze of her eyes told me she felt a bit off-kilter, too. "Thank you, and thanks again for everything, Hudson."

She turned once more to walk out of my office, and as she stepped over the threshold, a bizarre sense of panic washed over me.

"Stella, wait..."

She again halted and looked back.

Before I could stop myself, the craziest shit tumbled out of my mouth. "Have dinner with me."

4

Stella

"**H**ave you heard from Prince Charming yet?" Fisher opened my refrigerator and took out a container of yesterday's dinner, even though it was only 7AM.

I shook my head and tried to hide my disappointment. "It's probably for the best."

"What's it been, like, a week now?"

"Eight days. Not that I'm counting." *I'm totally counting.*

He looked me up and down. "Why are you dressed so early?"

"I just got back from watching the sunrise."

"You know, you can set the background of your laptop to some pretty nice sunrises and sunsets and sleep in." Fisher popped off the Tupperware lid and forked a full breaded chicken cutlet as if it were a lollipop. He bit off a piece.

"That's not quite the same, but thanks. Umm...do you want me to heat that up for you? Give you a plate

40

and knife to cut it up? Or better yet, make you some eggs for breakfast?"

"No need." He shrugged and took another bite. "Why don't you call him?"

I looked at my best friend blankly. "I can't call him."

"Why not?"

"Because he probably changed his mind. Are you forgetting how we met? I'm shocked he even asked for my phone number. I'm thinking he had a temporary lapse in sanity and thought better of it after I left. Besides, I have a date tomorrow, anyway."

"With who?"

"Ben."

"The guy you met online? That was a few weeks ago, wasn't it?"

"Yeah. I was supposed to go out with him a few days ago, but I canceled."

"How come you canceled?"

"I don't know." I shrugged. "Just had a lot to do."

Fisher gave me a look. "Nice try. But I ain't buying it. You were hoping Prince Charming would call and wanted to keep your calendar free."

"I wasn't waiting for Hudson to call."

"Have you checked your phone for missed messages more than once this week?"

"No," I said—*waaay* too quickly and sounding completely defensive.

I totally had, a few times a day, actually. But I knew how Fisher operated. He was relentless. It's what made him such a good lawyer. If he found one little string hanging, he would keep pulling and pulling until the entire sweater unraveled. So I wasn't about to hand him that thread on a silver platter.

He studied me. "I think you're full of shit."

I rolled my eyes.

"You know, you can go out with more than one person at a time…"

Luckily, our conversation was interrupted by my landline ringing, my business phone.

"I wonder who's calling Signature Scent on a Saturday. I guess it could be a vendor in Singapore. It's still Friday there, right?"

Fisher chuckled. "Wrong way. It's Sunday there."

"Oh."

I found the phone in the living room, where it sat on top of a box of samples. I cradled the receiver on my shoulder as I picked up the box, too. "Hello?"

"Hi, is this Stella Bardot?"

Returning to the kitchen, I opened the box and took out one of the small glass jars packed inside. "It is. Who's this?"

"My name is Olivia Royce."

The jar slipped from my hand. It hit the kitchen tile with a loud clank, but luckily, it didn't break. I fumbled to grab the phone from where it was balanced on my shoulder. "Did you say Olivia Royce?"

"I did. I hope you don't mind me calling. I couldn't find a website, but when I Googled the name of your company, this number came up, so I took a chance."

"Umm… No, not at all. Of course not."

"I received your note and gift. When I mentioned what you'd sent me to my brother, he told me you were starting a new fragrance company that made custom scents. I would love to order some perfumes for my bridal party, but I couldn't find you online."

"Uhh...the website isn't up yet."

"Darn. Can I possibly order them directly from you, then?"

"Sure. Of course."

"Eeep! That's great. I've been struggling to figure out what to get each of the girls. I want something personalized and special. This is so perfect. I absolutely love mine, by the way. Thank you for doing that."

I couldn't get over this conversation. Olivia was calling me to place an order, not ream me out for crashing her wedding? Was it possible she didn't realize I was the same person? I didn't think so, since I'd mailed her gift and an apology note in the same box, and she'd obviously had a conversation with Hudson about me.

"Thank *you*. I, uh, I can send them some kits and make their orders a priority once they tell me what they like."

"Oh no. I want it to be a surprise. I know a lot about them—maybe I could just tell you what they normally wear and a little bit about them and you could come up with something?"

I wasn't sure that would be as effective as the way I normally did it, but there was no way in hell I could say no to her. "Sure, that sounds good."

"How's Monday at twelve thirty?"

My forehead wrinkled. "Umm... Twelve thirty is fine."

"Okay. Would Café Luce on Fifty-Third work? Is that too far for you? Do you live here in the City?"

My eyes bulged. She wanted to meet in person? I'd assumed she meant she was going to pencil me into her calendar for an email or a call.

"Yes, I live in the City. And Café Luce sounds good."

"Perfect! It's a date. Thanks, Stella! I can't wait to meet you."

Ten seconds later, the line was dead. I stared at my phone. Fisher had been watching the entire conversation play out on my face.

"Who was that?" he said.

"Olivia Royce."

"And she is?"

"The bride whose wedding we crashed."

The next day, I arrived twenty minutes early at the coffee shop. Ben had wanted to pick me up for our date, but I preferred to meet people I didn't know well in public so I was always in full control of when I could leave. I bought a decaf latte and took a seat on a couch off to the side of the counter. My local coffeehouse always had newspapers and magazines for people to browse while they drank their overpriced coffees, so I picked up *The New York Times* and started to flip through the Sunday Style section. Halfway through, I froze when I saw a photo. After blinking a few times to make sure I wasn't imagining things, I lifted the paper closer to read the announcement.

Olivia Paisley Rothschild and Mason Brighton Royce were married on July 13th at the New York Public Library in Manhattan. The Rev. Arthur Finch, an Episcopal priest, officiated.

Mrs. Royce, 28, whom the groom calls Livi, is a vice president of marketing. She graduated from the University of Pennsylvania and received an MBA from Columbia.

She is the daughter of Charlotte Bianchi Rothschild and Cooper E. Rothschild, both deceased, from New York City. The wedding was hosted by her brother, Hudson Rothschild.

Mr. Royce, also 28, founded his own IT firm and specializes in security and compliance. He graduated from the University of Boston and received an MS in Information Technology from NYU.

I couldn't believe I'd stumbled on their wedding announcement. What were the chances? I hadn't read the Sunday *New York Times* in years, so it felt like a freaky coincidence. Fisher always said if you put positive thoughts out there, positive things would come back to you. That might explain this. I'd certainly done enough thinking over the last week and a half about a certain man who had asked for my number, but then never called.

Earlier this week, I'd been flipping through the channels and happened to pass *Dancing with the Stars*.

Even though I never watched it, for some reason I kept it on. When the couples slow danced, I reminisced about how it had felt to be in Hudson's arms at his sister's wedding. That had led to me remembering how much rhythm he'd had, which in turn made my mind wander to *other things* his good rhythm might be helpful with. Then, on Friday night when Fisher came over after work, he'd brought me a bottle of Hendricks gin. It reminded me of the way my arms had broken out in goose bumps when Hudson whispered in my ear, *"The night's young, Evelyn. Dance with me."*

I'd never in a million years expected him to ask me out when I showed up with my tail between my legs at his office to pick up my phone. But once he did, I'd let my imagination run away with itself. I'd even put off my second date with Ben. But after spending more than a week waiting for my phone to ring, I finally realized it was dumb to avoid a perfectly nice guy—one who *had* called multiple times—just because another guy might possibly dial my number.

Ben walked in a few minutes before the time we were supposed to meet. I took one last glance at the wedding photo in the newspaper before closing it. I was determined to not ruin my date by letting thoughts of another man sneak in.

"Hey." Ben kissed me on the lips.

It was only our second kiss, since our first had been at the end of our last date, but it was nice enough. There was no tingle, and goose bumps didn't run down my arms or anything, but we were in the middle of a coffee shop, so what did I expect? When Ben pulled back, he handed me a box of Godiva chocolate I hadn't noticed in his hand. "I was going to get you flowers, but I figured you'd have to carry them with you all night. This you can probably toss in your purse."

I smiled. "That's very thoughtful of you. Thank you so much."

"I made a reservation at a steak house. After, if you're up for it, there's a comedy club next door with an open-mic night tonight."

"That sounds great."

"You ready to go?"

"Yup."

I picked up my empty coffee cup and tossed it in the garbage on the way out. When I reached for the door handle, Ben beat me to it. "Please, let me."

"Thank you."

Outside I looked left and then right. "Which way are we heading?"

"The restaurant is a few blocks from here. It's on Hudson."

"Hudson Street?"

"Yeah, is that too far to walk in heels? I can grab us an Uber."

"No, no. That's fine." *But seriously...Hudson Street?*

We started to walk. "I haven't tried the place yet," Ben said. "But it has incredible reviews, so I hope it's good."

"What's it called?"

"Hudson's."

I had to stifle my laugh. *Hudson's on Hudson Street?* So much for not letting thoughts of someone else creep in tonight...

5

Stella

I arrived at the restaurant a few minutes late on Monday, even though I had left my apartment super early. The uptown local train I'd taken had decided to become an express and skipped my stop.

When I entered, Olivia was already seated at a table. She looked so different out of her wedding garb that I almost didn't recognize her. But she waved and smiled like we were old friends.

I had this wild notion stuck in my head that she didn't really want to order any perfume, but was luring me here so she could give me a piece of her mind in person—or worse yet, have me arrested. Her inviting smile did a lot to diffuse my paranoia.

"Hi." I set the box in my arms down on an empty seat and pulled out the chair across from her. "I'm sorry I'm late. My train skipped the stop."

"No problem." She reached out and tilted the breadbasket in my direction, showing me it was empty.

"As you can see, I kept myself busy. I hadn't eaten a carb for six months before my wedding. So I've spent the last few weeks making up for lost time." Setting the basket down, she held her hand out to me. "I'm Olivia Rothschild, by the way. Damn it, no, I'm not. I'm Olivia Royce now. I still can't get used to that."

I smiled, though I was a nervous wreck. "Stella Bardot." Figuring the best thing to do was clear the air, I took a deep breath. "Listen, Olivia, I'm so sorry about what I did. I'm usually not the type of person to crash a wedding."

She tilted her head. "You're not? That's a shame. I thought we were going to get along so well. I crashed a prom once."

My eyes widened. "You did?"

Olivia chuckled. "Yup. And I made out with some girl's date and came home with a fat lip."

My shoulders loosened. "Oh my God. You have no idea how relieved I am to know you're not mad."

She waved me off. "Nah. Don't give it another thought. I was pretty impressed with the story you told. Did someone really pee their pants for you?"

I smiled sadly. The memory of the truth was bittersweet now, considering my sister and I no longer spoke. "Actually, it was me who did that, and it was in preschool. My sister is a year younger and had an accident during practice for the Christmas pageant. A boy pointed at her wet backside and made fun of her. I couldn't let her stand there alone."

"Nice. My brother's older. He's always been ridiculously protective of me. But I'm not sure he would

50

have gone as far as peeing his pants to save my face." She sipped her drink. "On second thought, he probably would. He would just never admit he'd done it to protect me. He'd say he pissed his pants and I copied him, probably."

We laughed.

"Hudson filled me in on how you came to be at the wedding. I wasn't surprised when he told me what Evelyn did to you—taking off in the middle of the night and sticking you with the unpaid rent. She's always been unreliable. First year of college, we went on spring break together. She met some guy who was ten years older than us and only spoke French. Two days into the trip, I woke up to a note saying she'd left for France to meet the guy's family because she was in love. She left me in Cancun all by myself. The bitch took my favorite pair of shoes with her."

"Oh my God. She took *my* favorite shoes when she moved out, too!"

We laughed again, and Olivia continued. "She also stole something from Lexi, my brother's ex-wife. The two of them had a falling out and stopped speaking. Then I talked my hard-ass brother into giving her a job, and after a few months, she stopped showing up. He's never going to let me live that one down. The man can hold a grudge forever."

"Hudson definitely doesn't seem as forgiving as you do."

"That's putting it mildly. He's super overprotective. When I was sixteen and had my first boyfriend, Hudson used to sit outside on the steps and wait for me to come home at night. Of course, that meant I got a peck on the cheek instead of a nice goodnight make-out session. I feel bad for Charlie. She probably won't be allowed to date until she's forty."

"Charlie?"

"Hudson's daughter."

I nodded. I have no idea why, but I didn't expect him to have a child. Though of course, I didn't know much about the man other than he was handsome, smelled divine, knew how to dance, and hadn't called in the *ten days* since I'd given him my phone number.

"How old is his daughter?"

"Six going on sixteen." She laughed. "He's so screwed."

The waiter came over to take our order, and I hadn't even looked at the menu yet. Olivia ordered a pear balsamic salad with chicken. That sounded good, so I did the same.

"So..." She sniffed her wrist. "Tell me how you managed to make me the best perfume I've ever smelled in my life. I'm completely obsessed with it."

I smiled. "Thank you. I took my clues from your wedding. You had gardenias as your centerpieces and in your bouquet, so I used that as my starting point. I overheard one of the women at the table where I was sitting say you were going to Bora Bora on your honeymoon. So I guessed you must like the beach and added some calone, which gives it that hint of sea breeze. And then your dress was traditional, but with a bright red silk belt, so I thought you might have a bit of an edge to you."

"That's amazing. Even the bottle was perfect."

"That design was one I fell in love with, but we won't actually be selling. It's imported from Italy, and I couldn't make it work with my shoestring of a start-up budget."

"That's a shame. It's so pretty."

"I'm hoping down the road I might be able to add it."

For the next hour, I explained how Signature Scent worked. I gave Olivia the full demo—she sniffed all twenty of the little samplers and rated them, and then I asked her all of the questions that would eventually be up on the website as part of the ordering process. She asked a ton of questions, seeming very interested in the business side of things. I wrote notes on each of her bridal party members, and she picked out the bottles for each of them.

"So when does Signature Scent officially launch?" she asked as we finished up.

I frowned. "I'm not sure."

"How come? It seems like you have everything all ready to go."

"I do—planning wise, anyway. But I ran into some financing issues. It's a long story, but I had a partner and needed to buy him out. I'd used a good chunk of the business funds we had to purchase inventory, so buying him out drained every penny of what I had left. Though it was fine, because I had a business line of credit large enough that I'd still be able to launch. I'd applied for the loan almost a year earlier, just in case I ran short. But when I went to draw on it the first time, the bank told me I needed to do an annual update to keep the line of credit open. I hadn't been aware of that. I'd just left my job at Estée Lauder, and when I wrote down that I'd had a change in employment, they yanked my line of credit. If I'd done it a few days earlier, I wouldn't have had to write that, and I would have been fine."

"Oh, that sucks."

I nodded. "It does. And no bank wants to lend to someone who's unemployed. I applied with the SBA. They're pretty much my last hope."

The waiter brought the check. I reached for it, even though I hated to waste a dime these days. It was the absolute least I could do for this kind woman whose wedding I'd crashed.

But Olivia beat me to it. "This lunch is on me. I invited you."

"I can't let you do that. I already owe you one meal."

She waved me off and grabbed her wallet from her purse. Sticking her credit card in the leather check folio, she folded it closed. "Absolutely not. I insist."

Before I could argue further, she held up her hand and the waiter swooped in and took the bill.

I sighed, feeling like a loser. "Thank you. I appreciate it."

"Anytime."

We walked outside together. I was going uptown to run some errands, and she was heading downtown back to work, so we said goodbye. Olivia pulled me in for a hug like we were the old friends I'd said we were at her wedding.

"I'll have your scents ready next week," I told her. "I can ship them to you or to each individual person, if you prefer."

She smiled. "Call me when they're ready, and we'll figure something out."

"Okay. I will."

A week later, I was up to my eyeballs in cardboard.

"That's the last of it." Fisher stacked the last carton on top of an already five-foot-high mountain of boxes. He pulled up his T-shirt and used the bottom to wipe sweat from his forehead. "You better be making stuffed manicotti soon for all this lifting you had me do today."

"I promise I will. I didn't realize how much I'd accumulated in that storage unit. I can't believe there were two-hundred boxes in there." In my ongoing effort to cut costs, I'd enlisted Fisher to help me relocate everything from my pricey self-storage unit to my apartment. Since I no longer had a roommate, I had the space here.

Fisher reached behind him into the waistband of his shorts. "I almost forgot. I picked up our mail on my last trip in. This package you got is falling apart. It looks like the mailman ripped it when he jammed it in your box to make it fit."

Everything was damp from his back sweat. My nose wrinkled. "Gross. Put it over there for me, please."

Fisher tossed the pile on the kitchen table, and the envelopes fanned out. The logo on the corner of one caught my eye. *The SBA*. I picked it up and examined it.

"Oh my God. This is a small envelope. That's not a good sign."

"Who's it from?"

"The Small Business Administration—I was supposed to get a decision on the loan I applied for in two to three weeks. It's barely been two."

"That's great. They probably loved your business so much, they couldn't wait to approve you."

I shook my head. "When you apply for something and you get back a thin envelope, it's never a good sign. It's like finding a regular-sized white envelope from the college you applied to in your mailbox instead of the big brown one they send with all your welcome stuff inside. If they were approving me, this would be thick."

Fisher rolled his eyes. "Most things are done online these days. Stop being so negative and open the damn thing. I bet there's a login and password for you to go online and sign whatever they need you to sign."

I blew out a deep breath. "I don't have a good feeling, Fisher. What am I going to do if they decline me? I've applied at three banks already. No one is giving an unemployed person a loan. I was an idiot to quit my job and think I could make a go of this business. They already filled my job at Estée Lauder, and most of the decent jobs for perfume chemists are overseas now. What the hell am I going to do? How am I going to pay my rent?"

Fisher put his hands on my shoulders. "Take a deep breath. You don't even know what's in the envelope yet. For all we know, it might be a form letter just thanking you for applying or telling you there's a delay in processing."

I was too nervous to open it, so I held the envelope out to my friend. "You do it. I can't."

56

Fisher shook his head, but tore open the envelope. I watched, holding my breath as his eyes scanned the first few lines. The frown that formed at the corners of his lips told me everything I needed to know.

I shut my eyes. "Oh, God..."

"I'm sorry, Stella. They said you don't have enough time in the business or a strong enough positive cash flow. But how the hell are you supposed to have either of those if they don't give you the loan to help you get the business up and running?"

I sighed. "I know. That's basically what all the banks said, too."

"Can you just start really small and get some experience and apply again?"

I wished it were that easy. "I don't have the packaging and enough of some of the samples I need to put into the boxes people would use to order."

Fisher raked a hand through his hair. "Shit. I have about nine grand in the bank I was saving for a rainy day. It's yours. You don't even have to pay me back."

"I love you for offering that, Fisher. I really do. But I can't take your money."

"Don't be ridiculous. You're my family, and that's what families do."

I didn't want to insult my friend, but nine-thousand dollars wouldn't be nearly enough to launch. "I'll figure something out. But thank you for the generous offer. It means the world to me that you would even consider doing that."

"You know what this calls for?"

"What?"

"Dom. I'm going to go get one of those expensive bottles of champagne we have left from that wedding."

"This calls for a celebration? Are we celebrating my loan decline, or the fact that my apartment is now a warehouse?"

Fisher kissed my forehead. "We're celebrating that this is all going to work out. Remember, if you don't think positive, positive things won't happen. I'll be right back."

While he disappeared to his apartment next door, I looked around. My living room was a total disaster, which felt appropriate right about now since my life matched it. One year ago, I'd been engaged to be married, had a great job making six figures, savings most twenty-seven-year-olds didn't accumulate until they were forty, and the dream of an exciting new business venture. Now my ex-fiancé was engaged to someone else, I was unemployed and broke, and my new exciting business felt more like a noose around my neck.

I stared down at the loan-denial letter on the table for a minute, then wadded it up into a ball and pitched it toward the kitchen garbage can. Of course, I missed. In a daze, I shuffled through my mail, which was mostly just advertisements, and then decided to open the ripped package that had come. I assumed it was yet more of the product samples I'd ordered before the bank closed my line of credit—product I'd now never be able to afford. But when I opened the box, it wasn't perfume-ingredient samples. Instead, it was a diary I'd ordered off eBay. I'd actually forgotten all about it since I'd won the auction almost three full months ago. Shipping from overseas could take forever, and this one had come from Italy.

Normally, when a new diary arrived, I could hardly wait to read the first chapter. But this one was just a reminder of two-hundred-and-forty-seven dollars I'd wasted. I set it down on the coffee table in the living room and decided to go wash up before Fisher returned with the champagne.

Ten minutes later, when I emerged from the bathroom, I found my best friend sprawled out on my couch, drinking bubbly and thumbing through the new diary.

"Uh...you know this woman didn't write in English, right?" Fisher held out a glass of champagne for me.

I took it and plopped down on the chair across from him. "It's Italian. And it's a man's. Which means I overpaid for it and still need to have it translated."

Men's diaries always went for a premium on auction sites because they were so rare. Last time I bought a French one, it cost me three-hundred dollars, plus a hundred-and-fifty bucks for a translator.

I sipped the champagne. "It'll be collecting dust for a while. Splurging for a translation isn't as high on my priority list as eating next month."

Fisher shook his head and tossed the beat-up, old diary on the coffee table. "I thought you quit reading them after what happened last year when you got too caught up in it."

I sighed. "I fell off the wagon."

"You're a strange bird, my Stella Bella. You know that?"

"This coming from a man who collects the stickers you peel off bananas on the inside of his coat closet door."

My cell phone started to ring in my pocket, so I slipped it out and read the name flashing on the screen. "Well, this is appropriate. It's the woman whose champagne we stole."

"Tell her to send more."

I laughed and swiped to answer. "Hello?"

"Hey, Stella. It's Olivia."

"Hey, Olivia. Thanks for calling me back. I wanted to let you know I have the perfumes done for your wedding party."

"I'm so excited to see them. Or smell them. Or see and smell them. Whatever."

I smiled. "I hope your friends like them."

"I told a few people about what you do, and they're all interested in having scents made. Do you know when your website will be up and running yet?"

I frowned. "Not in the foreseeable future, unfortunately."

"Oh no. What happened?"

"The SBA turned down my loan application. I just received the letter today."

"Idiots. I'm sorry."

"Thanks."

"What are you going to do?"

"I don't know."

"What about taking on a partner? Someone who comes with a cash infusion in exchange for an interest in the business."

I'd actually considered that, but no one I knew had much money. "Maybe. I'm going to give it some thought. Tonight I'll have a few drinks to forget. Tomorrow I'll start formulating a new game plan."

"Good. That's the right attitude."

"Thank you. So where do you want me to ship your perfumes?"

"I could meet you tomorrow, if you're free? My maid of honor is leaving in two days to go work in London for a few months. I'm meeting her for dinner tomorrow night. I'd love to give it to her then, if it's not too much trouble for me to pick them up."

"No, no problem at all."

"Okay! I have a meeting in the morning. Is it alright if I text you when that ends to let you know a time? I should be able to come to wherever you are."

"Sure, that's fine. Talk to you then."

After I hung up, Fisher said, "Only you would make friends with the woman whose wedding we crashed."

I shrugged. "Olivia's actually really great. I'm going to give her all the perfumes I made for her wedding party as an apology gift, rather than charge her. I figured it's the least I could do."

"See if she has any more parties we can crash." He held up the bottle of champagne before refilling his glass. "We can't go back to the cheap stuff after this." He sucked half a glass down and let out an exaggerated *aaah.* "By the way, I take it you haven't heard from Prince Charming or you would have said something?"

I frowned. "Nope. When I had lunch with Olivia, she didn't mention that she knew he'd asked me out. So

I didn't either. Though she did tell me he tended to hold a grudge."

"His loss."

I didn't say so, but it felt like a loss to me, too. Something about Hudson had gotten under my skin, and I'd been excited to go out with him. In fact, I couldn't remember the last time I'd anticipated a call from a man the way I had his. Which was why when he hadn't followed through, it had weighed on me a bit more than it should have. *But, oh well.* Ben was...nice.

Over the next two hours, Fisher and I polished off that bottle and a bottle of wine I'd had open in my fridge. At least one thing had gone right this week—I'd managed to get sufficiently loaded as intended. When I yawned, Fisher took the hint.

"Alright, I'll leave. You don't have to fake yawn to get rid of me."

"It wasn't fake."

"Sure, it wasn't."

He stood and took our glasses and the two empty bottles into the kitchen. When he came back, I was debating sleeping in the comfy chair where I was currently slouched.

Fisher leaned down and kissed my forehead. "I love you. Everything will be better tomorrow."

Considering I'd probably be waking with a headache, I doubted that. But I hated to be a Debbie Downer. "Thanks again for everything, Fisher. Love you, too."

He picked up the diary still sitting on the coffee table. "I'm taking this and having it translated for your birthday next month."

"Uh, I won't be twenty-eight for a long time. *Your* birthday is next month. Are you doing what you did last year?"

"Yes, all the treats are for you, because *you're* my best gift ever. Plus, making you happy makes me happy, Stella Bella. Just don't let this diary take over your life."

6

Stella

Fifteen years ago

I picked up a brown leather book and brought it to my nose for a sniff. *God, I love that smell.* It reminded me of Spencer Knox. He carried a football everywhere he went and always tossed it into the air and caught it while talking. Every time the calfskin smacked against his palms, the faint smell of leather wafted and made me smile.

The lady running the garage sale was older and had an orange fanny pack around her midriff. Her frizzy gray hair stuck out in all different directions, making me think she might've recently stuck her finger into a socket, instead of the plug of the lamp she was positioning on a folding table.

I walked over to her. "Excuse me. How much is this?"

She glanced down at my hands. "It's fifty cents. But I paid ten dollars for it fifteen years ago at someone else's garage sale. That's what happens when you buy crap you don't really need. You end up getting rid of it like the person before you did. You write in a diary?"

I hadn't actually noticed the word *Diary* embossed on the front cover until she pointed it out. I shook my head. "I've never had one before."

A thin woman wearing a sweater set with her hair slicked back into a neat ponytail walked up the driveway carrying a boxed coffee maker. "I'll give you five dollars for this."

The old lady pursed her lips. "Can you not read? The sticker says it's twenty."

"I'm only willing to pay five."

"Well, then you can walk your skinny little ass right back over to the table you got it from and put it back."

The sweater set woman gasped. "How rude."

The old lady grumbled something about the woman going back to her country club and returned her attention to me. "So, do you want that diary or not? I need to pay attention to the browsers. Some people don't think the prices at a garage sale are low enough, so they help themselves to a five-finger discount."

I'd been thinking I should offer twenty-five cents since she'd started out at fifty. My mom always said we should haggle at these sales. But this woman didn't seem like the negotiating type. Besides, I had the fifty cents, she'd paid ten dollars, and I was a little afraid of her. So I dug into my pocket and pulled out two quarters. "I'll take it."

A few days later, I went to my room after dinner and locked the door before digging out the diary. I didn't want my sister bursting in and finding out I was writing down the things on my mind. She'd most definitely try to read it when I wasn't home—*especially* if she knew the type of stuff on my mind lately.

Two days ago, Spencer had asked me to be his girlfriend. I'd had the biggest crush on him since fifth grade. Of course I'd said yes, even though my parents had told my sister she couldn't date until high school when she'd asked, and I was only in seventh grade. Before Spencer became my boyfriend, I'd never been nervous around boys. But now I was freaking out whenever he and I so much as talked. I knew the reason—he'd gone out with Kelly Reed before me, and they'd made out. I'd never kissed a boy before, and now I worried I might do it wrong when the time came. So I thought it might be a good first entry in my new diary. Maybe it would help me work out how I was going to handle things by putting my fears down on paper.

Lying on my stomach on my bed, I swung my feet in the air behind me as I chewed on the top of my pencil and decided how to start. *Do I just write* Dear Diary *or is that geek city?*

"Stella?" My father's voice and the sound of him attempting to turn my door handle startled me.

I jumped up, and the diary bounced off the bed, landing pages down on the floor. "Uh, who is it?"

"It's your father. What other man knocks on your bedroom door, and why is it locked?"

"Ummm...because I'm getting changed for bed."

"Oh. Alright. I was just popping in to say goodnight."

"'Night, Dad!"

"Goodnight, pipsqueak."

I listened for his footsteps to fade into the distance before I scooped the diary off the floor. Some of the pages in the middle had wrinkled, so I went to smooth them out. But when I turned the book over, I found words written on the pages. Lots of them. Confused, I read a few lines and then flipped a few pages back. My eyes widened as I read the top of one of the pages.

Dear Diary,

Oh my God!

I flipped back more pages. Two or three were filled with words, but then there was the same start.

Dear Diary,

Pages and pages were filled. How could I have not noticed? I could've sworn I'd opened it at the garage sale. But as I flipped to the beginning, I realized why I hadn't spotted all the blue ink. The first five or six pages of the diary were completely blank.

But whose diary was it? The woman said she'd bought it at a garage sale years ago. So had she not noticed either?

Maybe I should go back and return it.

Or give it to my mom and see what she thought I should do?

Though...

Maybe I could read a little first and see if it gave me any idea who the book belonged to.

I didn't have to read the entire thing.

Just one little entry.

That would be it.

I flipped through from the first page to make sure I was at the very beginning, and then scanned the two simple words on the first line.

Dear Diary...

Just one little entry.

It couldn't do any harm.

I had no idea then just how much those words would come back to haunt me.

Stella

"Hello?"

"Hi, Stella. It's Olivia."

I switched the phone to my other ear so I could finish putting on my earrings. "How are you, Olivia?"

"I'm good. But my day is a little busier than I'd thought. Do you think you might be able to come by my office today with the perfumes? I'm not sure where you live, but if downtown is a giant pain in the ass for you, I can send a car."

My apartment was on the Upper East Side, so getting downtown was actually pretty inconvenient. But I owed Olivia, so I wasn't about to complain. "That's fine. I have some errands to run downtown anyway."

"Oh, that's great. Thank you. Is around two o'clock okay?"

"Sure, that's perfect."

"Okay. I'll see you then."

It sounded like she was about to hang up. "Wait—I need the address."

"Oh, sorry. I thought you had it."

Why would I have her office address? Did she think I'd stalked her thoroughly before showing up at her wedding? Jesus, just when I'd started to get over being embarrassed. "No, I don't."

"It's Fifteen Broad Street. Fourteenth floor."

I shut my jewelry box. *Broad Street?* That's where Hudson's office was. "You work in the same building as your brother?"

"Oh, I assumed you knew. Hudson and I actually work together. Rothschild Investments was our father's business."

I hadn't known. And it shouldn't have made any difference, but I'd be lying if I said the thought of possibly running into Hudson didn't make my pulse race.

When I went quiet for a minute, Olivia wrongly assumed why.

"It's a pain in the ass to get to, isn't it? Let me send a car for you."

"No, no—it's absolutely fine. I'll see you at two."

"Are you sure?"

"I'm positive. But thank you."

After I hung up, I looked in the mirror above my dresser. I'd gotten out of the shower and put my wet hair into a ponytail. Suddenly I thought I might be in the mood to take it down and give it a nice blow-dry.

"Hey!" I stood from my seat in the reception area, and Olivia swamped me in a big hug. "Sorry to make you wait. I've had an awful morning."

I wished I looked as bright-eyed and chipper as she did having a bad day. "It's fine. I wasn't waiting long."

She waved toward the inner sanctum. "Come on back. Do you have to leave right away? I was hoping we could talk. I ordered us some salads in case you were hungry."

I still couldn't get over the turn of events—that the woman whose wedding I'd crashed wanted to be my friend. "Sure. I'd love that. Thanks."

I followed Olivia, turning left and then right. I knew from my visit to pick up my cell phone that the last door on the end of this hallway was Hudson's office. As we walked closer, my mouth grew dry. His door was open, so I attempted to sneak a look inside without getting caught. Disappointment set in as we passed, and I saw it was empty. But it was probably for the best. I'd wasted enough time on a man who hadn't called.

Olivia's office was located around the corner from her brother's. It was large and sleek, but not quite the proverbial corner office with the floor-to-ceiling windows looking down on the city like her brother had. Don't get me wrong, I'd be thrilled to sit in a closet in this building. But I found it interesting that his space made it appear he was higher on the corporate food chain when Olivia had said they worked together—not that she worked *for* her brother.

"I skipped breakfast. Do you mind if we eat before I take a look at the perfumes? I'm dying to get my hands on it, but I'm also diabetic and shouldn't skip meals."

"Sure, of course."

Olivia and I sat across from each other. I unfurled the cloth napkin that held the utensils and laid it across my lap.

"This looks great."

"I hope you like it. I ordered a chopped salad that had some of the same ingredients that were in your lunch the last time we got together. Just to be safe."

God, she was so thoughtful.

We dug into our salads. "So any better news about Signature Scent?" she asked.

I forced a smile, trying not to let on how miserable I was. "Not really. The launch is going to be more delayed than I'd hoped since the SBA loan fell through."

She frowned. "I'm sorry about that. I kind of thought it might not get approved when we talked at lunch. But I didn't want to say anything and jinx it. I've worked with them before, and they're not really as start-up friendly as they claim to be."

"Yeah. They basically said come back once you're up and running and have some sales history."

"Would you...consider taking on a private-equity investor? It's part of what we do here. Rothschild Investments is a wealth-management company. We offer typical money-management services, like managing stock-investment portfolios, but we also have a pool of investors who invest capital in exchange for a piece of a new or expanding company."

"So, you're selling a piece of your company to a bunch of different people?"

She nodded. "Yes, sort of. But you usually keep controlling interest. And since the investors have a vested interest in your success, they don't just hand you the check. They also provide management help, like using their buying power and other resources. Our venture-capital division has a whole team whose sole responsibility is to support the businesses they invest in."

"Hmmm... Would I even qualify for something like that? I've invested a ton of my own savings, but I don't have a steady income anymore. To be honest, I'm going to have to get a job soon if I don't start turning over some of the inventory I bought."

"Working with a VC is different than a bank. It's not based on an owner's income, but on the potential of the business itself. I could set you up with an appointment if you wanted to explore it as an option."

"Could I...think about it a bit and get back to you? It's very generous of you to even consider my business for such a thing. I just want to make sure it's the right decision for me."

"Of course. Absolutely."

Olivia and I finished our lunch, chatting away like old friends. After, I showed her all of the perfumes I'd made for her wedding party, and she literally squealed over each one. Her excitement was contagious, and as I got ready to leave her office, I felt more pumped than I had in weeks—at least since the bank had yanked my line of credit.

"Thank you for lunch, again, Olivia."

"Anytime. It was fun."

"And I'll get back to you as soon as possible on the private-equity investment possibility. Just out of curiosity, if I decided to try that route, what would be the first step?"

"You'd meet with the VC investment team and tell them about your business, do a little dog-and-pony show here at the office, and answer whatever questions they might have."

I nodded. "Okay. Thank you."

Olivia walked me back out to the reception area, and we hugged goodbye. "Let me know what you decide, and I can probably get you on the calendar for next week. I think Hudson is going out of town, but not until Thursday."

"Hudson?"

"Yeah. He's the head of the VC investment team. Didn't I mention that?"

No, you definitely did not.

"I asked around and heard nothing but stellar things about Rothschild Investments," Fisher reported.

I poured a glass of wine and sat down at the kitchen table across from him. He'd come straight over after work, so he still had on a suit and looked all dapper.

Two days had passed since I met with Olivia, and I still hadn't come to a decision on the possibility of selling part of my business to an investment group.

The law firm Fisher worked at had a corporate division that did a lot of work with IPOs and financing, even though Fisher worked in entertainment law. So after he educated me on the realities of working with a venture capitalist, he put out feelers to get some references for Olivia's family's company.

"Prince Charming has a reputation for being tough," he said.

I sipped my wine. "Well, I guess there's a reason Evelyn used to call him GQ Prick."

"But he also has a pretty damn impressive track record of success for the businesses they take on. It's something you may want to seriously consider."

I sighed. "I don't know."

"What's holding you back?"

"Selling a piece of my business before it even gets off the ground."

Fisher nodded. "I get it. I really do. But realistically, what's your alternative? It will take you years of going back to work full-time to save the type of money you need to launch the way you'd planned. And you said yourself that a lot of the inventory you have won't make it that long."

"I could save for a little while and launch at a much smaller scale."

"But then you'd be working full-time while trying to make a go of a business that needs your full attention."

My shoulders slumped. "I know."

"You were going to borrow from the bank, so technically they would've owned your ass until you paid them back anyway. I spoke to the partner in charge of the business division at my firm. He said venture capitalists don't want to own the businesses they invest in forever. They're in it to make a nice return and get out—on to the next one. They need to liquidate or they'd wind up just owning a bunch of companies and no longer have capital ready for the next big thing that comes along. The average venture capitalist has an exit plan to be out within seven to eight years. And you can negotiate a first right of refusal, so when the time comes for them to sell, you get first crack at buying their ownership back."

"Really?"

Fisher nodded. "A bank loan would take you that long or longer to pay off anyway."

He had a good point. The reasons to not go this route were quickly shrinking. Though I still couldn't imagine that the man who had called me out for crashing his sister's wedding, only to ask me out and not call, had any desire to go into business with me.

I sipped my wine and juggled my thoughts. Basically a venture capitalist was my only choice left. Of course, I'd found out there were thousands of them when I'd done some research on my own. I could give a shot to working with another firm. I was certain Rothschild Investments wasn't the only game in town with good references. But on the other hand, they had Olivia, who seemed almost as excited and passionate about my business as I did. That was a huge plus. Then there was Hudson. At this point, he went into the minus column. However, what was that old saying? Better the devil you know than the devil you don't—or something along those lines.

I took a deep breath and looked across the table at Fisher.

"What would you do?"

My cell phone sat in the middle of the table. He reached out and slid it over in front of me. "I'd make a call before your new friend changes her mind."

8

Hudson

"**W**hat the hell, Olivia?"

"Calm down. Calm down. This is why I didn't tell you until now. You overreact to things."

I tossed the file I'd been working on to the side of my desk. "I'm overreacting? A woman opens someone else's mail and crashes your wedding—a wedding that cost me a small fortune, I might add—and you want us to go into business with the loose cannon? I think it's more like you have a couple of screws loose than I'm blowing things out of proportion."

I left out that I'd asked said loose cannon out on a date. Luckily, it seemed Little Miss Wedding Crasher hadn't shared that tidbit either when she'd talked to my sister.

I shook my head, still digesting that my sister had invited Stella to present for the investment team. "No, Olivia. Just no."

"My God, Hudson. I remember when you weren't such a perfect person. If my memory serves me right,

Dad had to bail you out after you were arrested for breaking and entering once."

"I was seventeen and drunk and thought it was our house..."

My sister shrugged. "What about the time you blew up a porta potty on a construction site? The only reason you didn't get arrested that time is because Dad agreed to buy the contractor three new ones."

"I was also in high school. It was the Fourth of July, and Jack lit the M-80, not me."

"You know what your problem is?"

I sat back in my chair and sighed. "No, but I'm sure you're about to enlighten me."

"You're no fun anymore. Five years ago you would have laughed if someone had crashed a wedding you went to. Now you're uptight and bitter. Your divorce sucked the sense of humor right out of you!"

My jaw flexed. A woman I'd recently dated a few times had told me I didn't smile enough. I'd been polite and refrained from telling her she just wasn't very funny, but her comment had nagged at me. The week before, Charlie had drawn a picture of her family at school. Everyone was smiling—her, my ex-wife, the babysitter, even the damn dog—except for me. I was frowning.

I shook my head and picked up my pen. "Go away, Olivia."

"She's coming in to do her presentation for the team at two o'clock today. They can vote with, or without you."

I lifted my chin toward my office door. "Shut the door behind you."

"Evelyn." I nodded as I walked into the conference room.

Stella frowned, and my sister glared at me.

"What?" I shrugged.

"You damn well know her name."

I smirked and looked to Stella. "Ah, that's right. Evelyn is your alter ego, the one who commits crimes. Apparently Stella is an upstanding businesswoman I have yet to meet. Do you change in a telephone booth or something?"

Since they hadn't started yet, I took my usual seat at the head of the conference room table. I was curious to see how Stella would handle my jabs. She surprised me by walking over with her hand extended.

"Hi, Mr. Rothschild. I'm Stella Bardot. It's very nice to meet you. I appreciate the opportunity to present to you today."

I shook her hand and held her eyes. "Can't wait."

After telling myself I wasn't going to bother showing up for this meeting, I went to the front reception area a little before two o'clock. I'd gone to put some mail in the outgoing bin, but as I walked down the hall near the conference room, I caught a whiff of perfume and knew Stella had arrived. She smelled even better than I remembered. The scent brought back some other memories I didn't care to recall—her phenomenal smile, a spunky personality, and the way I couldn't take my eyes off the slight hint of a pulse I could see in her neck when she laughed. The woman made me feel like a vampire, I wanted to suck on it so badly.

Back in my office, I'd attempted to ignore what I knew was about to start in the conference room. But ten minutes later, I gave in, knowing I wouldn't get any work done anyway. Plus, I never missed a pitch meeting, and it was probably best that I kept an eye on my sister. Someone had to keep her bleeding heart from giving away the kitchen sink.

Stella returned to her seat. I could tell by the way she kept shifting in her chair and twisting her ring that she was nervous. Though she did her best to pretend she wasn't, which I respected. The VC investment team was comprised of three senior analysts, the director of marketing, Olivia, and myself. But I generally led the team and did most of the questioning.

From the other end of the table, my sister caught my eye and gave me what I knew was a warning look. She wanted to remind me to be on my best behavior.

"Why don't we get started, shall we?" I asked. Looking to my left, I gave Stella a curt nod. "The floor is yours, Ms. Bardot."

She took a deep breath, not unlike the way she'd steadied herself after taking the mic in front of the crowd at my sister's wedding—and not unlike the image I'd conjured up on more than one occasion over the last few weeks while in the shower...

Those gorgeous green eyes, full, pink lips, and innocent face—Stella Bardot was beautiful. There was no doubt about that. But it was the way she rose to a challenge, pushing through to say *screw you* at the end, that made me want to sink my teeth into her flawless, ivory skin.

Today her hair was up, pinned into some sort of a twist in the back, and she wore those thick, dark-rimmed glasses. I had the strongest urge to push her up against a stack of books, rip her hair down, and toss her glasses over my shoulder.

Mature, Rothschild. Very mature thoughts.

Not to mention professional, too.

Luckily, at least one person in the room seemed to have their head screwed on straight.

Stella cleared her throat. "I brought a few sample kits, a demo of the website, some details of what I've invested so far, and a report of the inventory on hand. It's probably best if I start with the sample kit."

I nodded once, but said nothing.

For the next half hour, I listened to her presentation. Surprisingly, for a woman who acted on impulse, her business planning had been well thought out. The website was professional, with good branding and simple navigation. Most of the time when new business owners came in, they'd get *the pretty* right, but hadn't given any thought to the importance of remarketing. But not Stella. She talked about metrics and follow-back advertisements, demonstrating that she was thinking long term instead of short. The amount of capital she'd invested was also impressive, though it made me wonder where she'd gotten that kind of cash.

"Does the business owe anyone money or have existing investors?" I asked.

"No. No debt at all. I had one partner who had invested funds, but I bought him out last year."

"So the two-hundred-and-twenty-five grand you've put into it so far... That came from...?"

"My savings."

I guess the skepticism showed on my face, because she added, "I made a hundred-and-ten thousand as the senior chemist in my last job. It took me six years of saving and turning the small office in my apartment into a bedroom and taking on roommates. But I put away almost half of my net income every year."

Impressed again, I nodded. Half the people who presented before us had gotten handouts from Mommy and Daddy, or owed a big chunk of money before they even got up and running. I had to give her credit for the perseverance it took to get this far. Though I wouldn't be giving her that credit aloud.

When Stella got to the demonstration part of her presentation, I could tell my sister was already familiar with everything. She basically acted like her sidekick, helping Stella sell the product. They seemed to jell really well, and one picked up where the other left off. Olivia added anecdotal comments about how much all of her friends loved their creations. At one point, the two of them were laughing, and I found myself watching Stella, focusing on the pulse in her neck. I couldn't seem to take my eyes off the damn thing. Olivia glanced over and gave me a funny look.

"So what do you think?" My sister asked after the presentation was over. "Isn't it an amazing product?"

A strong murmur went around the room, each of my staff nodding and giving some sort of praise. The marketing manager talked about the profitability of the perfume industry and how much beauty supplies sold in general. For the most part, I remained quiet, until my sister looked at me.

"Hudson? What do you think?"

"The concept is interesting enough. Though I'm not sold on the idea that rating some smelling samples and completing an online survey equates to consistently making a product the consumer will like."

"Well, I love mine," Olivia said. "And the seven women in my bridal party all went crazy over theirs."

Stella turned and looked at me. "Would you like to give it a test run yourself? Perhaps have a woman in your life try it out."

My sister snorted. "Should he have his cleaning lady or his six-year-old daughter test it out?"

I scowled at Olivia.

"Actually," Stella said, "he can try it out himself."

"I'm not really much of a perfume wearer. But thanks."

"I didn't mean you had to put it on. You know what smells you like and which ones you don't, right? If you go to the perfume counter at a store, you smell a bunch of samples until you find the one that appeals to you. Signature Scent just skips the unnecessary steps. If you go through the process, the scent I create for you should be appealing enough that you would've bought it in the store for a woman." She shrugged. "Men like perfume as much as women. They just don't spray it on themselves."

As much as I thought her presentation had gone well, and she had a good product and unique marketing, I wasn't sure she was a person I wanted to partner with. Something didn't sit right, even without considering the wedding fiasco, or that she seemed to be the star of my pathetically frequent showers lately. I just couldn't put my finger on what it was. Though my sister would drive me nuts if I didn't have a legitimate business reason to decline investing, so perhaps this sampling could be my out.

Standing, I buttoned my jacket. "Fine. Give me a kit, and we'll see how this pans out."

Olivia clapped her hands like it was already a done deal. I gave her a warning glare not to get her hopes up, which she, of course, ignored.

"I have a meeting to get to," I lied.

Stella stood. She motioned to the crap all over the table. "I'll put this sample box back together before I go and leave you a copy of the questions that will be up on the website."

"Sounds good."

As I went to walk out, Stella called after me. "Mr. Rothschild?"

I turned back to find her again extending her hand. "Thank you for your time. I really appreciate you considering this, especially with the way things started out between us."

I looked down at her hand and back to her face before shaking. "Good luck to you, *Evelyn*."

Stella

I couldn't get over the letter in my hands.

Ten days had passed since my presentation at Rothschild Investments. Like I'd promised, I'd left the sample kit behind for Hudson. The following day, Olivia had called to let me know she made sure he completed everything, and she messaged me over his ratings and completed survey. When the package arrived, I was floored to find it also included a ton of gorgeous graphics Olivia had gotten her marketing department to mock up. She'd even created a few catchy taglines I thought would be perfect on the outside of the custom boxes I still needed to have made.

I'd called to thank her, and we spent almost two hours on the phone talking about all of our ideas. We'd also talked a half a dozen times since then. Her excitement was palpable, but after the last few letdowns I'd suffered with my financing, I was trying not to get my hopes up again—though Olivia made it impossible.

When we'd spoken two days ago, she told me she'd received the perfume I'd created for Hudson. He'd been traveling for business, but she'd placed it on his chair and left him a note, so he'd see it as soon as he returned. Her husband's father had to have emergency heart surgery, so Olivia was leaving for California for a week, but she'd said she wanted to get together when she got back.

I'd honestly been lulled into thinking Rothschild Investments was a done deal, which was why the letter I'd just read for the second time still shocked me.

Dear Ms. Bardot,

Thank you very much for your interest in working with Rothschild Investments. While your product was impressive, we regretfully must advise you that we will not be able to extend an offer at this time. We wish you the best of luck in your future endeavors.

Sincerely yours,

Hudson Rothschild

Disappointment was an understatement for what I felt. *Again.*

Still shocked, I reread the letter once more. I didn't want to call Olivia and ask what had happened since she was dealing with her father-in-law's health. Besides, Hudson had been the one to sign the letter, and if I had to wait a full week until she got back, I'd climb the walls. So I decided to call Hudson directly. I needed to at least find out what had made them change their minds, because I knew for certain it wasn't the perfume I'd created for him.

My fingers shook as I punched in his number on my cell. The cheery receptionist answered on the first ring.

"Good afternoon. Rothschild Investments. How may I direct your call?"

"Hi. May I speak to Hudson Rothschild, please?"

"Let me put you through to see if he's available."

I held for a minute until a voice I recognized as Helena, his assistant, answered. I'd met her on the two occasions I'd visited the office. She'd been super friendly and loved the idea of Signature Scent.

"Hi, Helena. This is Stella Bardot. Is it possible to speak to Hudson?"

"Hi, Stella. He just came back from a meeting. I think he has a lull in his schedule, but let me double-check if he's available."

She came back on the line thirty seconds later. Her voice wasn't as upbeat.

"I'm...sorry, Stella. He's on another line. Can I have him call you back?"

Something told me he wasn't on the phone, and he'd told her to blow me off. But I was upset, so that could have just been my paranoia.

"Yes, of course."

I left her my business phone number and waited patiently. But no return call came. So the following afternoon, I called and again got Helena. This time when she told me Hudson was unavailable, I blew out a frustrated breath.

"Would you let him know I just need two minutes of his time? I'm sure he's very busy, but it won't take long."

"Sure, I'll let him know. Is everything okay?"

"Not really." I sighed. "I received the letter he sent me declining to invest in Signature Scent, and I wanted to ask him the reason. The letter didn't say, and if nothing else, I want to learn from it."

"Oh wow. I'm sorry. I wasn't aware."

That was interesting. I would've expected his assistant to be the one who'd typed it up. "I don't want to be a pain. I'd just like a few minutes of his time."

"I'll pass along the message. And I'm sorry it didn't work out, Stella. I was really looking forward to this one."

"Thanks, Helena."

That day, I tried to keep myself busy. But I checked my phone a dozen or more times. By six that evening, I'd all but given up hope—until my phone rang while I was out for a run. I wiped my hands on my shorts and answered, panting.

"Hello?"

"Hi, Stella. It's Helena."

"Hi, Helena."

"I'm sorry Hudson didn't call you back. He was, uh, busy today. I passed along your message, and he told me to let you know the reason he decided not to go forward with the investment was because he didn't care for the sample he received. It made him uncertain of the product, I guess."

"Oh, I see." That was complete bullshit. Because I'd made him the same scent I'd been wearing the night of Olivia's wedding. And he'd told me *twice* how good I smelled. A few weeks ago, I'd been ready to give up and accept putting everything on hold for a long time. But I no longer felt ready to accept defeat. All of my planning talks with Olivia had gotten me too pumped up to let it go so easily this time. I wanted to give it one last-ditch attempt since I knew he was lying about the reason.

"Do you think it would be possible to make an appointment to speak to Hudson in person?"

Helena's voice lowered. It sounded like she might be cupping the receiver so no one would hear. "I don't want to get in trouble, but I'll be honest, I think if I ask him, he's going to say no."

I sighed. "Okay, thanks, Helena. I get what you're saying."

"But...I've worked for Hudson for a long time now. His bark is much worse than his bite. Now, if you were to just show up... He might not have a choice. And he does respect people who fight hard for what they want."

I smiled sadly. "Thanks, Helena. I appreciate the advice. I'll give it some thought."

The next morning I arrived at Rothschild Investments at 8AM. "Hi. Is Hudson Rothschild in?"

The receptionist smiled. "He is. Do you have an appointment?"

I took a deep breath. "I don't. But I only need two minutes of his time. Would it be possible to get in to see him?"

"Let me see. What's your name, and what is this in reference to?"

"Stella Bardot, and it's in reference to Signature Scent."

She picked up the phone, and I listened to one side of the conversation.

"Hi, Mr. Rothschild. I have Stella Bardot here to see you regarding Signature Scent. She doesn't have an appoint—"

He'd definitely cut her off. I heard the boom of his deep voice through her headset, though I couldn't make out what he was saying. But when her face fell, I knew it wasn't a good sign.

"Umm...okay...would you like me to tell her that?" A pause and then she raised her eyes to meet mine. "Okay. Thank you."

She clicked a button on her keyboard and gave me a discouraging smile. "Mr. Rothschild said, 'If you have nothing better to do with your time, take a seat.' If he finds a spare two minutes in his busy day, he'll see you." She grimaced. "Sorry."

"It's fine—don't shoot the messenger and all."

She motioned to the waiting area. "Would you like me to get you some coffee while you wait?"

"No, thank you."

"Okay. I'm Ruby. If you change your mind, just let me know."

"Thanks, Ruby."

I sat down on the couch and took out my phone to catch up on emails. My instinct told me I was going to be sitting here for a while. I had a feeling Hudson would enjoy making me wait.

And I wasn't wrong.

Three hours later, the receptionist came out from behind the desk and walked over to me.

"I just wanted to let you know, I called back and reminded him, to make sure he hadn't forgotten you."

I smirked. "And how did that go?"

She laughed and looked over her shoulder to make sure no one was around. "He was sort of snippy."

"I bet. But it's okay." I waved to the glass coffee table in front of me. "At least you have all these great magazines."

By five o'clock, I figured he was going to make me stalk him on his way out of the office, just to be a jerk. While I'd debated leaving after the first hour or two this morning, I now had so much time invested, there was no way I was giving in. I popped in my earbuds, settled back into the couch, and turned on some classical music to relax. I was going to outlast Hudson if it killed me. But at 5:30, the receptionist came back over.

She frowned. "I'm getting ready to leave, so I called back to Mr. Rothschild again. He said to let you know it turned out he didn't have two minutes to spare today."

What a bastard. That had been his game plan all along—make me waste the entire day. Well, lucky for me, I had no job and no place to go. So rather than get upset, I decided to dig in. I stood and lifted my pocketbook to my shoulder.

"Could you let Mr. Rothschild know I'll be back again tomorrow? Perhaps he'll be able to spare the two minutes then."

The receptionist's eyebrows jumped, yet she smiled. "Sure thing."

The following day I came more prepared. I brought my laptop, some snacks, a charger for my cell, and my to-do list. When the morning went by again, and Hudson still couldn't find a couple of minutes to speak to me, at least I'd knocked off a bunch of things from my list and cleaned out my emails—two things that were long overdue.

In the afternoon, I updated my resume and uploaded more than a thousand pictures from my phone to a storage website and organized them. I then spent an hour and a half online planning a dream vacation I could never afford—picking out luxury hotels and a private, captained sailboat to get me between the Greek Islands I wanted to explore. Again at 5:30, the receptionist came over.

"Good news. I think..."

"Oh?"

"I just called back and told him I was leaving and you were still here." She shrugged. "He didn't tell me to ask you to leave."

I chuckled because I'd clearly lost my mind now. "So I should wait?"

She pointed to the glass doors. "He has to walk out that door sometime..."

I nodded. "Okay. Have a good night, Ruby."

"You, too, Stella. Hopefully I won't see you sitting here tomorrow."

I smiled. "I hope not, too."

By 6:45, I'd watched most of the staff at Rothschild Investments leave, and a cleaning crew walked in and started to vacuum around me. I'd taken a break from dream vacation planning to text with Fisher for a while. When I was done, I again opened my laptop and went back to vacay-planning mode. Mykonos was the last island I still needed to find the perfect hotel on. As I sifted through photos of the incredible scenery, trying to decide if I wanted to be on the north or south side of the island, I must've become engrossed in what I was doing.

Suddenly, a deep voice scared the crap out of me, and I jumped from my seat. My laptop went flying to the floor, and my hand flew to my chest. "You scared me to death."

Hudson shook his head. "I should've just walked out the door. You wouldn't have even noticed." He bent and picked up my laptop, which luckily was still illuminated and not broken. Looking at the screen, he said, "Going on a vacation to the Greek islands? Good business plan. Have fun at..." He squinted. "The Royal Myconian. Looks expensive."

I snatched my laptop from his hands. "I'm *dream* vacation planning, not actually going."

Though he didn't quite smile, I could've sworn the corner of his lip twitched. Hudson pushed up the sleeve of his suit jacket, revealing a big, chunky watch. While I felt like punching the arrogant bastard for making me sit here for two days, I couldn't help but notice how sexy the damn watch looked on his masculine wrist. Shaking my head, I tamped down that feeling.

"Two minutes," Hudson said, folding his arms across his chest. "Go."

For the next hundred-and-twenty seconds, I rambled on—telling him I wanted to know the real reason he'd decided to decline investing, because it couldn't possibly be that he didn't like the scent I'd created. I even told him it was the same one he'd told me *twice* that he liked—once at Olivia's wedding and then again at his office when I'd come to pick up my cell phone. Then, for some insane reason, I started going into detail about the samples he'd rated and the chemicals I'd used... Somehow my diatribe morphed into a science lesson. I don't think I took a breath or used any punctuation during the entire two minutes I speed-talked.

When I finally shut up, Hudson stared at me. "Are you finished?"

"I guess so."

He gave a curt nod. "Have a good evening." Then he turned and walked toward the door.

I blinked a few times, sure he couldn't possibly be just leaving. But when he got to the door and pushed it open, it became apparent that was exactly what the jerk was doing. So I yelled after him. "Where are you going? I've been waiting for two days to have this conversation."

With his hand on the door, he didn't look back as he spoke. "You asked for two minutes. I gave them to you. The cleaning people will lock up after you leave."

If any evening deserved wine, it was this one.

Fisher had worked late tonight, but he'd been the lucky recipient of my rant earlier while I angry-marched from Rothschild Investments to the subway station. So he knew what he was walking into when he let himself into my apartment.

"Honey, I'm home!"

He held a large bottle of merlot in one hand and a flower he'd definitely just ripped out of our neighboring building's planter in the other—the bottom still had a root and dirt dangling.

I forced my sullen face to attempt a smile. "Hey."

"I passed a mounted police officer whose horse didn't have as long of a face as you do." Fisher kissed me on the forehead and pointed to the flower. "What do you think? The red vase or the clear?"

I sighed overdramatically. "I think that thing needs dirt more than a vase."

Fisher tapped my nose with his pointer finger. "The red one it is." He went to the closet and took out a vase meant for a giant bouquet, not one sad flower, then filled it with water from the kitchen sink and stuck the stem in. "I think you should call Olivia."

I drank the wine already in my glass. "I don't want to bother her. And what's the point? She told me herself that Hudson was in charge of the division. Plus, she's already been so generous to me. I don't want to make her feel bad."

"I can't believe that jerk asked you for your phone number and never called, then made you sit there for two days. This guy must get off on making you wait around for him. And here I had this gut feeling you two were going to wind up banging."

I scoffed. "Me and Hudson? Are you crazy? The man obviously hates me."

Fisher tugged at the knot of his tie as he walked to the couch where I sat wallowing.

"I watched you two together at the wedding. Even when he screwed with you and made you give that speech, there was a sparkle in his eye. There was real chemistry there."

I finished off my wine. "Some chemistry leads to explosions. Trust me, I know."

"But why ask you out and then never call?"

I shook my head. "To get even. Same reason he left me sitting in the lobby."

For the next hour, Fisher and I drank wine. Because he was the bestest friend of all best friends, he let me repeat everything I'd told him on the phone earlier without complaining.

But the long day of sitting around and consuming too much alcohol eventually got to me, so when I yawned for a second time, he stood to go.

"I'll let you get some rest. You have two days. Today was for being pissed off and drinking. Tomorrow is for wallowing. Thursday, we get back on the horse and figure out where to go from here. We'll make this work."

I didn't want to be an even bigger downer and say I had no place left to go, except maybe the unemployment line. Fisher meant well. "Thanks for listening to me."

"Anytime, my princess." He leaned over and kissed my forehead before heading for the door. Grabbing his suit jacket from the kitchen, he said. "Almost forgot—you had mail in your box. You want it on the couch?"

"Nah. I'll look at it tomorrow."

He set it down on the kitchen counter. "Get some sleep, my Stella Bella."

"Goodnight, Fisher."

After he closed the door, I forced myself up and walked around my box-filled apartment, shutting off lights. In the kitchen, a thick manila envelope on the bottom of the mail pile caught my eye.

I know that logo...

But it can't be...

Since I didn't have my glasses on, I picked it up to eye it more closely.

Sure enough, the circle with the R entwined through it was exactly what I'd thought it was. What the hell would Rothschild Investments be sending me? Another *go screw yourself* letter? Maybe this time with an itemized bill for the food and drinks I'd had at Olivia's wedding, along with an invoice for Hudson's precious time?

I'd had enough torture for the day and probably should've just left it for the morning. But leaving well enough alone was never my forte. So I slipped my finger under the seal and sliced open the envelope. Inside was a cover letter written on the same letterhead as the one I'd received a few days ago. Underneath looked like a bunch of legal documents...Term Sheet, Investor's Rights Agreement, Stock Purchase Agreement...

What the hell is all this?

Grabbing my glasses, I shuffled back to the cover letter to read.

Dear Ms. Bardot,

After careful reconsideration, Rothschild Investments is delighted to extend an offer of investment to your company, Signature Scent, LLC. The proposed structure, amounts, and terms can be found in the Term Sheet. Kindly go through the enclosed literature discussing the details of our proposal. As our offer affects the voting rights and your ownership stake within your company, we strongly suggest you have your attorney review all documentation prior to signing.

We are pleased to invite you to be part of the Rothschild Investments family and look forward to bringing your innovative product to market.

Sincerely yours,

Hudson Rothschild

Was this some sort of joke? Could what I had said during the two minutes he'd allotted me this afternoon have changed his mind, and he'd messengered over this letter? But how would a messenger have gotten into my locked mailbox?

Still feeling like there had to be some sort of mistake, I reread the cover letter before sifting through the documents. It seemed like a legitimate offer. Granted, I didn't understand most of the legal mumbo jumbo, but it appeared that Rothschild Investments wanted to invest in Signature Scent in exchange for a forty-percent stake in the company. And the first line did say *re*consideration and not consideration. I just couldn't believe it. I'd actually changed his mind today? In the measly two minutes he'd allotted me before walking out?

I stood in the kitchen with my mouth hanging open—until I noticed the date on the top of the letter. It wasn't today. *It was dated three days ago.* Grabbing the envelope I'd dropped on the table, I scanned the postmark. Sure enough, it had been mailed three days ago.

Which meant...

Hudson had sent this out *before* he let me sit in the waiting room for two days.

What the hell?

10

Stella

What a difference a week can make.

Instead of sitting in the lobby of Rothschild Investments, waiting for a chance to see the king of the castle, I was introduced around the office as *"our newest Rothschild partner."* The 180-degree turnaround still made my head spin, but I wasn't about to waste any more time dwelling on it. I had a product to launch in just a few months.

Olivia had called me the morning after I received the offer package. She was still in California taking care of her father-in-law, but said she wanted to check in to make sure I was happy with the terms of the deal. I gently broached the subject of the decline letter I'd received, and she'd apologized, saying it was a mix-up. Yet for some reason, I didn't think that was the truth. My gut told me there was more to it than just the wrong form letter being sent. But she was excited to move forward, so I decided to follow her lead and focus on what was to come, not look backward.

"Stella, this is Marta. She's the accounting manager," Olivia said. "FYI, Marta drinks her coffee black and prefers the Kenya blend from the little shop down the block, rather than Starbucks. Trust me, there will come a time when you'll need to come to her with coffee in hand and your tail between your legs because you're about to beg to get something approved that's over budget."

Marta laughed and extended her hand. "It's nice to meet you, Stella. And trust me, if your product is half as amazing as Olivia says, you wouldn't have to beg." She winked. "Just bring perfume."

I smiled, but to be safe, I also jotted down Marta's coffee preference as Olivia and I moved on to the next department.

After Fisher had had someone from his office review all the legal documents for me, I'd signed on the dotted line, and a couple of days ago Olivia and I had met for lunch to discuss basic logistics. Her role was head of marketing, but Rothschild Investments would also provide an array of assistance in everything from web development to accounting as part of their newly acquired stake in my company. All of it would save me a ton of money I didn't have.

But the first step had been deciding where my new corporate office would be. Olivia said many partners chose to set up an office in the Rothschild Investments suite since they utilized so many of the staff and services there. Considering my previous corporate office had been the couch in my living room, surrounded by wall-to-wall boxes, I figured it might look more professional to meet with people here—at least until I could afford something of my own.

At the end of the introductory tour, Olivia brought me to an empty office and handed me a key. "This is your new home. The ladies' room is at the end of the hall. I had my assistant set you up with basic supplies, but let her know what else you might need. I have an eleven o'clock meeting I have to run to. Maybe we can have a late lunch at around one thirty?"

I nodded. "That would be great."

After Olivia disappeared, I took a seat behind my big, modern desk and breathed it all in. Not only had Signature Scent gotten more funding than it needed to launch, it got staffing, systems, and a fancy office address downtown that I could only have dreamed about otherwise. It felt surreal. Each person I'd met today seemed genuinely happy about our new partnership and excited to get to work. Everything was almost too good to be true. Which reminded me, there *was* at least one person here who was likely *not* over the moon about my presence.

When I'd passed Hudson's office during my tour, his door had been closed. But I knew he was either inside or had recently left, because I'd smelled his cologne. He and I were long overdue for a discussion, so after I went to the ladies' room, I took a detour down the hall that led to his office. This time the door was open. My pulse quickened as I approached. He stood with his back to the door, reaching for something on a shelf, when I knocked.

"Just leave it on my desk," he said without turning around.

I assumed he had been expecting someone else. "Hi, Hudson. It's Stella. I was hoping we could talk for a moment."

He turned and looked at me. God, had his eyes gotten more intensely blue since the last time I'd seen him? I immediately began twisting the ring I wore on my pointer finger, something I did when I was nervous. But I caught myself and stopped. I couldn't let Hudson intimidate me.

So even though my insides felt queasy, I jutted out my chin and stepped inside the doorway. "It won't take long."

Hudson folded his arms across his chest and leaned against the credenza, rather than taking his seat at his desk. "By all means, come on in. You've already interrupted me."

Clearly he was being sarcastic, but I took the opportunity anyway. With a deep breath, I closed his office door behind me. Hudson remained quiet, but his eyes watched my every step as I walked to his equally intimidating, oversized desk.

"Do you mind if I have a seat?"

He shrugged. "Sure, why not."

I parked myself in one of the two guest chairs and waited for him to join me. But he never budged. "Aren't you going to sit?"

His eyes glinted. "Nope. I'm fine standing."

I took a moment to gather my thoughts, but the smell of Hudson's cologne wafted through the air. Did he have to smell so damn good? I found it very distracting. When I caught myself once again reaching for my ring to twist, I grabbed the arms of the chair to occupy my hands.

"Olivia said the decline letter I received was sent in error. Is that true?"

Hudson's eyes dropped to my hands white-knuckling the chair before meeting mine. "Does it matter? You're here."

"It matters to me. I've worked on my business for five years and put my heart and soul into it. Rothschild Investments is now a part owner, and I would prefer to clear the air of whatever issues are standing in the way so things can go as smoothly as possible."

Hudson rubbed his bottom lip with his thumb while he seemed to consider my words. Eventually, he said, "No."

My forehead wrinkled. "No what? You don't want to clear the air?"

"You asked if the first letter was sent in error. It wasn't."

That's what I'd suspected, yet it still hurt to hear. "So what made you change your mind?"

"My sister. She's a pain in my ass when she sinks her teeth in."

That made me smile. I really adored Olivia. "Did you not want to be in business with me because of my product or because of me?"

Hudson searched my face before answering. "Because of you."

I frowned, but appreciated his candor. As long as he was being real, I figured I'd keep going. "The date on the offer letter was the day before the first day I sat in the lobby waiting to see you. Yet you left me sitting there for two full days. Why?"

The corner of his lip gave the slightest twitch. "You asked for two minutes. I was busy."

"But you could've just told the receptionist to let me know you'd changed your mind, and an offer was in the mail."

This time, he couldn't contain the smirk. "Yes, I could've."

I squinted at him, which made him chuckle. "If that's your intimidating face, you might want to work on that."

His smile was dangerous. It made me feel a little breathless. Yet I straightened my back in my chair. "Are we going to have a problem working together? Olivia said you're pretty involved with all the start-ups."

Hudson again considered me. "Not if you're a hard worker."

"I am."

"I guess we'll see about that."

The intercom on Hudson's desk buzzed before the receptionist's voice came over the speaker. "Mr. Rothschild?"

His eyes never left mine as he responded. "Yes?"

"Your eleven-thirty appointment has arrived."

"Tell Dan I'll be with him shortly."

"Will do."

She buzzed off, and Hudson tilted his head. "Was there anything else?"

"No, I guess that's it."

As I stood and turned to walk out, he spoke again. "Actually, I have one more thing."

"Okay..."

He folded his arms across his chest. "As Olivia mentioned, I'm pretty involved with the launches of the new businesses we invest in. So you should probably give Helena your real cell phone number on your way out—just in case I need to reach you."

"What do you mean my real number? I gave it to you the day I came to pick up my phone."

His mouth formed a grim line. "The number you gave me was for Vinny's Pizza."

"What? No, it wasn't."

"It was. I called."

"You must've written it down wrong. I did not give you the wrong number."

"You typed it into my phone."

I wracked my brain, trying to remember that afternoon. Hadn't he written down my number? Then it hit me—he'd asked for my number and immediately after, his assistant had buzzed into the office. While they spoke, he'd reached into his pocket and handed me his cell. *Oh my God.*

"Can I see your phone?" I asked.

Hudson was quiet a minute. Eventually he reached down to his desk and picked up his cell. I felt him watch me as I typed my name into his contacts and read the number I'd entered. My eyes went wide. The last digit of my number was a nine, yet I'd typed a six—the digit above the nine on the keypad.

I looked up at him. "I typed in the wrong number."

His face was perfectly impassive. "I'm aware."

"But I didn't mean to."

He said nothing.

My brain seemed to be in slow motion as I processed what this meant. "So...the reason you didn't call me was because you thought I had intentionally given you the wrong number? But your sister called me. She was able to find my business number."

"I'm not in the habit of stalking women who give me a wrong number when I ask them out."

"I would never do that."

We stared at each other. It was like the missing puzzle pieces had finally clicked into place. "And that's why you enjoyed leaving me to sit out in the waiting room for two days. You thought I'd blown you off, and you were blowing me off in return." I shook my head. "But I still don't understand. What made you change your mind about investing?"

Hudson did that scratching-his-chin thing he often seemed to do. "My sister's very passionate about your business. She's had a rough time at work since our father died. When I stripped everything else away, your business is one I would've been interested in under different circumstances. I figured it wasn't fair to hold the fact that you blew me off against you and disappoint Olivia."

"But I didn't blow you off. I was disappointed when you didn't call."

Hudson looked down at my feet. I got the feeling he was as uncertain about what to do with this new information as I was. Again the phone on his desk buzzed.

"Yes, Helena?" he said.

"You have Esme on line one."

He sighed. "I'll take it. Just tell her I'll be one minute, please."

"Okay. And I'll grab Dan some coffee and put him in the conference room. I'll let him know you'll be a few more minutes."

"Thank you, Helena."

Hudson finally lifted his gaze, but he did so by working his way slowly up from my toes. By the time our eyes met, my body was tingling all over. The devilish hint of a smirk on his face didn't make things any better. "So you were saying...you were disappointed I didn't call?"

I swallowed, feeling a bit like a deer caught in the headlights. "Ummm..."

Hudson's ghost of a smirk turned to a full-blown grin. "Esme is my grandmother, so I have to take this call. To be continued?"

I nodded slowly. "Umm...yeah...sure."

I turned and headed for the door. But before I could open it, Hudson's voice stopped me. "Stella?"

"Yes?"

"I gave the perfume you made for me to my grandmother. She'd like more."

I smiled. "No problem."

Later that night, the cleaning crew knocked on my office door to ask if they could come in and empty my garbage can.

"Oh. Of course." I wouldn't have guessed it was time for them already, but I'd gotten engrossed in typing up my vendor list and making notes on which products I bought from who and the terms. It was definitely going to be a task to move all of the knowledge from where I currently kept it—in my head—to the different systems Rothschild Investments offered. But in the end, I knew it would be for the best. I picked up my cell and was shocked to find it was already 6:30. I'd looked at the time after Olivia said goodnight, and it had been a little before five o'clock. That felt like only ten minutes ago.

A smiling older woman dumped the contents of my wastepaper basket into a bigger garbage can in the hall and came back in carrying a vacuum. "Would you mind? It will take less than five minutes."

"Oh, not at all. I need to stretch my legs and use the ladies' room anyway." I shut my laptop and made my way down to the bathroom. As I approached, I found Hudson leaning against the wall right next to the door, looking down at his cell phone.

"Waiting to jump out and scare someone when they exit the ladies' room?" I teased.

He frowned and pointed to the door. "Are you going in there?"

"I was about to." My brows drew together. "Is there a reason I shouldn't?"

He pushed off the wall and dragged a hand through his hair. "My daughter's in there—Charlie. She gets lost in a bathroom, says she likes the *clue sticks*."

"Clue sticks?"

"Acoustics. I correct her, but she says it sounds better her way."

I chuckled. "Do you want me to hurry her along?"

He looked at his watch. "I have an important call with an investor overseas at six thirty."

"Go. I'll make sure she's okay and walk her back to your office."

"You sure?"

"Of course. No problem."

Hudson still looked hesitant.

I rolled my eyes. "I crashed a wedding once, but I promise I won't lose her."

He blew out a deep breath. "Okay, thanks."

Walking into the bathroom, I was absolutely curious. Charlie was nowhere to be seen, but one thing quickly became apparent—why she was concerned about the *clue sticks*. The sweetest little voice was singing... Was that "Jolene"? The old Dolly Parton song? Why yes, yes, it was. And little Charlie seemed to know all the words.

I noticed her little legs swinging underneath the first bathroom stall. I stood quietly, listening with the biggest smile on my face. She really could sing. Her voice was tiny, but by the size of her legs, I suspected it fit the body. Yet she sang on key and put in a vibrato that didn't usually come out of a little girl.

When the song ended, I didn't want to be standing there staring and scare her, so I gently knocked on the stall door.

"Charlie?"

"Yes?"

"Hi. My name is Stella. Your dad asked me to walk you back to his office when you're done in here. I'm just going to go to the bathroom. But don't leave without me."

"Okay."

I went into the stall beside hers and started to relieve myself.

Mid-pee, Charlie said, "Stella?"

"Yes?"

"Do you like Dolly?"

I stifled my laugh. "I do."

"Do you have a favorite song?"

"Hmmm. I do, actually. I don't know if it's a very popular one, but my grandmother lived in Tennessee and the song 'My Tennessee Mountain Home' always reminded me of her. So I'd have to say that's probably my favorite."

"I don't know that one. But my dad's is 'It's All Wrong, But It's All Right'. He won't let me sing that one, because he says the words are too old for me. But I memorized them anyway. You want to hear it?"

I most certainly did—even more so now that she'd told me her father said she couldn't sing it. But I stopped myself from telling her to belt it out. The last thing I needed was Hudson thinking I'd corrupted his kid.

"Hmmm... As much as I'd love to hear it, we should probably mind your dad."

The sound of the toilet flushing was her response, so I hurried and finished up so she couldn't run out of the bathroom without me.

Charlie was at the sinks washing her hands when I emerged from the stall. She was absolutely freaking adorable with sandy-blond curly hair that looked like it wasn't easy to tame, a button nose, and big brown eyes. She wore purple from head to toe, including tights, sneakers, skirt, and T-shirt. Something told me Charlie picked out her own clothes.

"Are you Stella?" she asked.

Again, I had to rein in my laugh. We were the only two in the bathroom. "I am. And you must be Charlie."

She nodded and watched me behind her in the mirror. "You're pretty."

"Why, thank you. That's very sweet. You're beautiful yourself."

She smiled.

I walked over to the sink next to her to wash up. "Do you take singing lessons, Charlie? Your voice is really amazing."

She nodded. "I go on Saturday mornings at nine thirty. My dad picks me up to take me because my mom needs her beauty sleep."

I smiled. This kid was hysterical and had no clue. "Oh, that's nice."

"I also take karate. Mom wanted me to take ballet, but I didn't want to. Dad took me to sign up for karate lessons without telling her, and she wasn't very happy."

I laughed. "I bet."

"Do you work with my daddy?"

"I do, actually."

"Do you want to come to dinner with us? We're taking the subway."

"Oh, thank you, but I still have some work to do."

She shrugged. "Maybe next time."

I could not stop smiling at everything that came out of this little girl's mouth. "Maybe."

We both dried our hands, and then I walked her to her dad's office. Hudson was still on the phone, so I asked her if she wanted to come see where I sat. When she nodded, I gestured to let Hudson know I was taking her down to my office.

Charlie plopped herself on a guest chair, with her feet dangling and swinging. "You don't have any pictures?"

"That's because today is my first day. I haven't had a chance to decorate yet."

She looked around. "You should paint your office purple."

I laughed. "Not sure that would go over so well with your father."

"He let me paint my room purple." Charlie sniffed a few times. "Your office smells good."

"Thank you. I'm actually a perfumist. I make perfumes."

"You *make* perfumes?"

"Yup. It's kind of a cool job, isn't it?"

She nodded fast. "How do you do it?"

"Well, it's a lot of science, actually. But what your dad and I are working on together is making a perfume based on how much people like a bunch of different smells. Would you like to try out some of my samples?"

"Yes!"

I'd brought a few sample kits with me today, so I grabbed one from my desk drawer and sat next to her on a guest chair. Opening the box, I took out one of the smelling jars and offered it to her. It was calone, which told me if a person had a penchant for a sea-breeze-type smell.

"What does this smell remind you of?"

Her eyes lit up. "Mmm...chocolate-banana ice cream."

My brows knitted, and I lifted the jar to smell it myself, even though I'd smelled the ocean the second I twisted off the cap. "That smells like ice cream to you?"

"No. But Dad took me to the beach last week, and afterward we got ice cream on the boardwalk. I got a banana split because that's my favorite. That smells like the beach, but now the beach just makes me think of that yummy ice cream."

I had asked her what the scent reminded her of and not what it smelled like. So her answer was right. I picked up the banana that had been sitting on my desk all day. "You're a banana fan, too, huh? You want to share this one?"

"No, thank you." She swung her legs. "My dad writes on my bananas when he packs my lunch. Sometimes oranges and tangerines, too. But never apples because those you don't peel the skin off of."

"He writes on your fruit?"

She nodded.

"What does he write?"

"Silly stuff. Like '*Orange* you glad it's Friday?' Sometimes he writes a joke. On Halloween he wrote 'What is a ghost's favorite fruit? A boo-nana.' Get it?"

I found that very interesting. I wouldn't have envisioned Hudson doing something goofy like that.

"Can I smell some more?" Charlie asked.

"Of course."

I opened another jar. This one smelled like sandalwood—oil from the Indian sandal tree.

She scrunched up her little nose. "That smells like a bellyache."

I had no idea what that meant. I brought it to my nose to try to figure it out. "Really? Does it make your belly hurt just by smelling it?"

She giggled. "No. Sour ice cream does. That smells like the man at the ice cream store around the corner from my dad. We don't go there anymore because the ice cream might have been bad."

Ohhh, well, that made more sense. Sandalwood was in a lot of popular men's colognes. Charlie had a knack for this. She was also apparently really into ice cream. "You know..." I said. "That's the second answer you've mentioned with ice cream. I'm sensing a pattern."

A deep voice from behind me chimed in, "Figured that out already, huh?"

I turned to find Hudson leaning against the doorframe to my office. It looked like he might have been eavesdropping for a while.

"Charlie here has a great sense of smell."

Hudson nodded. "She also hears things from a mile away, *especially* the freezer door. If I so much as crack it open, she comes running, thinking ice cream might be involved."

Charlie scrunched up her nose again. "He likes strawberry ice cream."

"I take it you don't?" I asked.

She shook her head. "It's gross. All lumpy."

"I'll have to side with your dad on this one. Strawberry is one of my favorites."

Hudson smiled, and I realized it might've been the first genuine smile I'd seen on his handsome face since the night of the wedding.

"You ready to go, Charlie?" He looked over at me. "We're going to dinner."

"I know. You're taking the subway."

Hudson's lip twitched. "The subway, Dolly Parton, and ice cream. She's not hard to please...yet."

"And notes written on fruit and the color purple." I motioned to my office. "Charlie suggested I paint my office purple. I told her I'd think about it."

Hudson smiled. "I wouldn't put it past you."

Charlie surprised me by jumping out of her chair to give me a hug. "Thank you for showing me your smelly things."

"You're welcome, sweetheart. Enjoy your dinner."

She skipped across my office and grabbed her father's hand. "Let's go, Dad."

He shook his head like her being the boss of him was a bother, but I could tell she was probably the only person in the world he enjoyed being bossed by.

Nodding at me, he said, "Don't stay too late."

"I won't."

After they disappeared, I could hear Charlie talking all the way down the hall.

"Stella's going to come to dinner with us next time," she said.

"Charlie, what did I tell you about inviting people you just met to things?"

"Doesn't she smell good?"

There was a pause, and I thought maybe they'd gone so far that I couldn't hear them anymore. But then Hudson grumbled, "Yes, Stella smells good."

"And she's pretty, too, right?"

Again there was a long pause. I moved closer to my door so I could be sure to hear the answer.

"Yes, she's pretty, but that's not how you decide who to invite to dinner, Charlie. We work together."

"But last month when Mommy dropped me off early at your house on Saturday morning there was a woman there, and she was pretty and smelled good. You'd said she was someone you had business with, and she'd come back in the morning because she'd forgotten her umbrella. I asked if she could come to lunch with us, and you said another time. But you never brought her."

Oh boy. I put my hand over my mouth. That Charlie was a whip, and I was curious how Hudson was going to talk his way out of this one. Unfortunately, instead of hearing his answer, I heard the lobby door open and close, and that was the end of the show.

I sighed and walked back to my desk—where it quickly became apparent that I could no longer concentrate. Today had been a whirlwind. Being introduced to so many people here at Rothschild Investments, a half dozen different meetings, new systems for accounting, inventory, orders, and an all-new, high-speed website interface. It was pretty overwhelming. But none of it was half as exciting as three little words Hudson had said earlier today.

"To be continued…"

Stella

I might've been a bit overeager the next morning.

Olivia had told me to meet her in the office at 8AM so we could start working with her team on the Signature Scent marketing plan. Yet the sun was barely up when I arrived at the offices of Rothschild Investments. Since I was so early, I went a few doors down to a twenty-four-hour deli and figured I'd get a cup of coffee and a muffin. Apparently, I wasn't the only one who'd gotten a head start on today. The line was ten deep with suit-clad men and women, every one of them with their noses buried in their phones as they waited.

When I finally arrived at the register, a kid who looked like he should be getting ready for high school instead of working took my order.

"What can I get you?" As he spoke, he took out his phone and stared down at it. I thought perhaps he had to type my order in for someone else to make it in the back.

"I'll have a coffee, light and sweet, and one of those crumb-cake muffins, please."

He held up one finger and texted into his phone. When he was done, he punched something into the register. "One coffee, light and sweet, and one blueberry muffin. That'll be six seventy-five. What's your name?"

"Well, my name is Stella, but I wanted a crumb-cake muffin, not a blueberry muffin."

The kid frowned as if I were annoying him. He hit some more buttons on the register, but then his phone buzzed, so his attention shifted there again. I took a ten out of my wallet and extended it to him, but he ignored my waiting hand. When a solid two minutes had passed and he still hadn't looked up from his phone, I leaned in and peered over at what he was doing.

Texting.

The kid wasn't putting my order in on his phone, he was texting someone named Kiara.

I flicked my wrist in an attempt to catch his eye. "Umm... Here you go."

Again, he held up a finger.

Unbelievable.

Eventually, he plucked the bill out of my hand and gave me change. Then he picked up a tall coffee cup, opened a marker, and scribbled a name on it. *Simone.*

My brows drew together. "Is that supposed to be mine?"

He huffed. "It's got your name on it, doesn't it?"

Rather than argue, I smiled. "Sure. You have a wonderful day."

"Next!"

I assumed that was his way of asking me to step aside so he could take the next customer.

A few people were milling around at the other end of the counter, so I went to join them and proceeded to do what everyone else was doing: look down at my cell phone. Fisher had texted a few minutes ago.

Fisher: Good luck working on the marketing today. I know that's your favorite part!

I texted back.

Stella: Thank you! I'm nervous but excited.

He then sent me a picture of a man from the newest dating site he'd joined. The guy wore only a pair of tight, gray boxers. His smile was nice, and he had good hair. But when I panned down to the rest of him, my eyes bulged. Now I knew why he'd sent it to me. Another text arrived underneath.

Fisher: You told me to stop picking men by their abs and look for a genuine smile. That thing is definitely smiling. ;)

Stella: That can't be real...

I lifted my phone closer and zoomed in on the bulge. No way was that all him. The guy had to have a banana stuffed in there somewhere. No, forget that, it was definitely a zucchini. Did penises even come in that size? Surely none that I'd ever seen.

A deep voice over my shoulder startled me.

"And to think I start my morning off by browsing *The Wall Street Journal...*"

I jumped, and my cell phone tumbled from my hands, hitting the floor. I bent to scoop it up and scowled. "Oh my God, why would you sneak up on me like that?"

Hudson chuckled. "How could I pass up interrupting when you're watching porn?"

"I'm not watching porn." I felt my face redden. "My friend sent me a picture of a guy from a dating site."

He looked skeptical. "Uh-huh."

Embarrassed, I tried to convince him it was the truth by holding up the phone to show him—only to realize I'd been zooming in on the guy's dick. "No, really..."

Hudson held up his hand to block the view. "I'll take your word for it. Thanks. But I'm glad to see you and your friend are both focusing on the important qualities in a man."

I shook my head. *Awesome.* I kept making one good impression after another with this guy. I sighed in defeat.

"Simone!" the barista yelled.

I heard him, but it didn't click at first.

"Simone!"

Shoot—that was me. I stepped up to the counter and retrieved my coffee and muffin. Hudson was shaking his head when I returned to where he stood.

"What?" I asked.

"A new alias?"

"The kid who took my order wasn't listening when I said my name."

Hudson gave a skeptical nod. "Right."

"No, really."

He shrugged. "What reason would I have to not believe you?"

I rolled my eyes.

"Hudson!" The barista yelled.

Hudson smirked. "He seems capable of getting *my* name right." After he grabbed his coffee, he nodded toward the door. "You heading to the office?"

"Yeah."

We walked out of the store and down the street side by side.

"Your daughter is absolutely adorable," I said. "She cracked me up without even trying yesterday."

Hudson shook his head. "Thank you. She's six going on twenty-six and has no filter."

"She sings beautifully, too."

"Let me guess, Dolly while sitting on the toilet?"

I laughed. "'Jolene'. I take it this is a frequent occurrence?"

"The toilet and the bathtub are her preferred performance venues."

"Ah," I said. "That's probably because of the great *clue sticks*."

Hudson smiled unguardedly. "Indeed."

A homeless woman sat in front of the building next to ours. She had a shopping cart full of cans and bottles and was rolling change from a plastic cup into paper coin wrappers. At our building, Hudson opened the door for me.

"Can you..." I dug into my purse. "Hang on one second."

I left Hudson holding the door open and walked back to the woman. Extending my hand with what I could offer, I said, "I'm sort of broke, too. But I want you to have this."

She smiled. "Thank you."

When I returned to Hudson, his forehead was wrinkled. "Did you give her money?"

I shook my head. "I gave her my Hershey bar."

He looked at me funny, but nodded before pushing the button for the elevator.

"So are you a big country-music fan?" I asked. "Is that where your daughter gets her love of Dolly?"

"Nope. And neither is my ex-wife or anyone else we know. She just heard one of Dolly's songs on the radio in the car once and liked it. She started singing the parts she could remember at home and then took it upon herself to ask her singing teacher to teach her the full song. Now it's the only artist she sings. She knows a dozen Dolly songs by heart."

"That's awesome."

"Last year for Halloween, when all the other little girls wanted to be Disney princesses, Charlie wanted her mother to stuff socks in her shirt and buy her a platinum wig."

"Wow, going platinum and stuffing. It's like she's thirteen already."

Hudson groaned. "I don't even want to think about that."

We got into the elevator together to ride up to the offices. The minute the doors slid closed, a familiar smell invaded my nose. Instinctively, I leaned toward him to get a better whiff.

Hudson raised a single brow. "What are you doing?"

"You have a smell on you that isn't cologne, body wash, or shampoo. I'm trying to identify it." *Sniff. Sniff.* "I know it. I just can't place it."

"I'm guessing you're the type of person who has an incessant need to know the answer to a problem. Will it drive you crazy if you don't?"

I sniffed again. "It absolutely will."

The elevator dinged, indicating our arrival on the fourteenth floor. Hudson held out his hand for me to exit first and then unlocked the door to the office. Once we were inside, he walked around the empty reception desk and flicked a bunch of switches to turn the lights on.

I waited on the other side. "So what's the smell? Some kind of a lotion, maybe?"

Hudson smirked. "Nope." He turned and began walking into the back with long strides.

"Wait... Where are you going?"

He spoke without turning. "To my office to work. You should try doing the same."

"But you didn't tell me what the smell is."

I heard him chuckle as he continued to walk. "Have a good day, Simone."

Olivia and I spent the morning going over some initial advertising plans, but her marketing manager really wanted to see how things worked in action. So I took them over to the lab that would be producing the perfumes and brought along a sample kit to show them the process each order would go through. I loved how excited they were to learn more about the product.

After we'd finished, Olivia had to go to a meeting, and the marketing manager was heading to meet a friend for a late lunch, so I stuck around the lab for a while before grabbing a train back to the office.

Hudson's door was open as I passed, so I knocked.

He looked up from a stack of papers, and I held up a box. "More of the perfume your grandmother liked."

Hudson tossed his pen on the desk. "Thank you. Are you sticking around late again tonight?"

I nodded. "I have a lot to do. Your team is full speed ahead, and they've given me a ton to review already."

"I've been going over your inventory and suppliers and have some ideas I'd like to run by you."

"Sure. That'd be great. When do you want to do it?"

He motioned to the piles of papers on his desk. "I need a little time to finish up. How about six?"

"Sounds good."

"Stella?" Hudson called as I turned to go.

"Yes?"

He motioned with his chin toward the box in my hand. "You forgot to give me the perfume."

I smiled. "Oh. No, I didn't. You'll get it when you tell me what the smell was this morning."

He shook his head with a smile. "Bring it to the conference room at six."

A little after five, Hudson's assistant called to ask if I liked Chinese food. Apparently Hudson and I were having a working dinner. I was definitely intrigued about spending some time alone with him. This would be my chance to correct my first—and second and third—impression and show him I wasn't actually flighty.

At six on the nose, I went into the conference room, armed with a giant file of inventory data, a notebook, and the perfume I'd made. Hudson was already inside with papers spread out, and cartons of Chinese food sat in the middle of the table, along with plates and utensils.

"You ordered garlic chicken, huh?"

Hudson shook his head. "How the hell do you do that? I haven't even opened the container."

I smiled. "Cardboard can't contain garlic."

Hudson was seated at the head of the table, so I settled into a chair on his left. "Plus, I was going back and forth between garlic chicken and what I ordered, so I had garlic chicken on my mind."

"What did you order?"

"Shrimp with broccoli."

"We can share if you want."

"Okay. Are we eating first or after?"

"Definitely first," he said. "I didn't eat lunch, so I'm starving."

Hudson and I dished food onto our plates. He lifted his chin to the perfume box and said, "Baseball glove oil. Now pass that over, smartass."

I smiled. "You play baseball at six in the morning?"

"No, but Charlie wants to join a peewee softball team. She only wanted the one purple glove they had at the store. Of course it's a piece of crap. So I've been trying to make it softer by massaging oil into it so she can at least open the damn thing with her little hand."

"Ah." I nodded and pushed the box of perfume over to him. "Lanolin. I don't know how I didn't identify it."

"Perhaps you should stick to gin."

Hudson winked, and I felt a little flutter in my belly. God, I was pathetic. Why couldn't a simple wink from Ben get me all hot and bothered? We'd had two dates and...nothing yet.

I popped a shrimp into my mouth. "Can I ask you something?"

"Would it stop you if I said no?"

I smiled. "Probably not."

He chuckled. "No wonder you and my sister get along so well. What's your question?"

"When exactly did you figure out I wasn't who I said I was at Olivia's wedding?"

"When you told me your last name was Whitley. Evelyn Whitley and my sister had been friends since high school. She was also close to my ex-wife for a while. The three of them travel in the same social circle. I suppose there could've been two women named Evelyn Whitley, but once you told me you'd worked at Rothschild Investments, it obviously confirmed my suspicions."

I nibbled on my bottom lip. "So before that...when we danced that first time, you had no idea?"

Hudson shook his head. "No clue."

"Yet you asked me to dance?"

A hint of a smile threatened at the corner of his lips. "I did indeed."

My heart sped up. "Why?"

"Why did I ask you to dance?"

I nodded.

Hudson's eyes dropped to my lips and lingered for a few seconds. "Because I thought you were interesting."

"Oh...okay."

He leaned close and lowered his voice. "And beautiful. I thought you were interesting and a knockout."

My cheeks flushed. "Thank you."

Hudson kept staring at me. I'd practically dragged the compliments out of the man, yet my face was beaming red.

He drummed his fingers on the table. "Anything else?"

"No."

He grinned. "You're sure?"

I nodded. But once again, after a minute of mulling things over, I changed my mind. "Actually..."

"Let me guess. One more question?"

"When I came to your office to pick up my cell, you asked me out to dinner, but I sort of got this weird feeling you were pissed off at yourself that you asked."

He tilted his head. "You're very perceptive."

I bit my lip, debating my next question. But I *really* wanted to know the answer.

"Would we have gone out if I hadn't accidentally given you the wrong number?"

The corner of Hudson's lip twitched again. "I called, didn't I?"

"Oh...yeah. Well, I guess everything worked out for the best anyway. We'll be working closely together and wouldn't want to muddy the waters."

Hudson's eyes flickered down to my lips again. "So if I asked you out right now, you would say no this time—because muddy water and all?"

Every part of my body wanted to go out with this man...except the part of my brain that had invested five years in my business. I just couldn't do it.

I frowned. "I almost didn't go forward with Signature Scent because of the mess I made with my last business partner."

"You mentioned during your presentation that you had a partner but you bought them out."

I nodded. "Yeah, it didn't work out."

Hudson seemed to be waiting for further explanation.

Sighing, I said, "My fiancé was my partner. When he became my *ex*-fiancé, I bought him out."

Hudson nodded. "Is he a perfume chemist, too?"

I scoffed. "Definitely not. Aiden is a poet. At least that's what he tells people. His paid occupation is teaching English at a community college."

"A poet? That doesn't sound like a very helpful business partner."

"He wasn't. He didn't help with the development at all, but he contributed to the start-up funds."

"What came first? The broken business partnership or the broken relationship?" Hudson forked a piece of shrimp and ate it.

"Hmmm... I guess what came first was him having sex with someone who wasn't me."

Hudson started to choke.

"*Shit*. Are you okay?"

He held out a hand and spoke with a strained voice. "Yes." He grabbed his bottle of water and washed the food down. "Just give me a minute."

Once his eyes stopped watering and he had an open airway again, Hudson shook his head. "Your fiancé was sleeping around?"

I smiled sadly. "Yeah, but everything turned out for the best—for my business anyway."

"How so?"

"Well, I don't know that I ever would have made it this far if Aiden and I hadn't split up."

"Why is that? Didn't buying out your partner cause the initial strain on your finances?"

"It did. Aiden had contributed a hundred-and-twenty-five-thousand dollars over the years. So the money I had saved for the rest of the start-up inventory went to buy him out. But I'm not sure I would have ever made it to launch, even if I still had all of that money. Aiden and I were young when we first got together. Back then, he was very encouraging, and we slowly started banking funds together in a joint savings account. At first it wasn't a lot, but as the years went by, the money started to add up. And by then, Aiden had gotten interested in using it to buy investment property. It probably should've been a red flag that he wasn't interested in using it to buy a house for us to live in *together*, even though we'd dated for years and still didn't share an apartment. But anyway, he said investment property was less risky than my business idea. He suggested we buy one property and *then* start saving for Signature Scent after that."

Hudson frowned. "Your ex sounds like a real dick."

I smiled. "He is. But I often let him sway me when I shouldn't have. A few months before we split up, we had started looking at rental properties. My dream wasn't his dream, and I was about to give up on mine and accept his. I had a good job, and he made me feel like I was selfish for wanting even more." I paused. "Our breakup was awful for many reasons, but the one good thing that came out of it was that I decided to take back my future."

Hudson contemplated me for a moment. Eventually, he nodded. "Good for you."

"I think so."

"Though I think there's more than one good thing that came out of your breakup."

My brows dipped together. "What else is there?"

"You're not marrying an asshole."

I laughed. "Yeah, I guess there's that, too."

My cell phone started to ring from its spot on the table, and Ben's name flashed on the screen. I reached for it and hit *Ignore*, but not before Hudson also read the name of the caller.

"If you need to take that..." he said.

"No. It's fine. I'll call him back later."

He waited a few seconds, and when I didn't offer more, he tilted his head. "Ben. Is that the guy you were with at the wedding?"

I shook my head. "That was Fisher."

"Right." He nodded. "Fisher."

Again awkward silence filled the air. Eventually he raised a curious brow. "Brother?"

"Nope. Don't have any. It's just me and one sister."

When I yet again offered nothing more, Hudson chuckled.

"You're going to make me ask, aren't you?"

I smiled innocently. "It's...new."

Hudson held my eyes for a few heartbeats before clearing his throat. "Why don't we get started? I can walk you through some of the things I wanted to discuss while you finish eating."

Hudson seemed ready to flip a switch and move on to business, but my head was too jumbled now. He started spouting off numbers and dates, and while I nodded and pretended I was following, everything seemed to go in one ear and out the other. I didn't even realize he had stopped to ask me something until I looked up and found him waiting for me.

"I'm sorry. What did you ask?"

His eyes narrowed. "Did you even hear anything I said?"

I jabbed my fork into a shrimp and shoved it in my mouth, pointing at my lips to show I was now unable to respond. I thought I was being cute and avoiding his question, but it only made Hudson zone in on my lips. It looked like he was hungry, only not for Chinese food.

Oh boy. My belly felt a familiar flutter, and when Hudson licked his lips, that flutter dropped lower.

I finished chewing and swallowed, clearing my throat. "Do you think you could repeat the question?"

That little twitch at the corner of his mouth was back. If I didn't know better, I might think he had a facial tic.

I was relieved when Hudson nodded and began to repeat what he'd been saying. This time around, I was able to focus on most of it. And I was blown away by how much he'd gotten done in such a short time. He'd had his buying team get multiple quotes on all of my sample materials and was able to save at least five cents per piece on the majority of items. It didn't sound like much, but with each box getting twenty different samples, and the freight discounts his buying power got on top of that, the total wound up being pretty significant.

"Wow." I sat back in my chair and smirked. "You're definitely better than Aiden."

His eyes gleamed. "I'm not going to touch that one with a ten-foot pole."

I laughed. "Probably a good idea. But really, the savings you've come up with will almost cover the cost of having a partner in year one already. I don't know what to say. And here I thought I'd done such a good job negotiating."

"You did. A lot of these savings are from prepaying and buying in bulk, which you weren't able to do before with your cash-flow restraints."

Hudson's phone buzzed a reminder. The word *Charlie* flashed on the screen, and he looked at his watch as if to double-check that the time was right on his phone. "I didn't realize it had gotten so late. Can you excuse me for a moment? I need to call my daughter to say goodnight."

"Of course. I need to run to the ladies' room anyway."

After I hit the bathroom, I went back to the conference room. Because Hudson was quiet, I didn't immediately realize he was still on the phone. When I did, I motioned that I'd wait outside, but he waved me in. So I took a seat and listened to one side of his conversation.

"I was only kidding when I said that. You shouldn't have repeated it to your aunt, Charlie."

A pause, and then he closed his eyes. "You told your whole class about it?"

This had me intrigued.

"Okay, well, I'm sure the teacher understood it was a joke, even if Mommy and Aunt Rachel didn't."

Hudson looked up at me. "Actually, tell your mom I don't have a minute right now. I'm still at work. I'll speak to her when I call tomorrow night."

Pause.

"Love you, too."

After he swiped his phone off, he shook his head. "I have to remember that a six-year-old won't always get my sense of humor."

I smiled. "What happened?"

"My ex-sister-in-law is pregnant. She's about to pop. Rachel makes my ex-wife seem like a ball of fun. Neither has a sense of humor. The other night, Charlie asked me what I thought might be a good name for her soon-to-be cousin. I have no idea why, but I told her Aunt Rachel was going to name the baby Homeslice, and then spent five minutes convincing her it was the truth when she doubted me."

My brows jumped. "Homeslice? As in the singular for *my homies*?"

He grinned. "I was obviously teasing, but then the food delivery interrupted our discussion, and I guess I failed to circle back and tell her I hadn't been serious."

"And she repeated it to her mother? I take it that didn't go over too well."

Hudson shook his head. "It gets worse. A few months ago, I was arguing with my ex-wife. She'd told me not to give Charlie ice cream anymore because her sister said being lactose intolerant was hereditary. I wasn't sure if that was true or not, but Charlie is most definitely not lactose intolerant—she eats enough ice cream that we'd know if she was. We got into words about her sister butting her nose in again, and I called Rachel *laugh*tose intolerant. After the argument, I didn't even remember saying it until Charlie mentioned it again. I'd had no idea she was listening. But she was." He took a breath. "Today it was Charlie's turn for show and tell in class, and she brought in a picture of the last sonogram of her aunt's baby. She told everyone her new cousin was going to be named Homeslice, and when the teacher said whoever told her that might've been joking around, Charlie said her aunt didn't tell jokes because she's laughtose intolerant."

I covered my mouth. "Oh my God. That's freaking hysterical."

Hudson grinned. "It is, isn't it?"

I nodded.

"Too bad my ex-wife lost her sense of humor a long time ago."

"Well, if it helps any, I think it's funny as hell. Most kids definitely overshare. In the ten minutes I sat with Charlie the other day, I learned you went to the beach last week, she once got a bellyache from an ice cream shop, and you write her notes on the fruit in her lunchbox. By the way, I think it's very sweet that you do that."

"When she first started kindergarten, she got really anxious at lunch because she wasn't sure who to sit with. I wrote her the notes to help her relax while she unpacked her food. It sort of stuck."

"I love that."

He smiled. "It's getting late. Why don't we call it a day, and we can pick up here tomorrow? I'd like the marketing department to be involved when we get to the next topics anyway."

"Oh, okay... Sure."

We went back to our respective offices. A few minutes later, Hudson walked by on his way out and stopped.

"Plans with Ben tonight?"

I smiled. "No."

"Good." He rapped his knuckles against the doorjamb. "Don't stay too late. You're the last one here, and the cleaning people already came and went, so I'll lock the door behind me when I leave."

"Okay, thank you. I just have a few more things I want to finish up before I head out, too."

He nodded and turned to leave, but then took a step back. "By the way, I heard you loud and clear earlier, so I won't be asking you out again."

The smile on my face wilted. "Oh...okay."

He winked. "I'll wait for you to ask me this time. Goodnight, Stella."

When Hudson left, my concentration went with him. But I needed to get some work done before I could head home. There'd be plenty of time for overanalyzing every word the man said later—maybe while I was naked in a hot bath or while I de-stressed with the vibrator I kept in my nightstand. Right now I needed to work on the spreadsheet I'd been procrastinating about finishing all day. I wanted to have everything ready to go over with the team first thing in the morning.

But Excel wasn't my jam to begin with, and it was getting late. So after I opened the spreadsheet, I just stared at the numbers. Unable to focus, I decided to dig my earbuds out of my purse. Classical music always helped me get into a zone. But as I worked, the office started to get really warm. The air conditioning must've been on a timer. Since I would use just about any excuse to take a break from working on a spreadsheet, I decided I needed to get some cold water from the lunchroom down the hall.

Vivaldi's "The Four Seasons" came on while I filled my big cup with crushed ice from the refrigerator door, and I couldn't help myself. Each and every time I heard it, I pretended to be the conductor. No one was around, so what the hell? I set my cup down on the counter, closed my eyes, and let the intensity of the music guide my arms as they waved around in the air. Nothing eased my mind like leading an orchestra. I got so into the moment that I became lost.

Until...

I felt someone grab me from behind. Startled, I spun around. Acting purely on instinct and adrenaline, I balled up my fist, leaned back, and swung with all my might.

I connected with what felt like a brick wall, though I couldn't be sure since my eyes were squeezed tightly shut.

But then I heard a voice over the music.

"*Fuck,*" it growled.

And my stomach dropped.

No.

Just no.

I couldn't have.

Please, dear Lord, let it be anyone but him.

My eyes flashed open to confirm what I already knew.

God hadn't been listening.

Because I'd just landed a punch square on the nose...

of Hudson.

Hudson

"**W**hat the fuck!" My hands flew up to my nose.

"Oh my God! Hudson! I'm so sorry. Are you okay?"

My eyes had started to water, so I assumed that was the wetness I felt. Until I took my hands away and realized they were covered in blood.

"Holy shit! You're bleeding!" Stella grabbed a roll of paper towels off the counter. Ripping off a bunch, she wadded them into a ball and attempted to shove it in my face.

I swiped it from her hands.

"I'm so sorry. I—You…you scared me!"

I pressed the paper towels to my gushing nose. "I said your name twice, but you didn't answer."

She plucked a wireless earbud from her ear. "I have these in, and the music was loud."

I shook my head. "You were flailing your arms around—I thought you were *choking*."

Stella frowned. "I was conducting."

"Conducting?"

"Yeah, you know, pretending to be the conductor in a symphony."

I stared at her like she had two heads. "No, I don't know. It isn't often that I conduct a symphony in the kitchen at the office."

"Well, that's a shame. You should try it. It's good for the soul."

"I think I'll skip giving that a shot considering how well your attempt just worked out." I pointed to the roll of paper towels. "Can you hand me those?"

"Oh, God...it's still not stopping."

I swapped out the bloody paper towels for some fresh ones. Stella began to look a little pale.

"You should sit down," she said. "Put your head back."

"I'm pretty sure you're the one who should be sitting. You look like a ghost. Sit down, Stella."

She held on to the table while she slipped into a chair. "I don't like blood. It makes me feel queasy. Maybe we should both sit."

Since it didn't seem like my nose planned to stop anytime soon, I sat down across from her.

Stella kept shaking her head. "I'm so, so sorry." She held her hand to her chest. "I can't believe I hit you. It was a gut reaction. I didn't even see who was there. It all happened so fast."

"It's fine. It's my own fault. I should know by now that you're jumpy. And you didn't know I came back. I misread the situation."

"Shouldn't you be tilting your head back?"

"No. That's the last thing you should do when you get a bloody nose. You pinch the soft part above the nostrils. Tilting your head back only makes you swallow the blood."

Her face wrinkled, and she covered her mouth. "That's gross."

For the first time, I noticed her knuckles were red. Two were starting to swell. I lifted my chin and pointed. "How does your hand feel?"

"Oh...I'm not sure." She stretched out her fingers, then made a fist before opening it again. It didn't look like they were broken. "It's sore, actually. I think the adrenaline was rushing through me, so I didn't feel it until now."

I stood and went to the refrigerator. The best I could find in the freezer was a Lean Cuisine. I wrapped it in a paper towel and handed it to her. "Hold this against your knuckles."

"Shouldn't you be using it?"

"Don't worry about me."

Ten minutes later, the bleeding from my nose finally started to subside. "You pack a pretty damn good wallop there for a little thing."

She shook her head. "I still can't believe I did that. I've never hit anyone in my life. I thought I was alone in the office."

"I did leave. But I forgot something for a meeting I have uptown early tomorrow morning, so I came back. I heard the icemaker when I passed the lunchroom and realized you were still here. I figured I'd let you know I would reset the alarm on my way out, but I guess you've got security covered with that right hook."

She smiled, but it quickly fell to a frown as she looked at my nose. "I'm really sorry."

"I'm okay. The nose just bleeds a lot. I'm going to go to the men's room and wash up before I head out." I pointed my eyes to her hand. "You sure you're okay?"

Stella took off the makeshift ice and flexed her fingers. "Yeah, I'll be fine."

I stood. "Don't stay too late, Rocky."

"What the fuck happened to you?" Jack leaned back in his chair with a giant smile on his face. The fucker was enjoying this moment a little too much.

This morning I'd been going about my regular business, brushing my teeth, when I glanced up to the mirror and found two black eyes reflected back at me. It looked a lot worse than it felt. My nose didn't really hurt unless I touched it. But both eyes were swollen, with black and purple rings beneath them. I'd slipped on sunglasses before I left my house, so it was easy to forget the problem—until I'd taken them off in my friend's office just now.

"Who clocked you?" He leaned forward to get a closer look. "Whoever it was did a better job than I did that night we got into a drunken fight over who would win a drunken fight if we had one. I barely left a mark when I sucker-punched you, yet I had to get thirteen stitches when you got up off the ground and socked me back."

"The person who did this was definitely much stronger than you."

"Who was it?"

I smirked. "Stella...you fucking pussy."

Jack's eyebrows jumped. "A woman did that? Who the hell is Stella?"

"Remember the woman you met at Olivia's wedding? The one who sniffed the shots at the bar? I won two-hundred bucks from her being able to identify the brand of gin by smelling it."

"The hot one who turned out to be a crasher?"

"That's the one."

"Okay. What about her?"

"Her name is Stella."

Jack's face wrinkled. "I thought that woman's name was Evelyn."

I hadn't yet filled my friend in on the shit that had transpired since the wedding, even though I'd actually come today to discuss Signature Scent. Jack was the vice president of one of the largest media conglomerates—that happened to own the most popular home shopping television station. I thought perhaps he could introduce me to some of the bigwigs there to discuss the possibility of getting Stella's perfume featured as a product on one of their shows.

"She was a wedding crasher, dumbass. She wasn't using her real name."

"Oh, shit. Okay, that makes sense. So hot sniffer girl is really Stella."

"That's correct."

"And she punched you because..."

It was probably easiest if I backed up and explained from the beginning, so I did. Starting at the lost phone, I made my way through my sister's bleeding heart and finally wound up at the purpose of my visit today.

When I was done, Jack sat back in his chair and rubbed his chin. "You've had plenty of investments in companies you could have used my connections for. A few times I've even told you you were dumb not to come to me. Your response is always that you don't like to mix business with friendship. What's changed?"

"Nothing."

He tilted his head. "Yet here you are..."

"I'm asking for an introduction, not for you to go out on a limb."

Jack shrugged. "You've had a dozen products you could have asked for my help with over the years. Yet this is the first one you're sitting on the other side of my desk about. You wanna know what I think?"

"Don't really give two shits what you think, so no."

He smirked. "I think you're hot for the sniffer, and you want to impress her."

Why the hell does everyone in my life ask me if I want to know what they think and then when I say no, they tell me anyway?

I shook my head. "I'm *invested* financially in the company, jackass."

The last thing I needed was Jack knowing the woman who gave me two black eyes had basically shot me down. He'd still be busting my balls about it when we were making bets from our wheelchairs.

"You were invested in all the companies you could have come to me about," he said.

I rolled my eyes. "Are you going to help me or not?"

"Yes, but you know why?"

"Because you owe me four-thousand favors?"

"Maybe, but that's not why I'm doing it. I'm doing it because it's been a long time since you made an effort with a woman. You're used to just walking into a bar, showing that pretty face, and taking the pick of the litter home. This is good. I hate spending so much time with Alana's sister's husband. He's a tool."

"I'm lost. What does your wife's sister's husband have to do with this conversation?"

"Simple. If you had a goddamned girlfriend, we could go out to dinner with you and her sometimes, instead of Allison and Chuck. Who the hell under the age of sixty calls themselves Chuck, anyway?"

"I'm not going out with Stella." *Until she asks.*

Jack smiled. "We'll see."

My best friend might be a pain in my ass, but he had damn good connections. Over the next two hours, not only did he introduce me to the head of the shopping network's buying team, he also took me on set to watch the end of the show they were currently taping. By the time he was done, he'd managed to sell the famous host on the concept of Signature Scent *and* gotten her to invite Stella and me to lunch the next day.

"Thanks a lot for the introductions." I shook Jack's hand in the building's lobby. "I need to get back to the office, but I owe you a beer soon."

Jack smiled. "Nah. We'll call it even since you'll be saving me from listening to more of Chuck's stories about bunions. Couldn't he at least be a gynecologist rather than a podiatrist?"

"I'll call you next week for that beer."

"You mean dinner with me, Alana, and Stella?"

"Once again, I'm not going out with Stella."

Jack smirked. "We'll see about that..."

I had one hand on the door when Jack yelled again, "Maybe I'll join you at lunch tomorrow—get to know my wife's new best friend."

Stella rapped on my office doorframe. "Hey, do you have a second? I was going over these reports Helena brought by and—" Her eyes widened to saucers when I looked up. "Oh my God! Please tell me I didn't do that?"

I nodded. "Okay. You didn't give me two black eyes. I got into a fistfight with the kid at the deli down the block. He wrote my name wrong on my cup, and it pissed me off."

"Really?"

"No, of course not." I waved my hand at my face. "This is all your handiwork, Rocky."

Her eyes shut. "I'm so sorry. I feel absolutely awful. Does it hurt?"

"Yes, I'm in excruciating pain."

"Oh, God."

She looked pretty upset, so I had to put her out of her misery. "Relax. I'm joking. It looks bad, but I feel fine."

"I can't believe I did all that."

"How's your hand?"

She opened and closed it. "My knuckles are sore, but I'll live. Really, Hudson, I'm so sorry I hit you."

Stella had a white paper bag in her other hand and held it out to me. "Here, take this muffin. It's still warm. I just picked it up from the deli down the block."

Was she offering me a muffin to make up for two black eyes? "Out of Hershey bars?"

She grinned. "Actually, I am. I ate my emergency stash last night after you left. This is all I have to offer."

I chuckled and raised a hand. "I'm good. Thanks anyway."

"Please take it. It'll make me feel better."

This woman was something. She walked to my desk and set the bag down on the corner.

I shook my head. "Fine. Thank you. So what was your question?"

"My question?"

"Something about the reports Helena brought over?"

"Oh yeah—I have a few questions on the purchase orders Helena asked me to approve. Do you have some time?" She thumbed over her shoulder. "I can run back to my office and get them. I came by this morning, but you weren't in yet."

I looked down at my watch. "I have a call in a few minutes. It shouldn't be long—maybe about a half hour. Why don't I stop by your office when I'm done."

"That would be great. I'll see you in a little bit then."

After she walked away, I stared at the empty doorway for a minute. Was it just me, or had the energy in the office changed since she started working here? I had two black eyes and more work than ever, yet I felt more balanced than usual.

I sighed and went back to work. It was probably just the blow to the face.

After I finished my call, I headed down to find Stella. Her office door was open, but her face was mostly hidden behind a huge bouquet of brightly colored flowers on her desk. Her nose was also buried in papers, so she didn't immediately notice me.

"Nice flowers." I raised a brow. "Ken?"

"If you mean Ben, then no. The flowers are for my friend's birthday."

"You had them delivered here to bring to her?"

She shook her head. "Her is a he, and today's his birthday. But he sent me the flowers because he doesn't like to celebrate the day. Fisher's mom passed away two years ago on his birthday, so it's a hard day for him. Instead of celebrating himself, it seems he now sends me gifts."

That was unusual for most people, but sounded about right for Stella. "You ready to go through the reports you had questions on?"

"Yes, please."

I took a seat on the other side of her desk. While she turned to rifle through some papers on the credenza behind her, my eyes snagged on a leather book sitting in an open box next to the flowers—or more specifically, the word engraved on it.

"Writing down your fantasies about me?" I asked. "I already told you all you have to do is ask me out."

Stella's forehead wrinkled, so I pointed my eyes at the book with the word *Diary* across the front.

"Oh...no, that's not mine. The messenger who delivered the flowers brought it. It's another gift from Fisher."

"You keep a diary?"

"No, it belongs to someone else. Or at least it did." She reached across the desk and nabbed it, tucking it away in a drawer.

As usual when it came to Stella, I was lost. "And you have someone else's diary because..."

She sighed. "Can we just forget you saw it?"

I shook my head slowly. "Not a chance."

Stella rolled her eyes. "Fine. But if I tell you, you can't make fun of me."

I folded my arms across my chest. "This is getting more intriguing by the moment. I can't wait to hear this story."

"It's not a story, really. It's just a hobby of mine."

"Writing in diaries?"

"No. I don't write in them. I read them."

My brows shot up. "How exactly do you come across these diaries? Do you steal them or something?"

"Of course not. I'm not a thief. I usually buy them on eBay."

"You buy other people's diaries on eBay?"

She nodded. "There's a big market for them, actually. Some people are into watching reality TV. I prefer to *read* my drama. Reading someone's diary isn't all that different."

"Uh-huh...."

"No, really. Millions of people watch those *Real Housewives* shows and *Jersey Shore*. It's the same thing, if you think about it—people airing their dirty laundry and keeping secrets."

I scratched my chin. "How exactly does one get into this hobby?"

She sighed. "When I was twelve, I went to a garage sale. I saw a brown leather book on a table, so I picked it up to smell it."

"Of course you did."

She narrowed her eyes. "Don't interrupt or I'm not going to finish my story."

"Continue..."

For the next five minutes she rambled on about smelling a diary at a garage sale, her crush on some kid who played football, and how she'd had no idea the diary was written in when she bought it. By the time she took a breath, I even knew how much she'd paid for the damn thing fifteen years ago.

I just kept staring at her, trying to keep up and waiting for her to get to the point. Though Stella didn't seem to notice. Then she looked at me like she wanted to make sure I was following her. So I nodded. "Okay..."

"I realized I'd bought a used diary, and I wasn't going to read it, but my curiosity got the best of me. It turned out to be a thirty-year-old diary written by a girl a year older than I was at the time. In the first few entries, she wrote about a boy she liked and her first kiss. I was hooked and couldn't stop. I read the entire thing in one night. After that, I checked every garage sale I went to for six months, trying to find another diary. But I never did. I'd pretty much forgotten about diaries when I stumbled upon one on eBay a few years later. That's when I learned there was an entire market for used diaries. I've been buying them ever since. Most people watch a show or two before they go to bed; I like to read an entry or two a night."

"So your friend bought you a used diary for his birthday?"

"Actually, I bought the diary. But it's written in Italian. Fisher had it translated for me for his birthday."

I processed that for a moment. "Out of curiosity, what does a diary like that set you back on eBay?"

"It varies. If you buy a woman's diary, it's usually anywhere from fifty to a hundred dollars. Some people sell photocopied diaries, and those are cheaper since they can sell it to multiple people. Original diaries from the eighteen hundreds can go for a lot more, and men's, no matter how old they are, are always a premium."

"Men's? Men write in diaries?"

"Some do. But they're rare and can get pretty expensive."

I was dumbfounded. An entire world existed that I knew nothing about. I lifted my chin toward the drawer where she'd tucked the diary away. "Who does the one you have belong to?"

"His name is Marco. He lives in Italy."

"What's his story?"

"I'm not sure yet. I haven't started reading it. But I'm really excited to. I'm going to have to be strict about only reading an entry a night, or I'll wind up finishing it in one sitting. Italian diaries are the best. The people there are so passionate about everything."

"If you say so. You know your hobby is a bit strange, right?"

"I do. But so what? It makes me happy."

It struck a chord, the way something so simple could make her happy. There hadn't been much that had done it for me the last few years since my divorce—not even the women I went out with. Maybe I was a little envious.

Regardless, we had work to do. So I cleared my throat. "Why don't you show me what you wanted to discuss when you came to my office?"

Stella and I worked through her questions and fixed some errors the purchasing department had made while prepping product orders. I had an afternoon meeting to get to, so I told her to let me know if she needed anything else and stood to go.

At the door, I realized I hadn't told her the good news. "I almost forgot—I used a connection to talk about your product with the executives at a home shopping network."

"Really? Did they like it?"

"A lot, actually. Both the head buyer and the host of one of the shows loved the concept. They want to see it in person. Robyn invited us to have lunch tomorrow. I hope you don't have plans."

Her mouth hung open. "Robyn? As in Robyn Quinn? The queen of the Home Shopping Channel?"

"That's the one."

"Oh my God! This is huge! How could you have come in here and let me babble for the last hour and not mention that sooner?"

"I guess I forgot. Listening to your stories makes my brain power down."

She shook her head. "I'm going to let that slide and not punch you again since you scored an appointment that could be life changing."

I smiled. "Robyn's going to email me with the time and details. I'll forward it along when I get it."

"Okay! Wow. This is turning out to be a great day. I might have to celebrate by reading *two* entries from Marco tonight."

"You're a real wild woman."

She shrugged. "I might not be, but sometimes the people in my diary are."

13

Stella

Seventeen months ago

"It could be them."

I pointed to a couple sitting a few steps down from where we were eating our lunch on the library stairs.

Fisher's brows knitted. "They could be who?"

"Alexandria and Jasper."

His forehead wrinkled. "The couple from that new diary you're reading? The one your roommate gave you for your birthday?"

I nodded. "It was really sweet of her." I hadn't even realized she knew it was my birthday, yet she had given me the most incredible diary as a gift. I was obsessed with it.

Fisher unwrapped his sandwich and took a large bite. He spoke with his mouth full. "I thought you didn't know the boyfriend's name."

"I don't. But I decided to call him Jasper since she refers to him as J. It makes him feel more real in my head when I think about them."

"Honey, you know I love you. But most of the shit that goes on in your head isn't real."

I elbowed him playfully. Lately, I'd started coming to sit on the stairs at the library for lunch—the exact stairs where so much of the story playing out in the diary I was reading had occurred. I liked to read my daily entry allotments here and imagine that some of the people sitting nearby were the ones on the pages in my hands.

"This diary is the best thing I've ever read. One day last week, Alexandria's husband came home early from work to check on her. The night before she'd told him she hadn't been feeling well when he'd tried to initiate having sex. But the truth was, she'd had sex with Jasper just a few hours earlier, so she wasn't into sex with her own husband. Anyway...when he came home to check on her, she was taking a nap because that morning she'd gone yet again to meet Jasper, and she was physically wiped out. Her husband always works late, so she hadn't thought anything about leaving her phone out on the kitchen counter charging. But when he walked in, he happened to catch a text message popping up on her screen. It was Jasper telling her when to meet him the next day. Luckily, he was only in her phone contacts as *J*. When her husband asked her about the text, she told him it was related to a surprise for his birthday, and he bought it. The poor guy still seems clueless about her affair. But she's become paranoid about where she leaves her phone now."

Fisher shook his head. "Poor guy? You mean poor schmuck."

"I know. I feel bad for her husband. Their wedding was right here at the library." I held my hands out. "And now she sometimes meets Jasper on these very steps so they can go screw in the alley around the corner behind a dumpster. I don't get it. She seemed so in love with her husband last year before the wedding."

He took another bite of his sandwich. "What—did you buy multiple volumes of this person's diary or something? One diary doesn't span years, does it?"

"This one does, because she doesn't write in it too often. The time hops around—it's months between entries at some points. She wrote in it a lot before her wedding, describing everything she was planning. But then it mostly stopped after. I guess she had nothing exciting to write for a year or two...until she started sleeping with her husband's friend."

"You better take this one slow. Sounds like you're going to have withdrawal after you finish it."

"I know. It's because the woman it belonged to and everyone she writes about are all right here in the City. I've never read a local diary before, much less one that takes place right down the block from my work. It makes it all seem so real—like it's going on now instead of whenever she wrote it. I can't stop thinking about the people in the story and wondering if I might be passing one of them. The other day I was at Starbucks, and the barista's nametag said Jasper. I dropped my iced latte all over the floor because I got so excited, thinking it could be him. I sat inside the store until he finished his shift. Luckily, his boyfriend came to pick him up, so that ruled him out as the diary woman's paramour."

"Was the barista cute?"

"He was, actually. But I was stalking a man because his name was Jasper! I don't even know the real name of the guy the woman in my diary is having an affair with."

"What Starbucks was it? A hot, gay barista sounds more up my alley than yours."

I chuckled. "Seriously, Fisher. What was I going to do after waiting two hours for that poor guy to get off of work? Follow him all the way home?"

"You're starting to sound a little obsessive."

I sighed. "That's what Aiden said. We recently had a fight because my phone was dead. I'd forgotten to put it on the charger, and when I went to look for his cell to text you to tell you I'd be late for dinner, I realized he never leaves his phone around anymore. It made me suspicious because of how paranoid Alexandria is about getting caught, and Aiden and I wound up arguing. He'd done nothing wrong."

Fisher shook his head. "Maybe you should take a little break from reading."

I finally opened the container of salad I'd made for lunch. Stabbing a fork into it, I sighed. "Yeah, maybe you're right."

Fisher snort-laughed. "You're so full of shit."

14

Hudson

Our lunch meeting had turned into a party. Robyn, the host of the show, invited her co-host and a segment producer, the head buyer was bringing someone along, and Jack had also decided to grace us with his presence. With so many people, and Stella wanting to bring sample boxes for everyone, I drove to make it easier. My car was parked at a garage a few blocks away from the office, so I left early and told Stella to meet me downstairs in fifteen minutes.

She was waiting in front of the building when I pulled up to the light at the corner. It gave me a chance to watch her without her knowing. Two large flowerpots sat on either side of the main entrance to the office. They were old wine barrels, and I'd never given them much thought, though I passed them every day, other than to notice that building maintenance changed the flowers out every so often. I watched from a distance as Stella looked around, almost as if to see if anyone was paying attention, and then leaned over. I'd thought she was going to smell the flowers, but she bent lower and brought her nose to the barrel beneath. *Did she just smell the pot?*

I chuckled to myself at how nutty she was. Anytime I thought I knew what she was going to say or do, I quickly found my assumption wrong. It was oddly refreshing. Within five minutes of meeting most women, I could guess the salad they were going to order, or that yoga or tennis was their hobby of choice. But not Stella—there was nothing cookie-cutter about her.

She stepped over to the flowerpot on the other side of the doorway and again checked to see if the coast was clear before going in for a sniff. Only this time, she didn't bend at the knees. She bent in half at the waist. Which gave me an unobstructed view of her ass—her *phenomenal freaking ass.*

Great. Just great.

I nailed the gas as soon as the light changed and pulled up in front of the building. I'd brought the boxes downstairs to the lobby before I went to the parking garage, so I got out and headed inside.

"Why don't you get in since I'm double parked, and I'll grab the stuff from security?" I told her as I passed.

"Oh...okay."

After I finished loading the trunk, I slammed it shut and waited for traffic to slow enough so I could open the driver's side door and get in without being clipped.

"Thank you for taking care of that," Stella said.

"Of course."

I buckled. "We have an hour before we have to be at the restaurant, but it'll probably take us almost that long with this traffic." Looking over my shoulder, it took a while before there was a gap in the cars big enough to pull away from the curb.

Stella sniffed a few times. "Is this brand new?"

My car was actually three years old, but it looked new since I didn't drive very much.

"It's a few years old."

"It still has that new-car smell."

"Oh yeah? Do you like that smell better than the flowerpots outside the office?"

Stella sighed. "You caught that, huh?"

"I did indeed."

"I was curious if they were actually aged barrels once used for wine."

"Were they?"

"I'm not sure. All I could smell was dirt."

I smirked. "Large quantities of soil tend to smell that way."

"What kind of a car is this? The interior is so pretty."

"It's a Maybach S 650."

"Is that an impressive car?"

"I don't know. You tell me. Are you impressed?"

She smiled. "Not really. I don't drive, so I don't know too much about cars."

"You mean you don't have a car because you live here in the City?"

"No, I mean I don't have a driver's license. I had a permit once, and my ex tried to teach me years ago, but I hit a fire hydrant rounding a corner and, well, that was the end of that."

We inched our way uptown slowly. At one point, a car came out of nowhere and cut me off, so I had to slam on my brakes. Stella and I both had our seatbelts on, so we were fine, but her purse flew off the seat and dumped onto the floor. It landed upside down, and when she went to pick it up, the contents spilled all over the place.

"Sorry about that," I said.

When she leaned forward to collect her belongings, I noticed the box with the diary from yesterday.

"My ex-wife used to write in one of those every once in a while. I'd find her writing in it after we argued. Pretty sure all she did was bitch. Isn't that mostly what people use that for? To vent?"

"Sometimes they're like that," Stella said. She straightened the book in its box and put the top back on. "I've gotten a few of those. The seller usually posts some screenshots of pages to give you a sample. That helps me rule out a lot, but occasionally you can't tell from just a short excerpt."

"Have you started reading Nico's secrets?"

"It's Marco, and yes, I did."

"Well...how was it?"

Stella sighed. "I read almost half the diary in one night."

I laughed. "That good, huh?"

She held her hand to her chest. "He's in love with an older woman. Amalia is nineteen years his senior and the librarian for the small village they live in. He's a grape farmer. She thinks it's just infatuation and will pass, but he sounds like he's head over heels for her. He's thinking about bringing another woman around, hoping to spark some jealousy to make her admit she has feelings for him, too. But I'm worried it's going to backfire and push her further away."

"I think Amelia, or whatever her name is, is probably right. Marco is just a horny kid. It'll pass. Every young guy's fantasized about a hot librarian at some point. He's not in love with her. He's in lust."

"You didn't even read the diary. How can you know how he feels?"

I shrugged. "Most relationships end up in the same place anyway."

"Someone's extremely cynical..."

"I'm not cynical; I'm a realist. Even if they get together, what do you think the chances are that a guy at forty isn't going to be looking elsewhere when his librarian bride is sixty?"

"Not when he loves her as much as Marco loves Amalia."

I scoffed. "It all starts out as fun and games..."

"Whatever."

"You said your ex was sleeping with someone else. And yet you still believe in fairytales?"

"Just because I've been burned doesn't mean I don't believe in love. I was devastated when Aiden and I broke up. It took me a long time to move on and find happiness again. Heck, I'm still working on finding my happiness. But one of the things that keeps my spirits up is to believe we're all meant to have a happily ever after. Mine just wasn't supposed to be with Aiden."

My eyes flashed to hers and then back to the road. "Whatever you say..."

"If you're so bitter about relationships, why did you ask me out?"

"Do I have to stay celibate just because I don't think everything ends in hearts and roses?"

"Oh." She rolled her eyes. "So you just wanted to get laid. I'm glad we cleared that up. I actually prefer to get to know someone and spend time with him, in addition to physical intimacy."

"Don't put words in my mouth. I enjoy spending time with a woman, too. Sometimes we just have different expectations of where things will end up."

Stella shook her head. "You know what you need? To try my happiness system."

"Your happiness system?"

Stella nodded. "I know—it needs a better name."

I grumbled. "I can think of a few."

"I heard that, but I'm choosing to ignore it. Anyway, when I was struggling and feeling grumpy all the time, I made a list of things that make me happy. Small things—not things that were out of my reach and difficult to accomplish. For example, I try to give someone a compliment every day. That might not seem like much, but it causes you to find something good in at least one person each day. After a while, it helps change your mindset. Another thing I do is set aside ten minutes to meditate each morning. I also watch the sunrise or sunset at least once a week. And I try to do something I've never done before every single weekend."

I smirked. "If you need help doing someone you've never done this weekend, just let me know."

She rolled her eyes. "Some*thing*, not some*one*."

I chuckled. "Our happiness systems must work a little differently."

Traffic had lightened up, and we were already halfway to the restaurant. "As riveting as this conversation is, why don't I fill you in on the network before we get to lunch? We're going to be at the restaurant soon."

"I already read up."

"Okay, then. Tell me what you know."

Stella proceeded to rattle off facts about the ownership of the network, statistics on the types of products they sold, which were their best- and worst-performing items, and the qualities they looked for in partners. Then she detailed personal and professional information on both the host and co-host. She'd done more homework than I had.

"You're thorough," I said.

"Thank you."

We stopped at a red light, and Stella shifted in her seat. She uncrossed her legs and re-crossed them in the opposite direction. It had been innocent enough, likely done in an effort to get more comfortable since we'd been sitting in the car for a while now, but the way my eyes ogled her bit of exposed thigh was anything but innocent.

Happiness system. A little leg worked for me. Why did women always have to overcomplicate shit?

Who was the woman I'd sat next to at lunch?

The same woman who'd spent fifteen minutes telling me all the details of a garage sale she went to at age twelve when all I'd asked was how she'd gotten into reading used diaries, the same woman who'd been sniffing barrels just a few hours ago, had morphed into an astute businesswoman. Rather than ramble on with stories, she listened—really listened—and quickly found the hot button for each of the key players at lunch. Then she subtly steered the conversation to those areas when she spoke. She'd had the network bigwigs eating out of the palm of her hand. Robyn Quinn even invited her to a woman's leadership luncheon to talk about how she took an idea and made it into an innovative business.

The valet brought my car around first, so I shook hands with the group. Stella got hugs from the women. Once we were back on the road, she looked over at me.

"So...go ahead. Tell me what I did wrong."

I glanced at her and back to the traffic ahead of me. "Wrong? What makes you think you did something wrong?"

"You're quiet."

"So?"

"You usually get all quiet and do this staring-at-me thing before you say something snarky. But you're driving, so your eyes are stuck on the road."

"Actually, I was thinking about how well lunch went. You did a great job. I might've made the introduction, but you sealed the deal."

From my peripheral vision, I saw Stella blink a few times.

"Was that...a compliment? Are you giving my happiness system a test run?"

We stopped at a light, so I looked over at her. "Definitely not. Though I am capable of giving them when due."

Her lips curved to an adorable smile. "I *was* good, wasn't I?"

"I already gave you one compliment, let's not go fishing for another so soon."

She laughed. "Alright. I guess I'll take what I can get."

Three days later, my assistant buzzed in to my office. "Jack Sullivan is on the line for you."

"Thanks, Helena."

I leaned back in my chair and picked up the phone. "I know I still owe you a beer, but it's only eight in the morning."

Jack laughed. "Like we haven't had beer for breakfast before."

I smiled. "That was a lot of years ago."

"Speak for yourself. You didn't go to Frank's bachelor party a few months ago."

I chuckled. "What's going on?"

"I have some news that should get you big points with your little girlfriend."

I knew exactly who he was referring to, yet I said, "There's no woman in my life at the moment. Plus, if there was, I wouldn't need your sorry ass to help me earn points with her."

"So you must not want to hear the news then..."

"Spit it out, Sullivan. What's up?"

"There's good news and bad news. The good news is, the new Steamer-Beamer—some sort of contraption that lets you get the wrinkles out of your clothes while wearing them—caused second-degree burns on one of our producers."

"Someone you work with got burned? That's the good news? I hate to hear the bad news."

"Obviously it's bad news for that dude. But it's good news for you. The Home Shopping Channel had to yank the Steamer-Beamer from its scheduled spot, and that means they have an opening for a product with some immediate air time."

"Oh yeah? Think Signature Scent might have a shot?"

"Better than a shot. Spot's yours if you can be ready faster than you originally planned."

The launch was set for nine weeks from now, but we could definitely speed things up a bit if needed. "No problem. When would we need to be ready?"

"That's the bad news. You'd have to be ready next week."

"Next week?" I shook my head. "That's impossible."

"Well, the show would film then. It would air the following weekend. But they quote two to four weeks for shipping. So you'd have some time to get the goods out the door."

I blew out a deep breath. "I don't know if we can move things up that much."

"Have I mentioned the volume they're forecasting?"

"No, what are we talking?"

It took a lot to make my jaw drop, but the number that came out of Jack's mouth left me catching flies.

"Jesus. That's more than we anticipated selling the entire first year."

"Women eat up the products they hawk on that channel. Robyn needs an answer within an hour. If you can't do it, she has a list of anxious people with products who can. So you better figure that shit out."

Hudson

"**S**eriously? They think they can sell *that* many?" Stella sat down, as if the number was too big to digest while standing.

"According to Jack, their sales forecasting is pretty spot-on. They know their audiences and buying power."

"My God. That's crazy. But we can't be ready that soon."

"Yes, we can!" Olivia chimed in. "We have no choice. This is a once-in-a-lifetime opportunity. We have to be ready."

Stella raised a hand to her forehead. "But how? We just ordered some of the products we need, and they're coming from overseas. Shipping alone is almost two months. We won't have anything ready next week."

"Well, we have longer than next week," I said. "The show would film next week, but air the following Saturday. Then they allow two to four weeks for shipping. So we could stretch it before we'd have to start moving products out the door. We'd either have to expedite the stuff we're missing—put them on a plane instead of a slow boat. Or find suppliers locally to start shipping until the full stock comes in. Maybe both."

Stella shook her head. "That'll all be really expensive."

"We could increase the price point to help make it up," Olivia said.

Stella looked skeptical. "I don't know. Perfume is really price sensitive when you aren't a well-known brand or don't have a celebrity endorsement."

"The shopping channel sells their products on a three-payment plan," Olivia said. "So items aren't as price sensitive as they normally are. Something that's fifty-nine ninety-nine might be hard to swallow, but when it becomes *three easy payments of nineteen ninety-nine*, it's a lot more palatable for a consumer."

"Well, if you guys think we could make it work, it's obviously an incredible opportunity," Stella said. "Maybe we could spend the next day or so figuring out what it would take to make it happen?"

I shook my head. "We don't have a day. They need an answer sooner."

"How much sooner?" Stella asked.

I looked down at my watch. "We have about fifty minutes left."

We reconvened in the conference room five minutes before I was supposed to call Jack back with a decision.

Stella tossed a legal pad with shit scribbled all over it on the table.

"I can get half of what we need expedited from local suppliers, with the exception of two items—calone and ambrette. The price is much higher, but if we buy in bulk, it's not actually as terrible as I thought it would be. And the lab is available to mix ingredients as soon as the orders come in. With that kind of volume, it might take us a few days to fill orders, but it's doable within the turnaround time."

I nodded. "I can get the two items you can't source locally flown in with very little price difference by increasing the order size." We both looked to Olivia.

She smiled. "The printer said he can run the presses all night, if he has to. He just needs twenty-four-hours' notice for staffing, and of course, our finalized PDF files, which aren't ready, but can be shortly. And the website is a non-issue. There are some cosmetic things the team was working on, but we could go live in an hour if we needed to."

Stella couldn't hide the excitement on her face. "Oh my God, are we really going to do this?"

"Looks like it," I said. "Though I forgot to mention one small detail."

"What?"

"They want you on camera to sell the product with Robyn."

Her eyes widened. "*Me*? On camera? I've never done that before."

"Guess there's a first time for everything." I smirked. "You'll get to make good use of your happiness system."

"She's fucking hot."

Jack's head moved in tandem with Stella's legs as she walked out onto the stage. She bent so the sound guy could hook up her microphones, and I didn't give him a chance to say anything more.

My jaw flexed. "Don't be disrespectful, you dick."

He scoffed. "What? Like you weren't looking at her ass just now?"

I didn't answer.

"Nice rack, too."

A noise gurgled from my throat.

Jack turned with a knowing smirk plastered on his face. "Did you just growl at me?"

"Shut the fuck up."

"Admit it. You don't want me looking because you like her. You're already territorial about this chick."

"This chick? Is it nineteen eighty-five here in the studio? Do you refer to your employees like that?"

"Stop deflecting. You like this *woman,* and you know it."

Jack might be vice president of a big company now, but parts of him were eternally stuck in sixth grade. I knew if I didn't give him something, he'd never shut the hell up.

So I tried to pacify him. "She's turned out to be a hard worker and a nice person, yes."

"So you don't think she's hot?"

I rolled my eyes. "She's attractive, yes."

"But you don't want to bang her?"

"Stella and I have a business relationship."

"Oh...so it's the business relationship that's the problem? So if you *weren't* in business with her, you'd be trying to bang her?"

"I'm done with this conversation."

Jack shoved his hands into his pockets and shrugged. "Okay. So you don't mind if I bring Brent down to meet her, then?"

"Brent?"

"Fenway. You remember him from college, right? Tall, good-looking—probably the only one who gave you a run for your money back in the day. He works here now. Looks the same, except more jacked. Still single..."

My friend thought he was being cute, as if I wouldn't give him a set of black eyes to match my fading ones. "Fuck off," I said.

He grinned. "That's what I thought."

A little while later, Jack looked at his watch. "I have a meeting. You hanging around for the taping?"

"Yeah. Olivia couldn't be here, so I told her I'd stick it out."

"They're probably going to be a few hours."

I held up my phone. "I have plenty to do to keep me busy."

He stood and clapped my shoulder. "I'm sure you do. But I'd bet my bank account you don't take your eyes off that stage."

It was a good thing I hadn't taken that bet—not that I would've ever admitted I'd spent the last three fucking hours watching Stella's every move on the stage. When Jack had told me they wanted Stella on-air, a part of me wasn't sure that was a wise business move. Sure, she was gorgeous and the camera would probably love her, but she had no experience. Though after sitting around the last few hours and watching her, I completely understood what the host had seen that made her want Stella to be part of the pitch.

She was passionate and funny, and had an innocent quality that made you believe everything she said up there—as if she were too wholesome to lie. Hell, I wanted to buy the freaking perfume, and I owned part of the company.

A little after five o'clock, they finally wrapped shooting. Stella talked to the host and crew for a while, then turned to look out into the audience. She cupped her hands over her brows, shielding her eyes from the overhead light. Finding me still sitting in the fourth row back, she smiled and headed to the stairs at the side of the stage. I stood and walked down the aisle to meet her.

"Oh my God," she said. "That was so much fun!"

"You looked like you were having a good time."

"I hope I don't come off as a weirdo." She held up her hands and wiggled her fingers. "I felt...like I'd been electrocuted or something. Not in a cook-your-organs way, but like a nonstop jolt of energy racing through my body."

I laughed. "You did great—entertaining, yet sincere." I turned at the sound of the stage door behind us opening and closing. Jack was back, and the fucker wasn't alone. I was going to kick his scrawny ass.

He walked over, sporting the biggest, gloating smile. "Hudson, you remember Brent, right?"

I gritted my teeth and extended my hand. "I do. How's it going, Brent?"

We were still shaking when the asshole's eyes locked on Stella. He couldn't let go of my hand fast enough. "I don't think we've met. Brent Fenway."

Stella smiled. "Fenway like the park?"

"One and the same. Have you ever been there?"

"I haven't, actually."

"Maybe I can take you sometime."

Seriously? He'd been in the room less than thirty seconds, and he was already hitting on her? How long until he pissed on her like she was a fire hydrant?

Jack gave me a look and rocked back and forth on his heels. He seemed pretty damn proud of himself. "That sounds like a fun *date*. Don't you think, Hudson?"

I glared at him. "I'm a Yankees fan."

"I saw Robyn on my way back down. She wants to see us." Jack thumbed toward the door he'd just walked through. "She's in her office. It's just down the hall."

"Okay." Couldn't say I was upset to say goodbye to Brent so soon. I nodded at him. "Good seeing you." I extended a hand to Stella. "After you..."

Jack shook his head. "Actually, she only asked to see you and me, Hudson. Stella can hang back here. I'm sure Brent can keep her company."

Brent flashed a smile I wanted to punch. "Absolutely."

The minute we were out in the hall, Jack poked the bear.

"Brent looks good, doesn't he?"

I glared in response.

"They make a cute couple, him and Stella."

"You've made your point. Now go tell him to get the fuck back to work."

Jack smiled. "Can't do that. He doesn't work for me."

Luckily for my friend, Robyn walked out of her office. "There you are. I have some good news to share."

I had to plaster on a happy face when all I wanted was to kill my buddy and use his limp body as a bat to knock out the pretty boy back in the studio.

"We're here, and you just killed it up on stage taping the segment for Signature Scent," Jack said, "I think we're already floating in good news."

Robyn handed me a packet of papers. "We usually test potential products with a focus group before we take them on—to see if they appeal to our known audience and to find out what they'll want to know most about the product. We didn't have time for that with Signature Scent since it was a last-minute add, but we had a group here today for another project. I had Mike, the segment producer, sneak over with a few minutes of what we taped earlier in the day, and it tested through the roof. I think we need to increase our sales forecast."

I looked down at the numbers. She wasn't kidding.

How likely are you to buy the product – 94% said extremely likely.

Have you found a similar product anywhere else – 0% said yes.

How relatable was the guest host – 92% said she was relatable.

And on and on—three pages of numbers that were truly remarkable. I flipped through, scanning them all. "This is..." I shook my head. "It's incredible."

"You know what else it is?" Jack said. We both looked to him. "Cause for celebration."

That evening, Stella and I drove to the restaurant together. Robyn and Jack were meeting us there, and we were ten minutes early and the first ones to arrive.

"Drink at the bar?" I asked her.

"That sounds great."

We told the hostess where we were going and found two stools next to each other.

The bartender walked over and placed a napkin in front of each of us. "What can I get for you?"

I looked to Stella.

"I'll have a merlot, please."

"Would you like to see the wine menu to select one?"

She shook her head. "House wine is fine."

He looked to me. "And for you?"

"I'll take a Coors Light."

Once he walked away, I raised a brow at Stella. "No gin to sniff?"

She smiled. "Not tonight. I don't think it's a good idea to mix business with hard liquor."

"You also don't think it's a good idea to mix business with dating. Yet you're going to ask me out."

She laughed. "Oh, am I?"

I'd spent the entire day watching her from a distance. The makeup people had painted her with much more than she normally wore, including a bright red lipstick that still hadn't dulled after all these hours. I couldn't take my eyes off her mouth.

I swallowed, staring at her lips. "Some rules were made to be bent."

She let out a nervous laugh. "Are you a rule-bender, Hudson? I feel like you know so much about me, yet I don't know too much about you."

"What would you like to know?"

The bartender brought over our drinks, and Stella lifted her wine to her lips.

"I don't know. You're divorced. What happened there?"

I frowned. "This is supposed to be a celebration, not a funeral."

She smiled. "That bad?"

"I gave her my grandmother's ring when I proposed. A few days later, I came home and she had a different ring on. She'd sold the ring and bought one she'd liked better."

Stella's eyes widened. "Oh my."

I sucked back my beer. "Serves me right since I married her anyway."

"Why did you?"

That was a damn good question. People always asked why we broke up, but never why I'd married Lexi to begin with. "If you'd asked me that before the wedding, I would have said I was young and we had a lot in common—we both liked to travel, we ran in the same social circle..."

"But the answer isn't the same now?"

I shook my head. "Hindsight is a lot clearer. My mother had died the year before. I was working in the family business, taking on more and more responsibilities because my father had taken a step back from things after his first heart attack. It felt like what should come next. That sounds really ignorant saying it out loud today, but my family was falling apart, and I think I just wanted what I'd had, so I went about making my own. I'd been with Lexi for a few years, so I took the next steps. Basically, I was an idiot."

"I don't think you were an idiot. I think it's kind of sweet that you were trying to hold on to your family life. I take it your parents had a strong marriage?"

I nodded. "They did. Still held hands, and whenever one of them noticed the time was five thirteen on a clock, they wished each other a happy anniversary. They were married on May thirteenth."

"Aww...that's pretty romantic."

"What about you? Parents still married?"

"They are. But they have an...*interesting* marriage..." She hesitated. "My parents are polyamorous."

My brows jumped. "Wow. So your father is married to multiple people?"

She shook her head. "No, that's polygamy. They just have an open relationship. Always have."

"How does that work?"

"I grew up in a two-story house in Westchester. We had a small, two-bedroom apartment downstairs, and three bedrooms upstairs. On the main floor, life was normal. My sister and I each had our own room, and my parents shared a bedroom. But we always had a lot of my parents' friends come to stay in the guest rooms downstairs. They never really hid their lifestyle from us, but it wasn't until I was about eight or nine that I realized how different their relationship was. Our bathroom was getting redone on the main floor, and I'd woken up in the middle of the night. I needed to go, so I went downstairs. As I went toward the bathroom, a woman walked out in her underwear. I'd met her before, but I hadn't expected to see anyone, so I screamed. My father came running out from the bedroom down the hall in *his* underwear. The next day, my parents sat my sister and me down and explained things."

"That must have been difficult to grasp at that age."

She nodded. "I definitely struggled with it for a while. None of my friends' parents were like that, and neither were the couples on TV—especially not twenty years ago. So I didn't understand why my parents had to be different. It made me wonder if that's how my life would be. I remember asking my mom one day if what they had was hereditary."

My eyes widened. "You don't... You're not..."

Stella chuckled. "Definitely not. I've accepted my parents' marriage for what it is, but I knew early on that it wasn't a lifestyle I wanted. I'm a pretty jealous person when it comes to my relationships. I'm way too territorial to share."

I smiled, thinking about how I'd felt when Jack had brought Brent around. Hell, Stella and I weren't even dating, and I'd wanted to punch the guy. "I get it."

I remembered that she'd alluded to a bad relationship with her father the day she came to my office to pick up her cell. "Do they still live in Westchester?"

She nodded. "Same house. As far as I know, they have the same upstairs marital bedroom and the downstairs for their extracurricular activities. But I haven't been there in over a year." She sipped her wine. "We had a...falling out, I guess you could say. If you don't mind, I don't really want to talk about it. Today was such a great day, and I'm not ready to come down from the high of it all."

"Yeah, of course."

She sipped her wine. "How about your family? Do you have any siblings besides Olivia?"

I shook my head. "Just the one. Thank God. I couldn't afford another wedding."

"I'm sure having a wedding at the library must've cost a small fortune. One of the women whose diaries I read a while ago got married there, too. I fell in love with the way she described it. At the time I was reading it, I worked nearby, and I used to go sit outside on the library stairs for lunch every day and read a few pages. I always looked around and wondered if the man she'd married might be passing by, since they'd obviously lived local at one time."

"You told me the diaries are your version of reality TV. But it sounds more like romantic fantasy than reality, if you ask me."

"Actually," she said. "That particular diary turned out to be more like a horror story. It was part of the reason I found out Aiden was cheating on me."

"How so?"

"The diary had big gaps in time and spanned a few years. But after the over-the-moon wedding at the library, things apparently turned sour. She went from entries where she described the beautiful venue and her flowers, to entries where she described how she was covering up an affair. Some of the things she was doing hit home because I'd noticed the same changes in Aiden—like he'd started to work late and then shower as soon as he came home. The woman described how much she hated to wash the smell of her lover off, and she said she actually resented her husband because she had to shower right away when she came home after one of her dalliances. That led me to start asking Aiden questions. At first he made me think I was paranoid. He blamed the diaries I read for planting things in my head that didn't exist. But more and more, things made me suspect something was going on. I'm actually pretty ashamed of how crazy I became at the end."

"What could you have done to be ashamed of? Sounds like your ex is the one who should be ashamed."

Stella looked away for a moment. "How did we get to talking about me again? We're supposed to be talking about you."

"I think the mention of my sister's wedding at the library took us down a path. I don't think I told you, but I was also married there."

"Really? Your sister got married at the same place you did?"

I nodded. "Our parents were married there, too. Ever since she was little, Olivia had been saying both of our weddings were going to be there. I'm glad she didn't let my outcome take that away from her."

We finished our drinks, but neither Jack nor Robyn had shown up. I looked at my watch and realized they were twenty minutes late.

Stella noticed. "We were supposed to meet them at seven, right?"

I nodded and glanced over to the front entrance. No one was waiting. "Let me double-check. Maybe I got the time wrong." I took out my phone and clicked into the text message Jack had sent. We were in the right place at the right time, so I shot my buddy a text.

Hudson: Did you change the restaurant or something? Stella and I are the only ones at The NoMad.

Stella's wine was empty. I motioned to her glass. "You want another?"

"I shouldn't."

"But do you want one?"

She laughed. "I'll pass. I want to keep a clear head during dinner with Robyn."

A minute later, my phone chimed with a response from Jack.

Jack: Did I forget to mention that the celebration was canceled for tonight? Robyn couldn't get a sitter. She's going to let me know what works for her next week.

I typed back.

Hudson: WTF? Yes, you did.

Jack: Guess it must've slipped my mind. Go celebrate without us tonight. Unless you're not up for it? I can always text Brent to come take Stella off your hands...

I shook my head.

Hudson: You're such a dick. You did this on purpose, didn't you?

Jack: You're welcome, my friend.

I tossed my phone on the bar.

"Everything okay?" Stella asked.

"Apparently something came up and dinner's been rescheduled. My jackass of a friend forgot to let me know."

"Oh. Wow. Okay."

My buddy's tactics might have been underhanded, but I couldn't say I was displeased with the result.

"We're on the same side now, right?"

Stella's brows furrowed. "What do you mean?"

"You didn't want to have another drink because we were having dinner with business associates. But you and I aren't business associates, we're co-owners. So we're on the same side."

She smiled. "I guess I have less to worry about now, considering I've already made a fool out of myself in front of you multiple times."

"What do you say we have that second drink while we order dinner? We should still celebrate."

She bit her bottom lip.

I reached out with my thumb, rubbing until she released it. "Stop worrying. It's not a date. We're just business partners and friends having dinner. I won't maul you until you ask me out."

16

Stella

"**Y**ou're not going to have another?"

Hudson held up a hand. "I'm driving."

I hiccupped. "And I'm tipsy. Nice to meet you, driving."

He chuckled. "You're cute when you're drunk."

I shook my head. "I'm not drunk. I'm tipsy."

"And the difference is?"

"Tipsy, I'm still in control."

"So drunk you lose control?" Hudson stopped our waitress, who happened to be walking by. "Could we get another wine when you get a chance? And *really fill* the glass, please."

I laughed. "Tonight has definitely been more fun than my last date. Wait…" I waved my hand around. "This isn't a date."

"Of course not." He smirked and sipped his water. "Things not going so well with Ken?"

"Ben."

"Whatever. Trouble in paradise?"

I sighed. "He's a really nice guy. There's just no... chemistry, I guess."

Hudson's eyes dropped to my lips. "No chemistry, huh?"

The air in the room started to crackle so loudly I was surprised everyone eating dinner wasn't looking around to find the noise. This... *This* was what was missing between Ben and me. Hudson only had to look at me in a certain way and my body temperature rose.

I swallowed. "He brought me flowers on our first date and Godiva on our second. He's very thoughtful. I guess I'm hoping the connection might develop."

Hudson's eyes darkened. "It won't."

"How do you know?"

"Because you can't force chemistry to exist where it doesn't—the same way you can't stop it from existing where you don't want it. There are some things we're just powerless over."

I felt a little powerless at the moment. Like if Hudson were to slip his hand under the table and up my skirt, I wouldn't be able to bring myself to stop him. Luckily, the waitress brought my wine, which was practically filled to the brim.

She winked at Hudson conspiratorially. "Would you like to see the dessert menu?"

He nodded. "That would be great. Thank you."

When she came back with the menus, she said she'd give us a few minutes. I thought the interruption might help Hudson and me change topics, but he set his glass down and obviously had other ideas.

"So when are we dumping Len?"

I smiled. "*We*? Are you going to let him down with me?"

"I'll happily do it *for* you." He held out his hand. "Give me your phone."

I chuckled. "Thanks, but I think I can handle it on my own."

"But you will be handling it? Meaning bye-bye Benny boy?"

"Of course you're able to get his name right when we're talking about dumping him." I rolled my eyes. "Besides, you and I look at relationships differently."

Hudson's eyes narrowed. "How so?"

"You said yourself that you enjoy spending time with women, but you have different expectations of where things will end up."

"I meant I break things off if I can't see a future and the woman I'm seeing seems to be growing feelings. I'm not averse to a relationship, if that's what you're thinking."

"Oh."

He grinned. "With you and me, our feelings are mutual. So it's not a problem."

I chuckled. "So I take it you're not seeing anyone right now?"

"Not at the moment, but I'm working on it." His eyes sparkled.

"When was the last time you had a date?"

"I guess it was the weekend before my sister's wedding."

"And how was that?"

"Well, we went to a Mexican restaurant. She asked me if I'd like to share an appetizer and told me to pick one, so I ordered chips and guacamole they made tableside. When I was done, my date turned to the waiter and said, 'Guatemala. He means chips and Guatemala.'"

I laughed. "You're making that up?"

He shook his head. "I wish I was."

"I take it you didn't go out with her again?"

"No. Though I met someone who spiked my interest the next weekend, anyway. She's kind of hard to get out of my head, so it wouldn't be fair to go out with someone else, even if they did know the difference between Guatemala and guacamole."

I tried to cool the warm feeling in my belly with my wine. But the way Hudson was watching me didn't make it easy.

"Did you meet Miss Guatemala on a dating site?"

"No. I actually met her at a fundraiser. I'm not on any dating sites."

"Really? Then how do you meet people? The old-fashioned way?"

"Yes, I pay for prostitutes."

"Liar." I smiled. "You've never had to pay for it in your life. I meant bars. Is that where you meet women?"

"Sometimes. I don't know. Wherever."

I rolled my eyes and waved my hand at his face. "You have no trouble meeting people because you look like that."

"Are you saying you like what you see?"

"You know you're hot. You have a mirror at home, don't you? I'm sure all you have to do is walk into a bar and snap your fingers and women run over."

Hudson chuckled. "What am I, the Fonz?"

"Maybe?" We both laughed.

His smile faded as his eyes roamed my face. "You're really beautiful when you laugh."

I looked down, feeling a little shy. "Thank you."

Hudson was still watching me intently when the waitress came back. She seemed to have impeccable timing—for me, anyway. Because when Hudson's eyes dropped to my lips, I'd been a hair away from suggesting something that wasn't on the dessert menu.

"See anything you'd like to try?" she said.

Hudson's eyes blazed, and the slightest twitch at the corner of his mouth confirmed we were on the same page. "I'll leave it up to the lady to decide what she wants."

I swallowed and focused on the menu. "Umm... They have crème brûlée cheesecake. You want to share a piece?"

Once again his eyes flickered to my lips for a moment. "Whatever you're in the mood for."

This was *definitely* my last glass of wine. I nodded to the waitress.

Hudson took my menu and lifted it with his for her to take back. "Thank you."

After she left, I sipped my wine, and Hudson and I talked some more. I couldn't remember the last time the conversation had flowed so easily when I'd gone out with someone. I'd also smiled the entire night. Though of course, this wasn't a date. And I kept forgetting that.

By the time my glass was empty again, I'd entered the short hallway that led from tipsy to drunk. Which was probably why I'd lost my filter.

"How long is considered normal to go without sex?"

Hudson's brows nearly reached his hairline. "Are you asking because you think you've surpassed whatever the acceptable limit is?"

My smile was lopsided. "Maybe."

He groaned. "I said I wouldn't ask you out again. But I could offer some help taking care of that problem for you."

I laughed. "Seriously. What's normal?"

"I have no damn idea."

"Well, how long has it been for you?"

"I don't know. A few months now, I guess. How about you?"

I cringed. "More like a year."

"Not a fan of hookups, I take it?"

"Does Theo James count?"

"The actor? You hooked up with him?"

"Well, no—not the actual actor. But I sort of named my vibrator after him."

Hudson groaned again. "Don't tell me that shit."

"What? Is that too personal? Surely it's not a shock that a single woman has one."

"No, it's not that. But now I want to punch Theo James."

I laughed.

Hudson shook his head. "I take it you named it that because that's who you...envision?"

I bit my lip. Theo had been my go-to fantasy for years, although lately, my battery-operated boyfriend should have been renamed for the man whose eyes were currently growing darker as we spoke.

I was grateful the waitress was quick and returned with dessert. At least my big mouth would be kept busy for a while.

Some time later, I looked around the restaurant and realized it was almost empty. "What time is it?"

Hudson checked his watch. "Almost eleven. I didn't realize it was that late. No wonder the waitress has checked on us three times since she brought dessert. She probably wants to get the hell out of here."

"I think you're right."

We left the restaurant, and Hudson drove me home. As usual, there was no parking in front of my building, so he parked a few doors down.

"I'm going to walk you."

"That's not necessary."

"Yes, it is."

He got out and came around to my side of the car to open the door, then extended a hand.

"Thank you."

He nodded.

We were quiet as we made our way to my building. I debated whether I should invite him in for coffee or something, and I still hadn't decided as we entered the lobby and stood in front of the elevator. Of course, the run-down thing usually took ten minutes, but tonight the doors slid open immediately after I pushed the button. Hudson put one hand on the edge to stop it from closing and held the other out for me to enter—though he didn't follow me in.

"Congratulations again on today. You killed it."

I smiled. "Thank you. For everything, Hudson—taking a chance on me, getting me the opportunity at the network, all the things you've done to help make everything come together, and even celebrating with me tonight. I don't think it's fully hit me yet that I'm going to be on the Home Shopping Channel showing the world Signature Scent. And truly, I owe it all to you."

He shook his head. "I just cracked open a few doors. Everything else was all you."

We stared at each other until the elevator tried to close. Hudson's hand stopped it, but he took that as his cue. "Goodnight, Stella."

"Goodnight, Hudson."

He stepped back, removing his hand.

The longest fifteen seconds ticked by while I stood in the car, waiting for the elevator doors to slide closed again. A sense of panic washed over me when they finally started to move, and at the last second, I stuck my hand between them, causing them to bounce open again.

Hudson had turned to leave, but he looked back when he heard the elevator open.

"Would you...want to come up for coffee or something?" My heart pounded inside as I waited for him to speak.

"Coffee?" he eventually said.

I bit my lip and nodded.

Hudson searched my face. "You sure you want me to come up?"

When I took too long to debate my answer, he smiled sadly. "That's what I thought."

I let out a relieved exhale and shook my head. "I'm sorry."

"Nothing to be sorry about. I tease you that I'm waiting for you to ask me out, but it's not really about you making the first move. It's about your head being clear on what you want. This isn't over. I'm just waiting for that little whisper in your head to get loud enough for you to listen."

"What whisper?"

"The one that keeps telling you that despite your trust issues and concerns about our business relationship, you want me as much as I want you."

I smiled halfheartedly, and Hudson took both of my hands in his. He lifted his chin to the empty space in the open car behind me.

"Now why don't you get back in the elevator before I lose the last shred of self-control I have and join you." He raised one of my hands to his lips and kissed the top. "Go."

I nodded and stepped back in. Pushing the button on the door panel, I said quietly, "Thanks, Hudson."

He winked as the doors began to slide closed. "Enjoy Theo."

Stella

The rest of the week flew by. Olivia and I worked day and night to get all of the marketing materials finalized, while Hudson focused on the orders-and-financing side of things. By Saturday morning, only a few of the rushed shipments had come in, so it was pretty daunting that the segment I'd taped was going to air at three o'clock this afternoon, and then orders could start pouring in. At least *I hoped* they poured in. Everything was in motion, but I wouldn't breathe a sigh of relief until the warehouse was full of all the products necessary to start shipping.

To add to that stress, I was a nervous wreck about seeing myself on TV. The last couple of days, I'd started freaking out that Signature Scent might bomb. I knew the show flashed the quantity remaining like a ticker at the bottom of the television screen, and I'd had a recurring nightmare that throughout the segment I only sold three boxes and there were 49,997 left after my hour was up.

I'd really wanted to stay home and watch the segment today by myself while I alternated between chewing my nails and hiding my face under a cover. But Olivia had organized a viewing party at her apartment. She'd been so kind and supportive, it was impossible to say no. So now here I was, Ubering downtown with two-dozen homemade cupcakes on my lap to watch the show with a dozen people from the office.

I'd obviously known the Rothschild family wasn't poor, since their business was loaning money to other businesses, but when we pulled up to the address Olivia had given me on Murray Street, my breath caught. *Wow*. She lived in one of the new, fancy skyscrapers in Tribeca—a modern tower of curved glass that widened as it went up. The design was super sleek, the type of building featured in *Architectural Digest* or some other glossy magazine. Even the entrance was intimidating. It jutted out onto the street in an imposing way, as if to show people who had to move for whom. Stepping out of the Uber and looking up, I suddenly wished I hadn't baked the cupcakes I'd brought and had instead picked up something more professional-looking from one of the dozen overpriced cupcakeries that had popped up all over the City the last few years. I also really wished Fisher hadn't had to go out of town this weekend on business. I could use him by my side today.

I sighed and tried my best not to feel inferior just because I couldn't even afford the enormous plantings outside the front door. Olivia's apartment was on the fifty-third floor, but I had to check in at a desk in the lobby. The security guard gave me a keycard to slide into the elevator panel, rather than pushing a button. As soon as I inserted it, the doors slid closed and the fifty-three button illuminated. I took a deep breath as the fast-moving car climbed its way up, but with each floor that passed, my nerves became more and more frayed. When the doors opened, I'd expected to have a few minutes to collect myself in the hallway, but instead I stepped directly into Olivia's apartment.

She greeted me with her usual bubbly enthusiasm and swamped me in a hug. "Eeep! I'm so excited! I can't wait! You're the first one here."

"That makes one of us. I think I might throw up."

Olivia giggled as if I were joking, but my stomach did feel pretty queasy at the moment. She ushered me from the entryway into the kitchen. However fancy I'd thought her apartment would be based on the building from the outside, I'd underestimated. The kitchen was beautiful, complete with high-end appliances, sparkling granite, and two big islands. But the living room was the showstopper.

"Wow. Your view is just..." I shook my head. "It's incredible."

Floor-to-ceiling windows lined the adjoining living room, showcasing sprawling views of the water and city.

Olivia waved it off. "View-shmew—these cupcakes look delicious. Do you mind if I have a bite of one now?"

I laughed. "Of course not. And I think you can have more than a bite. They're actually sugar-free. I found the recipe on a diabetes website. I ate one for breakfast this morning while I was baking them, and they're pretty damn good, if I say so myself."

"You're an angel!" She popped the lid off one of the plastic containers and chose a vanilla one with chocolate frosting. Peeling the paper off the bottom, she motioned to the giant windows I couldn't take my eyes off of. "I used to think that was everything I wanted. And then Hudson bought his brownstone in Brooklyn last year. He has no view, but he has a little backyard, and the building has so much character. It feels like he lives in a real home. This place..." She shook her head and licked a line of icing off the top of the cupcake. "I don't know... It just sort of feels like I'm staying at a luxury hotel or something. Charlie only stays with her dad a few days a week, and she already has friends who live on their block. I've lived here for two years, and I don't know a single person in the building. I sort of feel like I live in an ivory tower up here." She laughed. "Don't tell Hudson I said that. I wouldn't want to mess with our delicate dynamic. He thinks it's his job to teach me about life, and I pretend I don't need him to."

I smiled. "Your secret is safe with me."

A bell sounded overhead, and Olivia walked to an intercom system on the wall and pressed a button. "I have a delivery from Cipriani," the voice said.

"Great. Send them up, please, Dave."

Just as she released the buzzer, a man I recognized—though I hadn't actually met him—walked out from a hallway on the other side of the living room. *Ugh.* I'd been so busy worrying about seeing myself on TV and how Signature Scent would do that I hadn't stopped to consider that Olivia's husband would be home on a Saturday afternoon. Of course I'd apologized to Olivia multiple times. For the most part, I didn't feel embarrassed when I spoke to her anymore. We'd somehow been able to put what I'd done behind us. But I'd never spoken to her husband, and I prayed it wouldn't be too awkward. Though the grin on his face as he strode toward the kitchen had me freaking out a little.

Olivia waved between us. "Mason, this is the guest of honor, Stella. Stella, this is my husband, Mason. Mase, the food is here. Why don't you make Stella a drink while I deal with the delivery?"

My face heated with renewed shame as he extended his hand. "Nice to finally meet you."

"Hi." I cringed and shook my head. "I'm really sorry about your wedding. I apologized to your wife, but I should have sent you a note, too."

Mason shook his head. "Totally not necessary. The whole thing was pretty funny, especially the story you told. Plus, Liv never stops talking about you, so everything worked out for the best. I don't think I've ever seen her so excited about something to do with work. She's really invested in what you've created."

I let out a relieved breath and smiled. "She is. I'm very lucky. To be honest, I was really unsure about going into business with an investor. But she's given me so much more than financial backing. I feel like I have a partner who cares as much as I do."

Mason nodded. "She does." He looked over my shoulder at her before lowering his voice. "She went through a funk after her dad died last year. The only thing that seemed to get her out of it was planning our wedding. So I was a little concerned about what would happen when it was over. But then *you* happened, and I feel like I've gotten my old Liv back lately. So while you might think you owe me an apology, it's really me who owes you a big thanks."

Wow. I shook my head. "I don't know what to say—actually, I do. You two were made for each other. You're both amazing."

He smiled and again glanced over my shoulder. "I see her searching in her bag for money for a tip. She never carries a dollar, so I don't know why she's looking. In about ten seconds, she's going to call my name so she can rummage through my wallet. So what can I get you to drink? A mixed drink, beer, wine?"

"I'd love a glass of wine. Merlot, if you have it."

"You got it."

Olivia yelled from the kitchen. "Mason?"

He grinned and pulled out his wallet. "I'll be back with your wine after I tip the delivery man. Make yourself at home."

I could have stood at the windows and looked at the view of the City all day, but the mantel over the fireplace caught my eye. There were half a dozen framed pictures on it, so I walked over to be nosy and take a look.

The large silver frame in the center featured a photo from their wedding day. Olivia was bent over laughing as she stood next to a multi-tiered wedding cake, a piece of which she'd obviously just smashed in her husband's face. Mason's tongue was out as he tried to lick the cake from his face through a smile. I loved that they'd chosen that photo to frame, rather than some perfectly posed one. It really showed their happiness, and their smile grew contagious as I looked at it.

To one side of the wedding photo was a picture of an older couple. They were standing in the rain wearing yellow rain slickers, but the smiles on their faces radiated sunshine. They had to be Olivia and Hudson's parents, because the man was basically an older version of Hudson. Next to that photo was a shot of Olivia and Mason at the beach—sporting backward baseball caps and drinking beer. Again, the smiles on their faces were positively contagious.

I skimmed over a few more photos of the happy couple with various friends, and then my eyes landed on the last framed photo at the end. That one I picked up to take a closer look at the two kids—a young Olivia and Hudson. The little boy was probably about nine or ten, but his gorgeous, bright blue eyes were unmistakably Hudson's. He also wore a smirk I'd become all too familiar with. He leaned forward, hovering over a birthday cake, about to blow out the candles. Olivia sat to his left, and his arm was extended, one of his hands covering her mouth.

A deep voice over my shoulder startled me. "Some shit never changes."

Hudson. "Jesus. You scared me. Didn't you learn your lesson about sneaking up on people? I didn't hear you come in."

"Rode up with the food. By the way, be thankful she ordered and didn't try to cook today."

"I'm sure she's not a bad cook."

"Last Christmas she made two trays of shrimp parmesan. We all got a big crunch when we bit in."

"She overcooked the shrimp?"

He shook his head. "She followed a recipe that called for shelled shrimp. She thought *shelled* meant to leave the shell on."

I laughed. "Ohhhhhh…"

He nodded his chin toward the photo in my hand. "I still feel like doing that at least once a week."

"Why were you covering her mouth?"

"Because she thought everyone's birthday cakes were for her and blew out the candles. My parents thought it was cute and let her do it. But that year, I'd made a wish I really wanted to come true, and I wasn't taking any chances."

I laughed. "What was your wish?"

"I wanted a sheepdog."

"Did you get one?"

He shook his head. "Nope."

"Well, it's an adorable picture."

"My mom had it framed on her nightstand. She said it summed up our relationship perfectly, and she wasn't wrong. My sister must've taken it when we cleaned out my parents' things."

Mason walked over and handed me a glass of wine. He passed Hudson a beer. Raising his own bottle, he tilted it to us. "Good luck today, you two."

Hudson clinked his beer, so I followed his lead. "Thank you."

The rest of the guests piled in shortly thereafter, and Hudson and I were pulled in opposite directions. I saw a couple of people on the marketing team who I knew had worked on things for us, but I hadn't gotten to spend much time with them. So I made sure to seek them out and say thank you for everything they'd done.

A few times, while Hudson and I were both talking to different people, my eyes caught with his. His lip would twitch and his eyes sparkled, but neither of us made any attempt to talk again. A few minutes before three o'clock, Olivia pointed the remote at the TV above the fireplace and then used it to clink against her glass.

"Alright, everyone. It's just about time! This is so much more exciting than a dumb Superbowl party, isn't it? Who needs a refill before kickoff?"

I was really damn nervous, so I headed to the kitchen to take her up on the offer before I had to see my face on her giant TV. Mason was standing near the wine and lifted the merlot when he saw me coming.

"You look like I felt when they started playing 'Here Comes the Bride'."

I opened and closed my hands. "Did your fingertips go numb from nerves?"

Mason filled my glass to the brim and handed it back to me with a smile. "Head-to-toe numb. Pretty sure that's why the person who gives away the bride lifts the veil, and the best man holds the ring. The groom's hands are too shaky to do anything."

I sipped my wine. "Well, I hope I can fake it as good as you did. Because you looked cool as a cucumber."

An arm hooked through mine. "Come on," Olivia said. "I want to sit next to you!"

I guzzled as much wine as I could as we settled into the couch together. Immediately after we sat, the music at the beginning of the show started, and the host, Robyn, strolled out, waving to a live studio audience. It was pretty funny to watch, because I had been there when she'd done that walk, and the only people in the audience were Hudson and his friend Jack. Yet now the camera panned to a clapping crowd.

Olivia laced her fingers with mine and squeezed. "Here we go!"

She turned up the volume, and the noise in the room settled down. Robyn did her usual introduction from the side of the stage, and then walked over to the counter where she always stood. Signature Scent boxes and samples were piled all over. It felt completely surreal. Adrenaline rushed through my veins, leaving me a little lightheaded.

For the next few minutes, Robyn did her best Vanna White impression, lifting the boxes and waving her manicured hands around, which I now knew was to keep the viewers' eyes on the product rather than the host. When she began to introduce her guest co-host for the day, I held my breath.

It was absolutely crazy to see myself on television, standing next to such a well-known personality. Robyn Quinn was a pretty big celebrity. During the taping, the director had made me do that walk out onto the stage while waving almost a dozen times. As I watched, I smiled directly into the camera and waved like my personal fan club was in the audience.

Oh my God, I look like such a ham!

Everyone from the office started to hoot and howl, and I dropped my face into my hands, too embarrassed to watch. I'd heard actors say they don't watch their movies and thought that was insane. But now I understood why. I was aware of all the little nervous habits I had, as well as how heavy my New York accent was, and it left me unable to focus on anything but my flaws—all of which seemed highly amplified at the moment.

I cringed and shook my head. "God, this is so hard to watch."

"Are you kidding me?" Olivia asked. "You're a natural and doing incredible!"

The moment of truth came ten minutes into the show. Robyn pointed to the corner of the screen, and the price and telephone number flashed a few times. Thirty seconds later, a countdown clock appeared, too.

"Alright, ladies—and gentlemen out there who want to impress their ladies—we're going to open up the lines now and let you start getting your orders in. We'll continue to talk about Signature Scent, but I think you all already know you want it. So here's what you've been waiting for, your countdown to the opening of our phones and online ordering. You know the drill... And five, four, three, two, one. We're open!"

Within seconds, the countdown of the quantity remaining started to scroll. Slowly at first, but then it began to fly. I couldn't tell you what Robyn or I talked about for the duration of the show—my eyes were glued to that countdown clock. When the *thousands* started to dwindle at a rapid pace, I thought I might hyperventilate, and I really needed a moment.

"Would you mind if I went downstairs to get some air? I'll just be a few minutes."

Olivia looked concerned "Of course not, but are you okay?"

"Yeah. It's just a bit overwhelming, and I need a minute. I won't be gone for long."

"Of course. Of course. But don't go downstairs." She pointed to the hallway her husband had come from earlier. "Last door on the left leads to a guest bedroom. It has a private balcony and a bathroom, too."

"You don't mind?"

"Of course not. Go. Take as long as you need."

"Thank you."

The cool air outside felt incredible. I shut my eyes and took a few deep breaths. After only a minute or two, I felt calm enough to open them and enjoy the stunning view. From this height, the City seemed unusually quiet, which had a real tranquilizing effect on my mental state. So I felt a little better when I heard the sound of the door sliding open behind me, and I turned to find Hudson.

"You okay?" he asked.

I nodded. "I just got a little overwhelmed watching that ticker, and my heart started to race."

"Understandable." He smiled and held something out to me. "Here."

I looked down and my forehead wrinkled. "A banana?"

"I stole it from my sister's kitchen. She didn't have any oranges. I'm more creative with those."

I was confused until I realized he'd written on it. *Your television debut is very appealing.*

Hudson shrugged. "Get it? A-*peel*-ing. Go easy on me—I didn't have very long to come up with something and still follow you out here."

I laughed. "It's very sweet. Thank you. I can see why Charlie likes your messages in her lunchbox so much."

We stood next to each other, staring out at the City. The little fruit trick he used on his daughter had actually helped me relax. Or maybe it was just Hudson's presence.

I sighed. "This is all so surreal."

"I would imagine it is." He smiled.

Yes, I was in the middle of a mental meltdown, but I still noticed how handsome Hudson looked. Not only was he dressed casually in a pair of jeans, he also had some stubble on his face that I really liked.

He'd been quietly watching me look at him, so I felt compelled to say something.

"This is the first time I've seen you unshaven and in street clothes."

He flashed one of his sexy signature half smiles. "And?"

I tilted my head. "I like it."

"Are you telling the truth or just trying to get in your daily compliment quota from your happiness plan?"

I laughed. "No, I like it. The scruff on your jaw gives you a sinister look."

He tilted his head. "Is that your type? Sinister looking? That's not exactly what I envisioned when you said your ex was a poet."

I laughed. "Oh, Aiden is as clean-cut as they come. That's always been my type. I never went for the bad boys. I don't think I've ever dated anyone with a scar or a tattoo."

"And you'd like to change that?"

I shrugged, playing along and teasing. "Maybe."

Hudson's eyes sparkled. "That's good. Because I can help. I have both."

"You do?"

He nodded.

"Where are they?"

"Ah...that's information I'll keep for another time."

I laughed. "Top secret, huh?"

A light gust of wind pushed a lock of hair onto my face. Hudson used his finger to move it. "Feel better?"

I took a deep breath and relaxed my shoulders. "I do. Thank you."

He tilted his head toward the door. "Why don't we go back in, then? As much as I'd rather be right here, I don't want you to miss anything."

I nodded.

Back in the living room, I took my seat next to Olivia on the couch and looked up at the countdown clock to see how things were going. I blinked a few times reading the number. I hadn't been gone for more than five minutes, yet we were already almost completely sold out.

"I've been watching this show every day for the last week and a half," Olivia said. "And they never sell out this fast. You're absolutely slaying it. I was worried you'd miss the part where Robyn says her big tagline—*Going...going and buh-bye!*"

Sure enough, only minutes later, the side of the screen with the countdown started to flash.

"Uh-oh," the host said. "We're about to sell out. Hurry up and get those orders in!" She paused and shook her head. "I better say it before it's too late. Going...going..." She raised her hand and waved. "...and *buh-bye*!" A big stamp appeared over the countdown clock on the screen.

SOLD OUT

Everyone in the room cheered. Olivia hugged me, and people took turns coming over to congratulate us. When I turned back to look at the TV, the next product was already being introduced. Relief washed over me that we'd done well, and I wouldn't have to see my face up on that giant TV anymore.

Olivia and Mason popped champagne, and she handed out glasses. As she extended one to me, my eyes met Hudson's across the room. He silently raised his glass and smiled.

Olivia looked between the two of us before hooking her arm around my neck. She turned us so our backs were facing Hudson and spoke with a low voice. "He really likes you."

"Who?"

She rolled her eyes. "Uh, the man who hasn't taken his eyes off of you since he walked in. Hudson, of course. I see the way he looks at you."

"He's excited about today...about Signature Scent."

She pointed her finger at me. "He's excited about *you*."

I glanced over my shoulder at Hudson, and our eyes met once again. I couldn't deny that I'd felt like the center of his focus today. He looked between his sister and me, and his eyes narrowed. He absolutely knew we were talking about him.

I sighed. "He's a great guy."

"So..." Olivia shrugged. "Why are you two still playing cat and mouse, then?"

"We're in business together. He's an investor in my company."

"And..."

"I don't know." I shook my head. "If it doesn't work out, it could be pretty messy."

Olivia sipped her champagne. "Life is messy. You know the only time it's not? When you're not living it—when you're just going through the motions."

"I know... But—"

She interrupted me. "What happened to the woman who crashed my wedding and ran out laughing and drinking champagne?"

I laughed. "God, that's a good example of being a mess."

"Maybe." She shrugged. "But look where that mess led you. To a new business and a new best friend—and if you ask me who the new best friend is, I'm going to punch you. We're having a moment here."

I chuckled. "I get what you're saying, but I told you what happened with Aiden. A lot of our fights centered on being in business together. He would question how I spent money, and we would argue over the direction things should go. It was really the beginning of our problems."

Olivia shook her head. "I think you're wrong. Not to be crass, but the beginning of your problems was him sticking his dick in another woman."

"Not that it's a valid excuse, but he turned to someone else because we weren't getting along."

"No, he didn't. He turned to someone else because he's a piece of shit. That was just the most convenient excuse."

I sighed. "I guess…"

"Did I tell you that Mason and I met at work?"

"Really? At Rothschild Investments?"

She nodded. "Hudson brought him on as director of IT. He was there for three years, and we were dating for two of them. We worked together on a few projects, and we didn't always see eye to eye."

"He owns his own IT firm, right? Is that why he left?"

"No. There was nowhere for him to grow at Rothschild. We only have a few IT people, and he wanted to keep growing. But my point is, we worked together and fought. That didn't lead him to cheat on me." Olivia looked over at her husband and smirked. "Occasionally it led to some hot, angry make-up sex on my desk, though…" She held up her hands and her face scrunched. "Oh God. Don't do that with my brother because my office is so close. I once walked in on our parents, and I still haven't gotten over it."

I laughed.

"Seriously, Stella. If you're not into Hudson, that's fine. But don't let what happened with your ex, or your fears of things getting messy, ruin what could be a good thing. Some of the best things in life are messy—buns, sheets after good sex, lava cake, watermelon. Do I need to go on?"

I smiled. "No. I get it."

Hudson walked over with a bottle of champagne and topped off both our glasses. Noticing the label, I said, "No wonder this is so delicious. It's the good stuff. I've run out of the bottles I stole from Olivia's wedding, so you might want to hide any you have left when I'm on my way out."

Olivia laughed. "I'm going to go help Mason put out more food. You two continue the celebration without me." She walked away but looked back over her shoulder so Hudson didn't see and winked.

I smiled. "Your sister is pretty amazing."

"She's not too bad," Hudson agreed. "But don't tell her I said that."

He'd walked over to fill our glasses, but didn't have one of his own. "Where's your champagne?"

"I have plans." Hudson looked at his watch. "I actually need to be going. I was coming over to say goodbye."

"Oh." Disappointment gripped me, along with maybe a tiny bit of jealousy. I forced a smile. "Well, have fun."

Hudson's eyes narrowed before he eventually grinned.

"Are you jealous because I have a date?"

"No," I said—*waaay* too quickly.

He tucked his hands into his pockets and flaunted a smug smile. "You are."

"Am not."

He leaned forward, his nose almost touching mine, and whispered, "Jealous."

"You're so full of yourself. You can't even tell the difference between happy for you and jealous."

He pulled his head back. "Oh yeah? You're happy I have a date?"

I plastered on a smile and pointed to my mouth. "Yes. See?"

The look on Hudson's face told me my attempt at a smile came out more like one reflected in a fun house.

He chuckled. "I'm picking up Charlie from some playdate. My ex went to a doctor's appointment with her sister who's pregnant and might not make it on time, so I told her I'd take her home."

"Oh. Okay."

"Happy it's not a real date?"

Yes. I shrugged. "Whatever. It's your business."

He rubbed his chin. "I was thinking of coming back after. Think you'll still be here?"

"Maybe I have a date tonight. Would that bother *you*?"

Hudson's jaw flexed. "I'm not the one who pretends I'm not interested, so I don't think you'll be surprised to know it would."

I'd been teasing, and it backfired. His face was too serious to screw around. I sighed. "I don't have a date. I'll probably be here."

Hudson shook his head. "You're a pain in my ass."

I sipped my champagne. "Well, apparently you like pains in the asses."

His eyes dropped to my lips. "You know I'm counting all the times you torture me. Eventually I'll get even."

"And how will you do that?"

He leaned in and kissed my cheek, then moved his lips to my ear. "With my mouth."

I blinked a few times, taking in Hudson's smirk as he walked away.

He spoke over his shoulder. "Hold that thought, Stella. Your whisper is getting almost loud enough that I can hear it."

Oh boy. I'm in trouble.

18

Stella

I'd started to think Hudson wasn't coming back. It had been hours since he left, though with the stress of the show over, I'd relaxed a lot and was able to have a good time. But I'd be lying if I said I wasn't watching the door constantly. Half the guests had gone, and a few more were getting ready to leave. I went to the bathroom and figured I'd soon call it a night, too. But when I came out, Hudson was sitting at the island drinking a beer.

"You're back. I thought maybe you'd changed your mind."

His eyes flickered to my legs before returning to meet mine. "Definitely not."

I felt that flutter low in my belly—lately it had turned into part of the man's greeting.

"Since I was picking up Charlie, my ex-wife figured she'd go get a massage too. Must've been a tough week of doing nothing."

I smiled. "I take it she doesn't work?"

He shook his head.

"Screw asking you out. Maybe I should propose. You sound like a good ex-husband."

He chuckled. "Welcome back." My forehead wrinkled, so he explained. "You've been stressed. Apparently that caused your inner wiseass to take a hiatus."

"Oh." I laughed. "Yeah, I have been stressed."

"Feel better now that today's over?"

"I do." I rubbed the back of my neck. "Though I could actually use a massage, too."

He wiggled his fingers. "I could help you out. I'm pretty good with my hands."

I smiled. "I bet."

"You up to continue the celebration?"

I was wired and nowhere near ready to go home. "What did you have in mind?"

"Let's go get a drink. There's a bar down the block."

I nibbled my lip. "Hmmm... Are you asking me out on a date?"

"Nope. Taking a colleague out to celebrate."

"I'll think about it."

Hudson frowned. "You'll think about it?"

"Yes."

He looked a little disgruntled, but shrugged. When he reached for his beer, I tapped him on the shoulder.

"I thought about it."

"And?"

"Let's go celebrate some more."

"I still can't get over that we sold fifty-thousand boxes of Signature Scent in under an hour today." I shook my head. "A month ago I was thinking I might never see the day one box was ordered."

"We got lucky," Hudson said.

"No. We didn't get lucky. Luck means something falls into your lap. You went out and made this happen."

"Couldn't have happened without a good product."

I sipped my wine. "You know, I wouldn't have expected you to be so humble."

"Trust me. I'm not. I just give credit when it's due."

We were seated at a table in a high-end bar a few blocks from Olivia's apartment. The waitress came over to check on us. She was gorgeous, but Hudson didn't ogle her at all. In fact, he barely seemed to look her way, which made me curious.

"Tell me about the last woman you dated. Not including Miss Guatemala. A woman you went out with more than once?"

His brows dipped. "Why?"

I shrugged. "Just curious. Do you have a certain type? A look you're attracted to?"

He smirked. "Yes, blond hair and glasses."

I laughed. "No, really."

"I don't know." He shook his head. "I guess the last woman I dated was a brunette. Tall. Dark eyes."

"How long did that last?"

"We went out a few times."

"Why did it end?"

He looked back and forth between my eyes. "You want the truth?"

"Of course."

"All she talked about was her sister who had just had a baby. It felt like she was on the fast track to get married and have kids."

"And you don't want to get married again or have more children?"

He sipped his beer. "I didn't say that. I just didn't see it with her."

"So if she had wanted something casual, things wouldn't have ended?"

"I don't know, because that's not what the situation was. But I'm not commitment-averse, if that's what you're getting at. I didn't stop seeing her because she was looking for a future with someone. I stopped seeing her because the right person for her wasn't me."

I nodded. "The waitress is beautiful..."

Hudson tilted his head. "Is she?"

"Very."

He scratched his chin. "Are you trying to set me up?"

"Do you want me to set you up?"

"Is there a reason we're only talking in questions?"

I smiled. "I don't know? Is there?"

After a few seconds of staring at me, Hudson ended our little game. "I have no interest in the waitress."

When I said nothing, he tilted his head. "Aren't you going to ask why not?"

The way he was looking at me, I already knew the answer to that question.

I finished off my wine and smiled. "Nope."

He chuckled. "How are things going with you and Ken?"

"It's Ben and you know it." I smiled and shook my head. "I'm not seeing him anymore. We didn't have a connection."

Hudson's smile stretched from ear to ear. "I'm sorry to hear that."

I rolled my eyes. "Yeah, it looks like you are."

Hudson stopped our waitress as she passed. "Excuse me. Can we get another round when you have a chance?"

"Of course."

After she walked away, he mumbled, "Doesn't hold a candle." Then he finished up his beer and stood. "Excuse me for a minute. I'm going to hit the men's room."

While he was gone, I texted Fisher and filled him in on the rest of the afternoon. We'd texted a few times earlier today, and I'd given him updates on how well Signature Scent did, but I hadn't taken out my phone in a while.

Fisher: How's The Rose?

Stella: How do you know I'm here?

Fisher: I tracked you on your phone a half hour ago when you didn't answer my text for two hours. You never take that long to respond, so I got worried. Guess the party moved there?

Some people might not like being tracked, but I'd given Fisher access to my phone's location for a reason, and I appreciated his concern.

Stella: Some of the party moved here...

I smiled, seeing the dots immediately jump around.

Fisher: Just you and the Adonis?

Stella: We went for a drink after the party.

Fisher: Are you going to jump his bones finally?

Stella: I don't think that's on the menu...

Fisher: Sweetheart, men are _always_ on the menu. It's simple. Just tell him you're in the mood for a cocktail—hold the tail.

I shook my head with a smile.

Stella: I'll keep that line in my arsenal. Thanks.

When Hudson returned from the men's room, I put down my phone. He slid back into the seat across from me. "So what's going on with Marco these days?"

"Marco?"

"The boy toy."

"Oh." I laughed. "He's reading _The Thorn Birds_. He asked Amalia what her favorite books were, and each week he goes to the library and turns one back in and takes out another. Then he strikes up a conversation with her about the book he just finished. He's trying to show her how committed he is and find things in common. It's so romantic."

"*The Thorn Birds*? Sounds familiar, but I don't think I've ever read it."

"Oh, you should. It's actually one of my favorites, too."

"So is what's-her-name falling for it?"

"Amalia...and I think she is. He's started to go on the nights she closes the library, and she lets him walk her home."

Hudson shook his head. "How old is this diary? Sounds like a lot of work. Guess they didn't have Tinder yet?"

I laughed. "Well, I suppose it's much easier to swipe left, or right—whichever it is. But that's probably why the people you meet that way aren't usually the love of your life."

"What ever happened with his other plan—to make her jealous by bringing some young girl around?"

"Thankfully, he decided to go the mature route and show her he's dedicated instead."

A cell phone started to buzz. I turned mine over thinking it was me, but it wasn't. "Is that your phone buzzing?"

"Shit." He dug into his pocket. "I didn't even notice." Reading the name on the screen, Hudson's brows dipped. He looked at his watch. "It's my ex-wife. I should answer it. She never calls this late."

"Of course. Go ahead."

He swiped and brought the phone to his ear. "What's up?"

I heard a woman's voice, but couldn't make out what she was saying.

"Where's Mark?" Hudson asked after a moment.

Pause.

"Shit. Okay. Yeah. I'll be there as soon as I can."

He swiped the phone off and immediately raised his hand to call the waitress. "I'm sorry. I need to go."

"Is everything okay with Charlie?"

"Yeah, she's fine. Lexi's sister started having contractions, and apparently her husband is in California for business. Lexi wants to go to the hospital with her, and she needs me to meet her there to pick up Charlie."

"Oh, how exciting. I bet Charlie can't wait to meet little Homeslice."

Hudson chuckled. "She's going to be begging me to stay at the hospital all night."

The waitress came over, and he handed her his credit card.

"Wait." I reached for my purse and took out my wallet. "Let me, please."

He shook his head and waved off the waitress, who didn't even wait for me to argue.

"You bought dinner the other night," I protested. "I wanted to pay for this one."

"I'll tell you what, I'll let you pay when you ask me out."

"But what if I never ask you out? That wouldn't be fair."

"Just another reason you should ask. Though, it's not at the top of the list of reasons."

"No?"

The waitress came back with his credit card and a receipt for him to sign. Hudson peeled a generous tip from his billfold and stuck it inside the leather check folio.

He tossed the pen on the table. "You ready?"

"Yes, but I'm also waiting to hear what *is* at the top of your list of reasons I should ask you out."

Hudson stood and held out a hand to help me up. I took it, but after I was on my feet, he didn't let go. Instead, he pulled me flush against him and lowered his lips to my ear.

"I'd much rather show you than tell you. Take a chance, Stella."

Stella

Hudson wasn't in the office the next two days.

Olivia told me his ex-wife's sister had given birth yesterday afternoon after a pretty long labor, so I figured he wasn't around because of that. Today I'd checked in with his assistant because I wanted to run the terms of an order by him, but she'd said he'd be offsite all day at a company they were invested in.

As much as I hated to admit it, I missed him when he wasn't in the office. I looked forward to seeing him, and it wasn't just because he was intelligent and a good sounding board for my business. So it was probably just as well that we had a little separation. I needed to get my growing feelings for him under control. Our relationship hadn't changed—we were business partners. Though I was having to work harder and harder to remember why that's all we could ever be.

"Hey, good news." Olivia walked into my office. "I was able to get Phoenix Mets to shoot the images we need for the last of the marketing pieces."

"Oh, that's amazing!" I smiled, but then couldn't help myself and laughed. "I'm sorry. I have no idea who Phoenix Mets is."

Olivia smiled. "He's a celebrity photographer. He did that picture of Anna Mills pregnant that was on the cover of *Vogue*."

"Oh. Wow. That was a beautiful photo."

"He's going to make you look even better."

"Me?" My nose wrinkled.

"Yup. After watching you kill it on the Home Shopping Channel, I made some tweaks to the proposed ads." She opened a folder and set some sketches on my desk. "I had Darby mock these up, but I don't think we should use a model."

I picked up the papers. It was a rough drawing, but the woman in the ad looked a lot like the person I'd seen in the mirror this morning. "You want *me* to be in the ads?"

She nodded. "You're the face of Signature Scent. People respond to you."

"But I'm awkward in photos. I've never done a professional shoot or anything."

Olivia shrugged. "You'd never been on TV before either and look how great that went."

"I don't know..."

"This campaign is about beauty and science, and who better to sell that than you?"

I kept staring down at the ads. The woman sketched to be me had on thick glasses and had her hair up. She sat in front of a lab table with all kinds of beakers and science equipment scattered about. Yet her leg was sticking out from behind the table, and she wore a red-bottomed shoe. It was definitely an ad I'd stop and look at—but then again, I'm a science geek.

"How about this..." Olivia said. "We'll shoot what we'd originally planned *and* these. You can make the final call." She pointed to the mocked-up ad. "But I'm telling you, this could be something amazing."

I couldn't say no after she offered that. Olivia had been wonderful, and I knew she must believe in her idea or she wouldn't be pushing it. She had nothing but the best intentions for making Signature Scent a success.

So I took a deep breath and nodded. "Okay. I'll give it a shot."

Olivia clapped her hands. "Great. The shoot is the day after tomorrow—Friday morning."

"Just let me know what I need to do to get ready. Do you want me to bring some clothes?" The photo had a white button-up blouse and what looked like a black pencil skirt. "I definitely have a white shirt and dark skirt."

"Nope. We're all set." Olivia smiled apprehensively. "I already ordered everything we need. The clothes, the science-y looking props, even the shoes. I wasn't sure of your size, so I ordered a few of everything."

I laughed. "Okay."

She stood. "All I need you to do is show up."

"I can handle that."

"I have my admin making us reservations right now. I'm going to book our flight home for Sunday, if that's okay—just in case we need a second day on Saturday."

My brows furrowed. "Flight? Where is the shoot?"

"Oh. The photographer is based out in LA. Didn't I mention that?"

"You didn't. But that's fine. I've never been to California."

"You're going to love it. We'll probably have a lot of downtime. I can play tour guide."

"Okay. That sounds great. Thanks, Olivia."

The following morning, I was up and ready early. I'd taken a melatonin before going to sleep last night, knowing I'd be anxious and toss and turn. It was bad enough my face was going to be plastered all over marketing materials; I didn't want to have bags under my eyes, if I could help it.

Our flight was at 9:30, but we had to leave for the airport by 6:30. At 6:15 I was drinking my second cup of coffee and staring out the window, watching the sun come up, when a black stretch limousine pulled up in front of my building. There was never any parking, so I rushed to the kitchen and dumped the rest of my coffee, then rinsed out my mug and grabbed my luggage. In the hallway, I pushed the button for the elevator, but realized I'd forgotten my other bag with my laptop. So I left my luggage and ran back to my apartment.

From down the hall, I heard the elevator ding its arrival as I locked my door for the second time. I didn't want the car to have to circle the block, so I hurried to grab my bag as the doors slid open. Not expecting anyone to be inside the elevator, I barreled in without paying attention and crashed right into someone trying to exit.

"Shit." I dropped the handle to the suitcase I'd been dragging behind me, and it tipped over and fell to the floor. Bending to pick it up, I continued, "Sorry! Are you oka—" I stopped in my tracks as I looked up. "Hudson?"

"I guess I should be grateful you didn't swing at me."

"What are you doing here?"

"I'm picking you up to go to the airport." He shrugged. "What else would I be doing here?"

I was thoroughly confused. "But where's Olivia?"

"Oh, that's right. I told Olivia I'd let you know I was going instead of her. It must've slipped my mind. Sorry about that."

"But why are you going instead of Olivia?"

"She had a change in her schedule. Is that a problem?"

Other than my heart already hammering after being close to this man for one minute—and now I'd have to spend *days* by his side—what could be the problem with that? I looked into his eyes, not quite sure what I was searching for. Then I finally exhaled. I was a professional; I could handle this.

Straightening my spine, I said, "No. No problem at all."

I could've sworn I saw a sparkle in his eye. But I didn't have time to explore it since Hudson grabbed my wheely bag and held out his hand for me to enter the still-waiting elevator car. "After you."

I felt very off-kilter, yet managed to step inside.

My mind raced with a million thoughts as we made our way down to the lobby, though one particular question stuck out. My building didn't have a doorman. We had a buzzer system, and visitors had to be buzzed in. "How did you get in?"

"Fisher. He was heading out for a run when I arrived."

I'd have to remember to thank my friend for the heads up. He knew I thought I was going with Olivia. He'd raided my refrigerator while I packed and told me all about my trip last night. But whatever—I had bigger fish to fry. Like how I was going to keep my distance from the man standing next to me in the elevator when he looked so damn good. Hudson had on a simple pair of navy slacks and a white dress shirt. I was standing a half step behind him, and it was impossible not to notice how nicely the material hugged his round ass. I bet he did a shitload of squats.

He looked over at me, and my eyes jumped to his in the nick of time. At least I hoped they had. Though the corner of his mouth might've said otherwise. *Great. Just great. This is going to be one hell of a long trip.*

Hudson had to take an overseas call on the ride to the airport, and then once we arrived, he was sent to a different line since he had security pre-check and I didn't. I was grateful for the reprieve. It wasn't until we boarded the plane that we really had time to talk. We were seated next to each other in row three of first class, which I hadn't expected.

"Well, this is comfy." I buckled my seatbelt. "I've never sat in first class before."

"I could do coach years ago when there was more space between the seats, but over the last ten years they've made it impossible for someone over six-feet tall to sit comfortably—especially on a six-hour flight to the West Coast."

A flight attendant walked over with a tray of orange juice in champagne flutes. "Mimosa?"

"Uh, sure," I said. "I'll have one."

She passed me a flute and then looked to Hudson.

He held up his hand. "No, thank you. But I'll take a coffee whenever you get a chance."

"Sure thing."

After she walked away, I held up my glass to Hudson. "Not a morning drinker?"

He smiled. "Not usually."

"I probably should have skipped it, too, but my nerves are shot."

"Nervous flyer?"

"No...not really. Though I sometimes get a little nauseous if there's turbulence."

"Great." He pointed to the aisle. "Tilt your head that way."

I laughed. "I'm guessing you're the type who doesn't even notice you're on a plane. You probably work through half of it and then close your eyes and take a nap."

"Close. I usually work through most of the flight."

The flight attendant came back to deliver Hudson's coffee. Service was definitely better up here than in coach.

"So what are you nervous about?" he asked. "If it's not the flight?"

"Oh, I don't know...maybe having my picture taken by a famous photographer so it can be plastered all over the Signature Scent marketing materials?"

Hudson looked back and forth between my eyes. "You want to know a secret?"

I smiled. "Sure."

He leaned close and whispered. "You can do anything."

I laughed. "That's the secret?"

"Well, technically it's not a secret since the only person who doesn't seem to know it is you."

I sighed. "That's very kind, but I'm not so sure it's true."

Again Hudson took a moment to look at me. It seemed like he was debating whether he should say something.

"Do you remember your first day working in the office?" he finally asked.

"At Rothschild? Yes, why?"

"You asked me why I changed my mind about investing in your company."

"You said your sister was very persuasive, or something along those lines."

He nodded. "That wasn't the whole truth."

"No?"

Hudson shook his head, and his eyes dropped to my lips. "I wanted to get to know you. The week after my sister's wedding, I couldn't stop thinking about you. It wasn't because you're beautiful—don't get me wrong, you are. But I was attracted to your strength. You're not a woman who needs a man. You're a woman a man needs. I'm not sure I even recognized the difference years ago. But you make it impossible to forget now."

I blinked a few times. "Wow. I think that might be the nicest compliment I've ever received."

He frowned a little. "I assumed that jackass ex of yours was an idiot for the crap he pulled on you. But now I'm positive he's a colossal moron."

The flight attendant interrupted our conversation to collect our drinks since we were about to push away from the gate. Then the safety check started, and we watched the woman standing a few feet away from us put on a plastic, uninflated life jacket and show us how to buckle the belts we were all already wearing.

As we taxied onto the runway behind a backup of planes preparing to take off, Hudson offered me a newspaper. I declined in favor of popping in my earbuds and trying to relax. Though the minute I shut my eyes, I knew that wouldn't be happening. Now I couldn't stop thinking of what Hudson had said. He saw me as beautiful and strong, two things I hadn't felt in a long time. And you know what? He was right—at least on the strength part, anyway. Lately I'd felt almost high from all I'd accomplished. I'd been nervous about taking on an investor, but that had turned out to be the best decision I'd made so far. And I'd been terrified about going on-air at the Home Shopping Channel, and that had been a resounding success. So why should I be afraid of getting a few pictures taken and putting my face on my company's marketing? I shouldn't. That was the answer to that question.

I took a few deep breaths and felt my shoulders relax. All I needed was some Vivaldi, and I might actually be one of those people who could take a nap on a flight. Who knew?

As the music started, I looked over at the man seated next to me. Hudson noticed my eyes on him and flashed an adorable face, one that was half crooked smile and half confused—as if he were trying to figure out what I was thinking, but glad whatever it was had me looking at him. I removed the earbud on his side and leaned over to him.

"Thank you," I said.

"For what?"

"For seeing me the way you do. I know I can be a handful at times."

Hudson looked into my eyes. "You *are* a handful. But don't worry." He winked. "I've got two big hands."

"Welcome to Hotel Bel-Air. Are you checking in today?"

"Yes, under Rothschild," Hudson said. "There should be two reservations."

The woman behind the reception desk clicked her long nails against the keyboard while I gawked around the hotel's lobby. I'd expected us to be staying in downtown LA in some trendy hotel, but this place was more like a hidden sanctuary in the woods. Hotel Bel-Air had an old-school Hollywood feel to it. It had all the standard luxury touches—marble columns and counters, limestone floors, natural wood ceilings—but something made it feel serene and private rather than flashy.

Hudson noticed me looking around. "The grounds are beautiful. You almost forget you're in LA. I've stayed here once before, but the photographer picked it this time. We're going to do the shoot here."

"Oh, wow. That's nice and easy. I can't wait to look around."

The hotel clerk raised two cardboard squares. She held up one. "This is for the Stone Canyon suite." She raised the other hand. "And this is for the deluxe room."

Hudson took the room key and handed me the suite key.

"What? No. I don't need a suite. You take it."

"You're going to have a hair and makeup team tomorrow morning. You need the space. Plus, the photographer plans to shoot some of the session on the patio of your room. He requested that specific suite."

"Oh..." I still felt funny about taking it, but I guess that made sense. "Okay."

Hudson walked me to my room. He wheeled my bag in while I went right to the two open doors in the living room. They led straight out to a private patio.

"Holy—there's a fireplace and a big Jacuzzi out here."

Hudson stepped outside behind me. He pointed to a seating area with a backdrop of lush plantings and greenery. "I think this is where he wants to set up tomorrow. He emailed over some mock-ups late last night with some furniture he rented for the day."

I pointed to the Jacuzzi. "I knew I should have brought a bathing suit."

"It's a private patio." He shrugged. "Don't think you need one."

"Ooohh. That's even better."

Another set of double doors led into a bedroom, so I went to check that out, too, before wandering into the most luxurious bathroom I'd ever seen. Hudson seemed amused at my enthusiasm.

"I never want to leave this room," I joked.

He glanced over to the bed and back to me. "That makes two of us."

I laughed, yet my eyes lingered on the bed. When my gaze lifted, I found Hudson watching me.

He cleared his throat. "I should get going. I have some work to catch up on. The photographer thought it would be a good idea to have dinner tonight, but I wasn't sure if you'd feel up to it."

"I'm fine. Dinner would be nice."

Hudson gave a curt nod. "I'll tell him five, since it will be eight New York time to us."

"Good idea."

We walked to the door. "Are you planning on going anywhere?" he asked. "Do you want the keys to the rental car?"

"Hmm...I have some work to do, but maybe I could go pick up a bathing suit. We passed a bunch of cute boutiques not too far away."

"On second thought," Hudson said. "I don't need to work. You probably need someone to model them for."

I laughed. "Think I'm good picking it out on my own."

He took the keys from his pocket and held them out to me. "Shame. But let me know if you want company in that hot tub when you get back."

"You brought a suit?"

Hudson grinned. "Nope."

Stella

I'd changed three times.

So when Hudson knocked on my door five minutes early for dinner, I wasn't ready.

"Hey..." I swung open the door. "Oh...you're wearing jeans."

He looked down. "Should I not be?"

I shook my head. "No, no. It's fine. I just wasn't sure what to wear. I had jeans on, but I thought I might be dressed too casually. So I went downstairs to the restaurant to see how fancy it is. It looked really nice, so I changed...twice."

Hudson looked me up and down. I'd settled on a simple, sleeveless little black dress with nude heels.

"I don't know what you had on before," he said. "But I can't imagine it could be any better than what you're wearing. You look beautiful."

I felt that warm feeling in my belly. "Thank you. You look nice yourself. I really do like you with a five o'clock shadow."

"I'll be tossing all my razors right after dinner."

I laughed and stepped aside. "I'll just be a minute. I need to put on lipstick and change my jewelry."

Hudson took a seat on the couch in the living room while I went to the bathroom to finish up. "I got shipping notifications for a bunch more products," I yelled as I lined my lips. "If everything works out, we could be ready to start shipping boxes even earlier than we'd expected."

"Well, then I guess we'd better get this photography wrapped up tomorrow," he called from the other room.

After I finished my lipstick, I clipped on a set of turquoise beads to add some color, along with a matching chunky bracelet. I ran my fingers through my hair one last time and took a deep breath, looking in the mirror. As if being around Hudson wasn't nerve-wracking enough, having dinner with a photographer who was used to shooting famous models and celebrities added another level of pressure. I didn't want him to look at me and think, *Oh shit...how am I going to make that look good enough to sell women perfume?*

But it was what it was, and five more minutes of primping wasn't going to change things. So I headed out to the living room and grabbed my purse from the coffee table. Tossing a few things inside, I snapped it shut. "Were you able to get all your work done this afternoon?"

Hudson stood. "I was. How about you?"

"I got most of it done. But then I couldn't resist trying out the Jacuzzi."

"Did you go get a suit?"

I shook my head and smirked. "I went commando."

Hudson's eyes swept over me, and he grumbled, "We should go."

His frustration gave me the boost of confidence I needed at the moment. Hudson was quick to open the door to my suite, which made me giggle. We walked side by side to the hotel's restaurant.

"Have you ever met Phoenix before?" I asked.

"No. I figured it wouldn't be too hard to find him. Photographers usually have a certain look to them, and he'll be alone."

When we checked in at the restaurant, the hostess said the other member of our party had already arrived and was having a drink at the bar. We went to join him, but there were a few guys sitting alone.

"Which one do you think he is?" I asked.

Hudson looked around and pointed to a guy at the far end of the bar. He had shaggy hair, a bright-colored shirt, and bracelets halfway up his arm—he looked totally trendy.

"Him." He pointed.

I could only see the two other men from the back, but one had gray hair and wore a tweed sports jacket, and the other guy had shoulders broad enough to be a football player, so I figured Hudson was probably right. But I let him take the lead, anyway.

He walked over and asked, "Phoenix?"

The guy shook his head. "Think you got the wrong guy."

"Sorry."

Hudson and I looked across the bar to the other men, both of which we could now see from the front—

and...wow, the guy with the linebacker shoulders was absolutely gorgeous. He noticed us looking and smiled.

I lifted my chin. "I think that's him."

"He doesn't look like a photographer," Hudson said.

"I know. He looks more like a model."

The guy got up and walked in our direction.

"I'm guessing you're from Signature Scent?" he said.

"We are." I smiled. I hadn't meant to sound so jovial or anxious, but I guess it came out that way, because Hudson gave me a weird look as I extended my hand. "Stella Bardot. Nice to meet you."

"Ah. My muse." He lifted my hand and kissed the top of it. "I can see this is going to be an easy job."

Hudson seemed to be going for an impassive face as he introduced himself and shook hands with the handsome man, but I saw the frown lurking in his eyes.

The three of us requested a table, and I went first, following the hostess to our seats. I noticed more than one woman turning her head to look at the men behind me. I couldn't blame them. Hudson and Phoenix were very different looking, but each gorgeous in his own right.

Hudson went to pull out my chair, but Phoenix beat him to it.

"Thank you," I said.

Once we were settled, Phoenix started the conversation.

"So, how long have you been modeling?" he asked me.

"Oh, I'm not a model. I created Signature Scent."

"Really? Could have fooled me."

Hudson picked up the drink menu and grumbled. "The information about who you'd be shooting was in the write-up marketing sent you. Guess you missed it."

I tried to make light of Hudson's comment. "How long have you been a photographer?"

"Professionally, about five years. I was a model for ten before that, so that's how I learned the business. Models age out pretty quickly. While I was still booking a lot of jobs, I took some classes so I'd have something to fall back on."

"Smart."

"So you invented the product *and* you're going to be the model? Beauty and brains. Your husband is a lucky man."

"Thank you." I blushed. "But I'm not married."

Phoenix smiled, and Hudson rolled his eyes.

I made a point to loop Hudson into the conversation and steer away from any more flirtatious exchanges. While I was flattered by Phoenix's attention, and it was fun to see a spark of jealousy from the man to my left, this was a business dinner. Plus, it didn't matter how nice-looking Phoenix was, I had no interest in him.

I wasn't sure if it was my efforts or perhaps the two scotches on the rocks Hudson knocked back during dinner, but he seemed to relax while we ate. We talked about Signature Scent—everything from how it was developed to the marketing plans Olivia had come up with.

When the waitress suggested coffee and dessert, Hudson declined, so I followed suit.

"How's nine o'clock tomorrow to start?" Phoenix asked. "Hair and makeup can get to you by eight. Is your wardrobe all set?"

Hudson answered. "Olivia texted me that the last of the packages were delivered to the hotel a little while ago."

"Perfect," Phoenix said. "I think we'll be able to wrap it up by early afternoon, so you can go out and enjoy some of the California sunshine."

I smiled. "Oh good. This is my first time here, so I'd love to see the city."

"I'm a born-and-raised LA boy. If you're up for it, I can show you around after the shoot wraps."

My eyes slanted to meet Hudson's. I could tell he was pissed, yet he refrained from saying anything.

"Actually..." I smiled politely at Phoenix. "I have plans already. But thank you very much for the offer."

The three of us walked to the lobby together. Hudson was quiet, but professional, as he said goodnight to our dinner companion.

"I need to stop at the front desk to pick up the packages Olivia had delivered for you," Hudson said once Phoenix had gone.

"Oh, okay." I nodded.

I couldn't tell if he was pissed at me or just in a piss-poor mood. He maintained his stern demeanor as he asked the hotel clerk about the delivery.

She punched some keys on her keyboard and looked at her screen. "It looks like it was delivered to your room. Room two thirty-eight."

"Okay, thank you."

Since room 238 was his, and I needed to try things on, I said, "Do you mind if I pick them up from your room now? I want to prep as much as I can tonight so I don't waste anyone's time in the morning."

"That's fine."

Again he was quiet as we made our way to his room. He unlocked the door and held it open for me to enter, but once the door closed, the silence grew deafening, and I couldn't take it anymore.

"Are you...mad at me?"

Hudson's eyes looked back and forth between mine. "No."

"Okay... Are you tired? It's been a long day with the travel and all."

He shook his head. "I'm not tired."

I nodded, intending to leave it alone. But that only lasted thirty seconds. I couldn't help myself. "When I said I'd never been to LA and wanted to check it out, I wasn't hinting that he should ask me out." I shook my head. "I don't even know if he was asking me out—but whatever he was offering, I wasn't trying to open a door for him to show me around."

Hudson's eyes seared into me. "Oh, he was asking you out. Make no mistake about that."

"But I—"

He interrupted me. "You were perfectly polite and professional. You didn't do anything wrong."

I shook my head. "So why does it feel like you think I did?"

Hudson stared down at his feet for what was probably only a few seconds, yet felt like an hour.

Eventually, his eyes met mine. "I'm just a jealous asshole. I don't mean to take it out on you. I apologize."

Oh...*wow*. I didn't think he'd be so honest. I smiled sadly. "Thank you. For what it's worth, if the roles were reversed and the photographer was a beautiful, female ex-model who asked to show you around, I'd be jealous, too."

Hudson looked into my eyes. "You know, we don't get jealous of things we don't want."

"Want has never been an issue for me. It's just...so much could go wrong."

"Or so much could go right." Hudson forced a smile and nodded. "But I get it." He glanced around the room. "I don't see the boxes in here. Let me check the bedroom. Do you have a list of what we should have received?"

"Yeah..." I sighed. "I can pull it up on my phone."

I sat down on the couch and dug my phone out of my purse. As I started to scroll, I noticed something sticking out of the corner of the couch, tucked between the cushions. It looked like a book. Without giving it any thought, I pulled it out and laid it on the end table so it wouldn't get lost. But when I caught the title on the front, I did a double take.

The Thorn Birds.

Hudson and I had talked about this book the other day. He'd said he hadn't read it.

I picked the book back up and began to thumb through the pages. About three-quarters through, one of Hudson's business cards was tucked inside like a bookmark.

"They delivered two box—" Hudson froze. His eyes rose to meet mine, but he said nothing.

"You're reading this?"

He set the boxes on the coffee table in front of me. "You mentioned you liked it the other day. I usually read a lot while I travel."

My heart swelled inside my chest, leaving me a little breathless. I shook my head. "You knew I thought Marco reading Amalia's favorites was romantic."

Hudson was quiet for a moment before tapping on the boxes. "How many were left to be delivered?"

"Umm..." I hadn't finished looking to find out. I swiped to my email and searched for the one Olivia had sent with the shipping confirmations. "I think those are the last two. All of the props are being delivered tomorrow morning from a local company."

He nodded. "I'll carry these down to your room for you."

I shook my head. "That's okay. It's just a few outfits. I can take them."

Hudson pushed his hands into his pockets and kept his eyes down. The shy demeanor was very un-Hudson-like.

So many emotions swam through my head, and I stood, not knowing what to say, though the conversation about the book felt unfinished. Eventually it became awkward, so I took the boxes and figured it was time to go.

"Thank you again for dinner. I'll see you in the morning?"

"I'll be down at your room by the time they get started."

"Okay. Thank you."

He opened the door and our gazes caught once more. Why did it feel like my heart was breaking? "Goodnight, Hudson."

I made it down to my room but couldn't bring myself to go inside. I had two boxes in my hands, yet I just stared at my door.

What the hell am I doing?

For the last few weeks, I'd been reading a diary and rooting for a man to get the girl because of all his sweet gestures. Yet in my personal life, I had a man who listened to me, a man who'd forgiven me for crashing his sister's wedding, and for giving him a black eye. I'd called him an asshole on more than one occasion, yet he'd done nothing but help me get my business off the ground and stand by my side the entire time. He was also an adoring father, which says a lot about a man. Not to mention, I was ridiculously attracted to him.

So why the hell don't I take a chance?

I'd told myself it wasn't a good idea to mix business with pleasure because of the way things had turned out with Aiden. But my business had already exceeded all my expectations, and we hadn't even made the website live yet for the general public. So it wasn't that. I thought back to my conversation with Hudson a few minutes ago.

"So much could go wrong," I'd said.

But maybe what he'd said was more important.

"So much could go right."

The truth was, I was afraid to take a chance. But I realized now that by not taking a chance, I might miss out on something really beautiful.

My palms started to sweat, because I knew what I needed to do. I also knew that if I walked into my room and started overthinking things, I might chicken out. So it had to be now.

Right now.

I dropped the boxes on the floor in front of my door and rushed back to Hudson's room. Standing in front of his door, my first instinct was to take a moment and pull myself together. But doing that would give me time to lose my nerve. So I forced myself to just do it and knock—though with all of the adrenaline and nerves rushing through me, my knock came out more like a bang, a very loud and fast pounding.

Hudson whipped open the door. His face was angry, but at the sight of me, he jumped into protective mode.

"What happened? Are you okay?" He took a step out of his room and looked down the hall, first to the right and then the left. "Stella, what's going on? Is everything okay?"

"Everything's fi..."

I forgot what I was saying mid sentence. When he'd whipped open the door and startled me, all I saw was an angry face. But now...

I couldn't take my eyes off him.

My Lord.

Hudson's dress shirt was unbuttoned. His belt was open, and the zipper to his pants was down, revealing dark boxer briefs. But it wasn't his state of undress that had me unable to form words, it was what was underneath the clothes.

248

I knew from our talks that he exercised, so I'd expected him to be in good shape. But Hudson was so much more. He was...magnificent. Beautiful smooth, tan skin, carved pecs, and an eight-pack of rippled muscles. A thin line of hair led from his belly button down into his boxers, the sight of which made me salivate.

"Stella? Are you okay?"

Hearing the concern in his voice, I blinked a few times.

"Oh...yeah. I'm fine." *Though not as fine as* you.

"You banged on my door like there was a fire or something."

"Sorry." I shook my head. "I was just anxious."

"Anxious about what? The shoot tomorrow?"

"No...yes...no...well, I am anxious about the shoot tomorrow, but that's not what I was anxious about when I knocked on your door."

Hudson still looked confused.

But of course, why wouldn't he when I was babbling like an idiot? So I took a deep breath and steadied myself.

"I...I...would you like to have dinner tomorrow night?"

"Dinner?"

I nodded and swallowed. "Yeah...like a date?"

All the confusion and anger disappeared from his face. He shook his head. "It's about fucking time."

I rolled my eyes. "Don't be all cocky about it. Do you want to or not?"

He smiled. "Yes, I'd very much like to go out with you, Stella."

My belly did a little somersault. I suddenly felt like I was in middle school and the most popular boy had told me he liked me back. Nervous, I looked down. "Okay, so tomorrow then? After the shoot. We'll have dinner or something?"

Hudson looked amused. "Yes, that's how it usually works—dinner or something."

I scowled at him. "This isn't easy, you know. You don't have to make it even more difficult by being a jerk."

His eyes sparkled. "I'll work on that."

"Good." I'd never asked a man out in my life, so I wasn't sure what came next. But when I caught myself grabbing for the ring I always twisted when I felt nervous, I figured the best thing would be to say goodnight. "Alright, I'll see you tomorrow, then."

I went to walk away, but Hudson stepped out of his room and grabbed my hand. "Hang on a second. You forgot something."

My brows dipped. "What?"

He yanked my hand so I stumbled and fell against his chest. Then in one quick swoop, he leaned down, lifted me up, and turned us so my back was up against the door to his room. My legs wrapped around his waist, and Hudson pushed into me, pinning me with his body. He cupped my cheeks and looked into my eyes.

"This, sweetheart, you forgot this."

Hudson's mouth crashed down on mine. The gasp that had been halfway through my lips was swallowed, along with any shyness I'd felt a minute ago. I threaded my fingers through his thick hair and tugged, wanting him even closer.

Hudson groaned. He tilted my head to deepen the kiss, and our tongues frantically collided. All hell broke loose after that. Hudson grinded between my legs as one of his hands snaked around to the back of my head where he grabbed a fistful of my hair. The roughness of his actions coupled with the feel of his warm, hard body pushing against me brought a moan from somewhere deep inside me.

"Fuck," Hudson growled as his mouth moved to my neck. He sucked along my pulse line before kissing his way back to my lips. "Do that again. Make that sound again."

It wasn't a sound I'd tried to make, so I wasn't sure I could repeat it. Though when he rubbed his cock up and down between my spread legs, I didn't have to worry about trying to make it, because yet again it came from somewhere deep inside me.

Hudson grunted. "Fuck, yes."

I wasn't sure how long we stayed like that—grabbing and pulling, grinding and groping—but when our kiss finally broke, we were both panting. I reached up and felt my swollen lips. "Wow."

A smile spread across Hudson's face as he leaned his forehead against mine. "Took you long enough."

I laughed. "Shut up. I had good reason to be scared."

Hudson pushed a lock of hair from my cheek, and his face softened. "Don't be scared. I won't hurt you. Except maybe a little biting."

A sound at the other end of the hallway interrupted the intimate moment. An older couple was headed down the hall toward us.

"Shit," Hudson said as he lowered me to my feet. In a really adorable move, he pulled my black dress down and straightened it for me.

I laughed and pointed my eyes down to his trousers. "Uhh... I don't think I'm the one you need to worry about looking obscene."

Hudson's forehead wrinkled until he glanced down and saw his erection bulging from his pants. "Shit."

"Don't worry," I said. "I got you." I stepped in front of him and angled myself to shield him until the couple passed. Then he pulled up his zipper and partially buckled his belt.

"Come on," he said. "I'll walk you to your room."

"You don't have to do that."

"It's on my way."

My brows furrowed. "On your way where?"

"To the front desk. I locked myself out of my room."

I chuckled. "Smooth, Rothschild. Smooth."

He responded by swatting my ass. "Be nice or I won't be a gentleman when we get to your door."

"Maybe I don't want you to be a gentleman."

He hooked an arm around my shoulder as we started walking. "I said I'd be a gentleman when we're *at* your door. Trust me, that shit will stay parked outside once we're somewhere less public, now that you're mine."

"Oh, I'm yours now, am I?"

When we arrived at my door, Hudson kissed me gently on the lips. "You have been for a while, sweetheart. You just finally admitted it."

I rolled my eyes as if what he said was arrogant, but it was the truth.

I grabbed his shirt. "Do you...want to come in?"

He stroked my cheek. "Yes, I want to. But no, I won't. You have to get up in the morning. Plus, you deserve a nice date, and I'm going to give you that before we take things any further. If we go into your room, I *will* wind up trying to get you naked. You're impossible to resist. Trust me, I've fucking tried."

I smiled and pushed up on my tippy toes for another sweet kiss. "Goodnight, Hudson."

"Glad you finally listened to the whisper, sweetheart."

"I didn't really have a choice. My whisper has been more like a scream lately."

21

Hudson

The next morning, I showed up at Stella's door at seven thirty.

She opened it wrapped in a towel. "Hey. You're early."

My eyes dragged up and down a shitload of creamy, exposed skin. I shook my head. "Looks like I came at the perfect time."

She giggled, and I swear the sound might've been even better than the view, and the view was pretty fucking spectacular.

Stella stepped inside. "The hair and makeup people are coming at eight, so I waited to take a shower so my hair would still be damp."

Being inside her suite felt completely different than it had when I was here just yesterday. For example, now I could do this...

The moment the door shut, I took her in my arms and crushed my lips to hers. Last night I'd fallen asleep thinking about the way she tasted, and this morning I'd awakened starving. The soft moan that almost did me in yesterday made an appearance again—it crossed from her lips to mine and traveled straight down to my cock.

Fuck.

She probably wouldn't stop me if I slipped the towel from around her, though that would only make things worse. If just a kiss made me feel like a savage, there was no way in hell seeing all of her would be enough. So I wrenched my mouth from hers.

Stella lifted her hand and rubbed two fingers along her bottom lip. "I don't think I've ever felt what was going on in someone's mind from just kissing them."

"What do you mean?"

"Your kisses. They say so much. Whether it's a sweet peck on the lips or what just happened, I just know what's going on in your head when our lips meet."

"Oh yeah?" I said. "What was going on in my head just now?"

"You wanted to take off my towel, but you knew that wasn't a good idea because people will be here any minute."

My brows shot up. "How the hell did you know that?"

She shook her head. "I don't know. I just did."

"That's dangerous—for me."

She smiled and adjusted the tucked-in corner of her towel. "I should go get dressed before people start arriving."

As much as I hated to see her cover up, there's no way I wanted to share the way she looked with anyone—especially the asshat photographer. I nodded. "Go."

Stella walked away, but at the bedroom doorway she yelled back.

"Hudson?"

"Yeah?"

She let the towel drop to the floor.

I groaned. This was going to be one long day.

Before Stella finished getting dressed, the first person arrived. Dig—at least I was pretty sure that's what he'd grumbled when he introduced himself—was a stylist. He rolled in a trunk on wheels and looked around for where to set up.

A minute later the makeup person knocked, followed by three guys delivering rented furniture, room service, a lighting technician, and some random guy whose accent was so strong I had no idea what the hell he said he did. They all pounced on Stella as soon as she emerged from the bathroom.

After forty-five minutes being surrounded by a team of people primping, she looked a little overwhelmed. So I made a plate with some fruit and a croissant from the breakfast spread and set it down in front of her.

"Did you eat yet?"

Stella shook her head.

I looked at the hairdresser who had just wrapped her entire head in rollers and then at the two guys flanking her on both sides. "Could you give her five minutes, please?"

"Oh...of course."

I nodded my head toward the trays of food. "Why don't you help yourselves to something to eat? There's a table outside on the patio."

Once she wasn't being prodded anymore, Stella let out a big exhale. "Thanks. How did you know I needed a break?"

I shrugged. "Same way you knew I was about two seconds from ripping your towel off during that kiss earlier."

She smiled and picked up the banana I'd put on her plate. As she went to peel it, she caught my scribble and read out loud.

"*I can't wait to show you my banana.* Ooh..." She giggled. "I think I'm going to like these notes much better now."

I smiled, but pointed to her plate. "Eat. They're going to be back in here painting shit on your face in a few minutes."

"On second thought, I'm going to save this for later." Stella set down the banana and picked up a piece of melon. "So what are we going to do tonight for our date? I know I asked you out, but it's my first time in California."

"I figured I'd feed you and show you around LA, since you've never been."

"Oh, that sounds awesome." She bit into the cantaloupe and made an *Mmmmm* sound. "This is really good melon."

"I have a call at four this afternoon that I couldn't postpone, but if we wrap things up here early enough, I can always do that from the road."

"If you're too busy to go out later..." She smirked. "I can always ask Phoenix to show me around."

My eyes narrowed. Stella lifted the piece of cantaloupe toward her lips for another bite, but I caught her wrist and redirected the fruit to my own mouth, nipping at her fingers as I took it.

"Oww..."

"You're lucky we have a crowd and I can't put you over my knee and smack your ass for that comment."

She giggled. "We could go in the other room..."

"Don't tempt me, sweetheart." My eyes dropped to her lips. "I'll absolutely clear this suite if you want to play that game."

Stella's eyes sparkled, daring me to make good on my threat. But a knock at the door interrupted our little chat.

It was an effort not to scowl, finding Phoenix on the other side. Yet I welcomed him with a curt nod. "Morning."

The fucker walked right to Stella without even acknowledging me.

Shutting the door behind him, I grumbled, "Good to see you, too."

Deciding it probably wasn't good to act like a jealous boyfriend before the first date, I thought I'd go see what was going on outside. The furniture and prop people had been working on the patio since they arrived.

The small outdoor area had been transformed into a scene from *Bill Nye: The Science Guy*, with the addition of some estrogen. There was a lab table set up with beakers and equipment, but also jars of bright red rose petals, sand, and various colorful flowers. The front of the table had been outfitted with the Signature Scent logo, and a mirrored tray displayed all the different bottles the perfume came in.

Dig walked over and wiped sweat from his forehead. "What do you think?"

"It looks great."

"Yeah, I wasn't sure what the hell it was going to look like from the list of stuff we were instructed to pull together. Seemed like a strange combination. But I get it now, especially once the model is in the shot."

I knew my sister would be awake and appreciate seeing everything set up, so I snapped a few shots and texted them to her.

Olivia: It looks awesome! I'm a genius.

I chuckled and texted back.

Hudson: A modest one.

Olivia: Where's Stella? I want to see how she looks.

I glanced back inside and saw the hair person taking out the rollers while a woman painted more shit on her face.

Hudson: They're still working on her.

Olivia: Send me some pics once they start! I bet she slays it.

Of course she will. I looked back into the suite again, and my eyes met Stella's. The corners of her lips curled with the sweetest smile, one she was trying to hold back but couldn't. I knew, because my face had felt the exact same way most days since I'd met her.

The rest of the morning was chaotic and flew by. Stella looked amazing in the shoot. Just ask good ol'

Phoenix—he'd told her enough times. I understood that photographers needed to encourage their subjects with compliments, coax them out of their shell for the shoot, but there's a difference between telling someone they're doing great and look beautiful, and cooing at the model how sexy she looks—while calling her *love* and *baby*. Every time he repositioned Stella's hair or fixed her collar, I watched the fucker like a hawk.

When we broke for lunch, the stylist suggested Stella change so she didn't get anything on her outfit. She went into the bathroom and came out wearing shorts and a tank top.

"How did I do? It's not easy to smile for that long. I started to feel like I might look like Joaquin Phoenix as the Joker."

"Nah. You did great. Maybe Heath Ledger, but not as bad as Joaquin."

Stella play-smacked my abs. Her back was facing me, so she didn't notice that Phoenix had taken a seat at a folding table outside on the patio, right on the other side of the sliding glass doors. But I definitely did. Catching her hand, I pulled Stella to me and stroked a piece of hair from her face.

"You're doing amazing. You look beautiful, and the ads are going to be perfect."

"You're just saying that because you want in my pants."

I slipped two fingers under her chin and tilted her head up. "I'm saying it because it's the truth. Though I do want in your pants. Kiss me."

She smiled and pushed up on her tippy toes, pressing her soft lips to mine. I would have preferred to kiss the shit out of her, but I'd do that without a full crew in the next room and out on the patio. When I looked up, my eyes found Phoenix, who had just watched the entire thing. *That takes care of that...*

The afternoon session went as smoothly as the morning, except the photographer was a hell of a lot more professional. I snapped a few pics of Stella set up with all the props and sent them to my sister. Though the one I took of her leaning over to smell a cluster of purple flowers hanging over the fence when she thought no one was looking? That one was for me.

At three o'clock, the photographer finally called it a day. Everyone started to clean up, and Stella went into the bathroom to get changed again.

Phoenix was disassembling his camera and putting the pieces into a case when he lifted his chin to me. "I got a lot of good stuff. I'll go through everything and do a touch-up on the ones I think are the best. But I'll also send you the unedited proofs to go through in case a shot I didn't pick catches your eye. I know you need it ASAP, so I'll have everything to you by Monday."

I nodded. "Thank you."

He snapped his camera case closed. "And...I owe you an apology. I didn't realize you and Stella..."

I could've said it was new or that last night at dinner she hadn't even agreed to go out with me yet—I could've let him off the hook. But instead, I simply said, "Not a problem."

"Thanks." He held out his hand. "She seems like a great girl."

I shook his hand, giving it a squeeze that was firmer than socially acceptable. "Woman. She's a great *woman*."

He held up both hands. "Got it."

By the time everyone left, it was almost four, and I had a call to make. I needed my laptop for it, which was back in my room.

I took one of Stella's hands. "You still feel up to going out tonight?"

"Definitely. But I'd like to take a quick shower, if you don't mind. I feel like I have a mud mask on with all this makeup, and my hair has ten pounds of hairspray."

"I have that four o'clock call to take. So why don't you come down to my room whenever you're ready."

"Okay."

Stella walked me to the door. "Where are we going tonight, so I know what to wear?"

"Wear something sexy."

"Oh, okay. So it's fancy then?"

"Not really. I just want you to wear something sexy."

She laughed. "I'll try my best."

I leaned down and kissed her cheek. "You don't even have to try."

"Wow. This is gorgeous." Stella settled into her seat, staring off at the ocean. I'd taken her to Geoffrey's in Malibu because it was a beautiful night, and dining on their back deck meant an unbeatable panoramic view of the Pacific Ocean. Scratch that—what she was looking at didn't hold a candle to what I was currently looking at.

"*You* look gorgeous."

Stella blushed. "Thank you."

I loved that she was so humble. The woman truly had no clue that she'd made every head turn when we'd walked through the restaurant.

"Have you eaten here before?"

"I have. A client took me here a few years ago. With most places, you get the view or the food. This is one of the rare places you get both."

She lifted the cloth napkin from the table and draped it across her lap. "I'm actually starving."

My eyes dropped to her lips, which were painted with the same bold red lipstick she'd worn at the shoot today. I guess I should be grateful she normally wore something more understated, because otherwise I wouldn't get any work done around the office.

I lifted my water glass, never taking my eyes from her. "I'm starving too."

Stella caught the suggestive tone of my voice, and her eyes met mine with a sparkle. "Is that so? Tell me, Mr. Rothschild, what's your idea of a *satisfying meal*?"

I could feel myself starting to harden under the table. Being around her made me feel like a horny, fifteen-year-old virgin. And her calling me Mr. Rothschild? I'd never been into role-playing before, but I saw a boss-employee scene in our near future.

I cleared my throat. "We better change the subject."

She looked at me with a truly innocent face. "Why?"

I glanced around us. The tables were close, so I leaned forward and lowered my voice. "Because I'm hard thinking about what I really want to eat."

She blushed. "Oh."

The waitress came to take our drink order. Stella perused the wine menu while I was relieved to get a minute to get myself under control. I seemed to have a one-track mind tonight, and I didn't want her to get the impression that sex was the only thing that interested me—though it had certainly felt like that lately. It was only our first date, so I probably should refrain from telling her that every time she blushed, I couldn't stop wondering what color her creamy skin turned when she came.

When the waitress disappeared to get our wine, I steered the conversation to safer territory.

"So, what are you going to conquer next now that Signature Scent is almost ready to go?"

Stella sat back in her chair. "You know, Robyn asked me the same thing during one of the breaks on set a couple of weeks ago. She wondered if I had plans to come out with complementing products, such as men's signature cologne or anything else beauty-related."

"Is that what you'd like to do?"

She shrugged. "Maybe. But I'm not in any rush. I'd like to make sure everything goes smoothly with Signature Scent for a while. I worked on it while working full-time for so long, and then after I left my job, I threw myself into it even deeper." Stella paused and looked out to the ocean. Smiling, she said, "I think I'd like to conquer happiness next."

The waitress brought over our wine. Stella dipped her nose into the glass for a sniff and smiled, so I knew it would be good. After, the waitress filled both our glasses and said she'd be back in a few minutes to take our order.

"Are you saying your happiness system isn't working?" I teased.

"No, not at all. I just...working fourteen hours a day might bring financial satisfaction, but that's not the only thing that matters."

My eyes roamed her face. "Yeah, I'm starting to realize that myself."

She smiled and tilted her head. "Are you happy?"

"At the moment, very much so."

She laughed. "I'm glad. But I meant in general, in your life."

I sipped my wine and gave it some thought. "That's a pretty big question. I guess there are things in my life I'm very happy with—my work, having financial stability, my friends, my family, my current dating situation." I winked. "But then there are things I'm not happy with, like not seeing my daughter every night when I get home, coming home to an empty house..."

Stella nodded. "I think a lot of the reason I've struggled to be happy over the last year or two has been that my life turned out a lot different than I'd envisioned it. I needed to let go of what I thought my life was supposed to look like in order to write a new story."

And to think when I first met this woman, I'd thought she was flaky. A few months later, I'm realizing she's the one with the firm grip on life, and it's me who has a lot to learn. Even crazier than that, I'm hoping that when she writes that new story, I get to be part of it.

Hudson

I couldn't help but kiss her.

After an entire day and evening looking at her with barely a touch, I'd begun to feel like a man who hadn't eaten in days, and she was a big, juicy steak. So when the kid at the valet jogged off to get my rental car, I tugged Stella's hand and pulled her to the side of the building.

"What are you doing?"

"Eating your face."

She giggled. "Eating it? That doesn't sound too romantic."

"Trust me." I wrapped one arm around her waist and pulled her flush against me, while my other hand gripped her neck and tilted her head where I wanted it. "I'll romance you—whispering in your ear, sending you notes to let you know I'm thinking about you. You just might want to shield your phone when you're around others before you open my messages."

She bit down on her bottom lip, and I groaned.

"Give me that." My mouth descended on hers, and she surprised the shit out of me when she caught my lip and bit down.

Pulling her head back just slightly with my flesh between her teeth, she flashed an evil smile. "I might eat your face first."

We were both still laughing as I sealed my mouth over hers for a long-ass kiss. The sound of a couple nearby was the only thing that kept me from feeling her up right outside the restaurant.

We returned to the valet station, and when our rental car pulled up, I waved the kid off as he went to open Stella's door. I handed him a tip while she climbed inside.

I was glad it was a long drive to show her all of the touristy crap, because I needed some time to recover after that kiss.

Settling in behind the wheel, I buckled. "I was thinking we could hit the Hollywood sign and then go over to Hollywood Boulevard to take a walk. That's where the Walk of Fame is. Maybe tomorrow we could check out Santa Monica Pier, Venice Beach, and a few other places."

"Would you mind a change in plans?" she asked. "I was thinking we could just go back to the hotel."

As much as I hated touristy crap, I'd been looking forward to showing her around. I definitely wasn't ready to call an end to our first official date. But today had been a long day for her, so I hid my disappointment.

"Sure. Of course. You must be tired. I wasn't thinking."

"Actually..." She reached over and laid her hand on my thigh. "I'm not tired at all."

And...the woman just kept on surprising me. I turned my head and caught her gaze. "You sure?"

She nodded with a shy smile. "How long is the drive back? I wasn't paying attention on the way here."

"It's about a half hour." I put the car into drive. "But I'll get us there in twenty minutes."

I replayed Stella telling me she wanted to go back to the hotel over and over in my mind as I broke a half-dozen traffic laws on the drive. She'd laid her cards on the table. She wanted to be alone with me, but I didn't want to assume that meant she wanted to have sex. I'd have to remember that, because I tended to go from zero to a hundred whenever my lips so much as touched hers.

We'd gone to dinner early since we'd planned to go sightseeing after, so when we walked into the hotel lobby it was barely eight o'clock.

"Do you want to get a drink at the bar?" I asked.

"I haven't touched the bar in my room, and it's stocked pretty well."

I smiled. "To your room then..."

Back in her suite, Stella slipped off her shoes while I walked behind the bar to see what she had. She hadn't been exaggerating; the thing had more choices than any hotel room I'd ever stayed in.

I lifted a bottle of merlot and a full-size bottle of gin. "Are you in the mood for more wine or something else?"

Stella was rummaging through her purse. She sighed with exasperation as she tossed it on the couch. "Do you have condoms?"

Okay, then. *Something else it is.*

I set the bottles down and stepped out from behind the bar, keeping a few feet of distance between us.

"I do."

"With you now?"

I chuckled. "Yes, with me now."

She swallowed. "I went back on the pill a few weeks ago, but you need to be on it a full month before you're protected."

I took a step closer to her. "We're good."

"How many do you have with you?"

My brows jumped. "Big plans for the night?"

She flashed the goofiest smile. "It's been a while for me. A *long* while."

I smiled and closed the distance between us. Brushing the hair from her shoulder, I leaned down and dropped a soft kiss on her creamy skin. "I have two with me. But I have more in my suitcase back in my room."

"Okay..." She looked away for a few seconds, and I could see the wheels in her head turning as her eyes lost focus.

"Is there something else you want to talk ab—"

I didn't get to finish the question because Stella launched herself at me. Caught off guard, I stumbled back a few steps but managed to keep her in my arms. I'd heard the saying *climbed like a tree* before, but never actually experienced it. In one swoop, she jumped up, wrapped her legs around my waist and arms around my neck, and her lips came crashing down on mine.

"I want you," she mumbled between our joined lips.

So much for being unsure where things were heading. Her eagerness was a total surprise, yet I fucking *loved* it. I would've gone slow, taken my time not to rush things. But this? This was so much better. We had all night for going slow. Taking long strides, I carried her through the living room and into the bedroom. Stella pushed her tits up against me and ground her wide-open legs up and down my already hard cock.

I groaned. "And here I thought you wanted romance."

"I think I'd rather have you eat my face off right now."

I set her down on the bed and dropped to my knees. "Sweetheart, that's not what I'm about to eat..."

I was so fucking consumed with the idea of burying my face between her legs, that I couldn't be gentle about getting her panties off. Reaching up, I gripped the flimsy material of her thong and tore it straight from her body. The gasp that spilled from her mouth was almost enough to make me come, and she hadn't yet laid a finger on me.

I nudged one of her legs wider and tossed the other up and over my shoulder. Her pussy was beautifully bare and glistening, making me salivate. I couldn't wait to devour her. Flattening my tongue, I dove in for a long stroke, licking from one end to the other. When I reached her clit, I sucked it into my mouth and drew deep.

"Ahh..." She arched off the bed.

The sound made me wild. I was so amped up that it wasn't enough to have my tongue in on the action alone.

So I pushed my entire face into her wet pussy, using my nose, cheeks, jaw, teeth, and tongue. And while I was in there, I stopped to take a deep inhale. Later, I'd have to remember to see if Stella could develop *this* as one of her custom freaking scents—for my private collection only.

Her hips bucked against me as I sucked and slurped, and when she cried out my name, I knew she was close to coming. So I slipped two fingers inside her. Stella's muscles clamped down tight as I pumped in and out.

When her back arched off the bed again, I reached up and pressed her hips to the mattress, keeping her immobilized as I continued my feast.

She moaned. "Ah...I'm...ah..."

I began to be concerned I might finish at the same time as she did. And if that were the case, my finale would take place in a pair of three-hundred-dollar slacks and be reminiscent of a teenage boy. But the sound of her losing control was just that fucking good, and I actually didn't give a shit if it came to that, because there was no way in hell I could stop.

Stella's nails dug into my scalp. She yanked my hair as she moaned louder and louder and then...all of a sudden she let go, and I knew she was coming.

"Oh, God... *Ohhhhhhh*...God..."

I kept at it, lapping at her until every last quake had rolled through her body. Then I wiped my face with the back of my hand and crawled up onto the bed, hovering over her.

Stella had squeezed her eyes closed tight, but the biggest smile stretched across her face. She threw one arm over her eyes to hide them. "Oh my God. I'm so embarrassed."

"What are you embarrassed about?"

"I basically attacked you."

"And it was the best fucking thing that's happened to me in as long as I can remember." I peeled her arm away from her face, and she peeked one eye open. "Attack away anytime the mood strikes."

She bit her lip. "You're...really good at that."

I smiled. "I'm really good at a lot of things. The night is just getting started, sweetheart."

She opened her other eye and her face went soft. "You called me *sweetheart*. I like that."

"Good." I kissed her lips gently before pushing up off the bed.

Stella leaned up on her elbows and watched me as I slipped into my shoes. "Where are you going?"

"To my room."

"Why?"

I walked back over and kissed her forehead. "To get the rest of the condoms. Two isn't going to be nearly enough."

23

Stella

I never slept this late.

Quietly setting my phone back on the nightstand, I recalled the *many* reasons I'd slept until almost noon. How many times had Hudson and I had sex? Three? Four? It had been years since I had sex more than once in a twenty-four-hour period. Even at the beginning of things with Aiden, I could only remember a handful of times we'd had sex twice—and it was certainly never anything more than that. A grin spread across my face as I remembered last night—and early this morning.

Hudson was insatiable. Actually, we both were. We'd done it with him on top, me on top, while spooning from behind... But my favorite had been early this morning while we were both lying on our sides and talking. I'll never forget the connection we had as he glided in and out of me and we looked into each other's eyes. It was quite possibly the most intimate thing I'd ever experienced. Even thinking about it now took my breath away.

Still smiling at the memory, I decided maybe I'd wake up Mr. Sleepyhead with my mouth. I turned over, expecting to find Hudson sound asleep, but instead all I found was an empty bed.

I leaned up on one elbow and called, "Hudson?"

No answer.

But now that I was awake, I needed to get up and answer Mother Nature. Climbing from the bed, my body ached. But I'd take a few aches and pains in exchange for the hours of pleasure any day of the week.

After I finished in the bathroom, I decided to get my phone to see if Hudson had left me a message. But as I rounded the foot of the bed, I noticed something laying on his pillow—a white box with a red bow and a yellow sticky note attached.

> Had a conference call at eleven thirty.
> Didn't want to wake you. I'll be back when it's over.
> Stay naked.
> H
> P.S. Let's start writing it.

Let's start writing it?

What the heck did that mean?

I wasn't sure, yet my smile beamed as I untied the red bow and slipped open the box. Inside was a beautiful, leather-bound book. It took me a minute to realize the significance, but when I did, my eyes welled up.

"Let's start writing it." Last night at dinner, I'd told Hudson I'd struggled to be happy because things hadn't worked out the way I'd envisioned them, that I needed to let go of the past and *write a new story*.

God, first the most beautiful sexual experience I'd ever had, now a beautiful gift. A girl could really get used to this.

For the next half hour, I practically floated while I took a shower and got myself ready for the new day. Just as I'd started to do my makeup, I heard the door to my suite open and close.

"Hudson?"

"Stella?"

I chuckled. "I'm in the bathroom getting ready."

Hudson walked in carrying two bags. He held up one and spoke to my reflection in the mirror. "Breakfast." He lifted the other bag. "Lunch. I wasn't sure what you would be up for."

"If you have coffee in either of those, I'll be your best friend for life."

He opened one bag and lifted a Styrofoam container. "I guess Jack's out. I'll have to let him know."

I smiled as I turned and accepted the coffee. "Thank you so much for the journal. It's beautiful, and the sentiment really means a lot to me."

Hudson nodded. He pulled a second container of coffee from the bag and lifted the plastic tab from the top. "They also had diaries. But I wasn't sure if you wrote in one or just preferred to snoop in other people's."

"I've actually never written in a diary myself. Which is funny, because I bought that first one with the intention of writing in it. It just took me on an entirely different path."

"Oh, you take a different path alright..."

I laughed. "Shut up. When did you get that anyway? You must've been up pretty early to go to the store and leave it there before I even woke up."

"I picked it up after I went for a run this morning."

"You went for a run? I'm lucky I made it from the bed to the shower."

Hudson chuckled. "Well, get done in here and come out and eat something so you have some energy. I want to get on the road to show you the sights so we can get back to the hotel early."

"Okay. I just need to dry my hair, so maybe ten minutes. Actually...better make that fifteen. I love it in this bathroom."

Hudson's brows drew together. "You love the bathroom?"

"Uhhh, yeah." I waved my hands around to what I thought was obvious. "It's about ten times the size of the one I have at home, has a *bathtub*, and look at all this beautiful lighting."

Hudson smiled. "I think you're going to like my house."

"Are you saying you have a big bathroom with a tub?"

He nodded.

"You're definitely my new best friend."

A hand holder.

I never would've guessed.

I smiled up at Hudson. He contemplated me suspiciously.

"What?"

"Nothing." I shrugged. "You're holding my hand."

"Should I not be?"

"No, I love it. I just wouldn't have taken you for a hand holder."

Hudson shook his head. "I'm not sure if that's a compliment, or I should be insulted."

We'd been walking along Hollywood Boulevard for the last half hour, reading the names of the stars on the street. So far today, we'd gone to Muscle Beach in Venice (I thought it would be fancier; the weights were actually all rusty.), the Hollywood sign (He tricked me into hiking...yuck.), and the Santa Monica Pier (Note to self—macho men would rather ride a rickety Ferris wheel than admit to being a little afraid of heights. Hudson's olive skin turns a lovely shade of green.).

"It's just a coupley thing to do."

"So?"

"I don't know." I shrugged. "Is that what we are?"

Hudson abruptly stopped walking. "Seriously?"

"What? I didn't want to assume just because of last night."

Hudson frowned. "Well, let me clear that up for you. We are."

I couldn't hide the smile that grew on my face. "Okay...*boyfriend*."

He shook his head and started walking again.

After another hour and a dozen or more blocks of walking, we went into the Roosevelt Hotel to a fancy-looking place that served burgers and the best truffle fries for dinner.

"What's your favorite food?" I waved a fry at him.

"Easy. Macaroni and cheese."

"Really?"

"Yup. Charlie and I have tried...I think we're up to forty-two different boxed kinds."

I laughed. "I had no idea there were forty-two different types of boxed mac and cheese."

"We make one most weekends she spends with me. We ran through the ones in the supermarket, so now I buy them online. She keeps a chart with our ratings."

"That's so funny."

Hudson sipped his beer. "What about you?"

"These truffle fries are a close second. But I'd have to say tortellini carbonara—the kind with peas and little pieces of prosciutto in it."

"You make it yourself?"

I frowned. "No, my mom used to make it for me. She actually also made an amazing baked mac and cheese. I don't have either of the recipes."

Looking down, I swirled the fry in the ketchup. It made me sad to think how long it had been since I'd spoken to my mom.

Hudson must have noticed I'd gone quiet.

"You mentioned you don't talk to your dad," he said. "Are you and your mom not close?"

I sighed. "We haven't spoken in more than a year. We used to be really close."

Hudson was quiet for a moment. "Do you want to talk about it?"

I shook my head. "Not really."

He nodded.

I attempted to go back to eating and not ruin the day. I hated thinking about what had happened, much less talking about it. But now that the topic had come up, I knew I shouldn't let the opportunity pass entirely. Telling Hudson at least some of what happened between Aiden and me and my family might help him understand my trust issues a little more.

So I took a deep breath. "I told you my ex cheated on me, but I didn't mention that my parents also betrayed me."

Hudson set down his burger and gave me his full attention. "Okay..."

I looked down. "They knew about Aiden's affair."

"And they didn't tell you?"

I looked down, feeling embarrassed. "No, they didn't say a word. It was a mess." I couldn't bring myself to tell the rest of the sordid story.

Hudson shook his head. "Shit. I'm sorry."

I nodded. "Thank you. Honestly, in hindsight, it wasn't Aiden who was so hard to get over. It was that I also lost my family at the same time." I frowned. "I miss talking to my mom."

Hudson dragged a hand through his hair. "Do you think you can forgive her and move past it at some point?"

For the last year, I hadn't thought that would ever be possible. I'd been so bitter and sad about everything that, on some level, I might've held my parents as accountable as I did Aiden. Maybe it took me being happy for the first time in a long time, but today I didn't feel so bitter, and I wasn't sure I should hold a grudge against my family forever.

I shook my head. "I don't know if I can forget. But maybe I could try to forgive. Would you be able to pretend it never happened if you were in my situation?"

"I've never been in a similar predicament to say for sure, but as someone who's lost both parents, I wouldn't want to have regrets when they were gone. I don't think forgiving your parents means you're excusing their behavior. I think forgiveness is more about not letting it destroy your heart anymore."

I felt his words *in* my heart. "Wow. Where did you come from, Hudson Rothschild? That was deep and mature. The men I usually seem to attract are shallow and immature."

He smirked. "I seem to remember you found me at a wedding you crashed."

"Oh yeah...I guess I did. Well, at least one of us is mature."

For the next few hours, we enjoyed the Malibu sunset, good food and wine, and each other's company. Now that I'd given in to my feelings, it felt like someone had put Miracle-Gro on them instead of just nourishing them with water. My heart was so full and content. And that feeling stayed with me throughout the night and all the way back to my hotel suite.

I laid on the bed, watching Hudson undress and admiring the view. When he unbuttoned his shirt and tossed it on a nearby chair, I wasn't sure where to look first—at his sculpted pecs, eight-pack abs, or the deep-set V that made my mouth water. Hudson unbuckled his belt and took down his zipper, causing my eyes to feast upon yet another of my favorite parts of his body—his sexy happy trail. There was so much to enjoy about this man, I thought maybe he should just stand there for a while, fully naked.

He bent to step out of his pants, and I caught a glimpse of the ink that ran up the side of his torso. I'd seen it last night, but at the time, we'd been too busy ravishing each other for me to ask about it.

I lifted my chin, pointing at the tattoo. "Is that someone's heartbeat?"

Hudson nodded. He twisted his body and lifted his arm to give me a better view. "My father had a great sense of humor and a very distinct laugh. It was a real belly laugh—sounded like it came from somewhere deep within him. Anyone who knew him recognized it, and it always made people around him smile—even strangers. He was in the hospital for the last week of his life. One day, I was visiting while he was getting a bedside EKG. He told some corny joke and started to laugh. The joke wasn't even that funny, but the sound of his laughter made all three of us—the technician, my dad, and me—crack up. For some reason, we just couldn't stop laughing. She had to redo the EKG because the reading had all these big spikes on it. The electrodes had picked up my dad's heart laughing. I asked the nurse if I could have the printout she was going to toss away, and I got this a few days after he died."

"That's so incredibly sweet."

Hudson smiled sadly. "He was a really good man."

"So where's your scar?"

"Scar?"

"Last week, I said I'd never dated anyone with a tattoo or scar, and you said you had both."

"Ah." He twisted his body the other direction and lifted his arm to reveal a jagged, three-inch line. "I have a few, but this one is probably the worst."

"How did you get it?"

"Fraternity party. Drinking, a slip and slide, and a stick hidden under the tarp."

"Ouch."

"Not my finest moment. It wasn't that big at first. Jack helped me bandage it up, and then it split open wider when I continued to dive on the slip and slide."

"Why didn't you stop after you got cut?"

He shrugged. "We had a bet."

I shook my head. "Did you win, at least?"

Hudson's smile was adorable. "I did."

He finished getting undressed, and I continued to admire his amazing physique.

Catching me staring yet again, Hudson squinted. "What's going on in that head of yours?"

I spoke to his body, unwilling to lift my eyes quite yet. "I wasted months going to bed alone when I could have been spending my time touching *that*. How would you feel about standing there for a while so I can take a good, long look? Maybe two or three hours? That should do."

He chuckled and finished taking off his pants before climbing onto the bed and hovering over me. Lifting my finger to his lips, I traced the outline. Hudson caught my hand and raised it for a soft kiss.

"Why did you reject me for so long? And don't insult me by saying it's because I'm an investor in your business. We both know that's a load of crap."

"You only asked me out once."

Hudson made a face that said *you know you're full of shit*. "Semantics. You knew I was interested from day one. I left the ball in your court, but I still let you know I was interested often enough."

I sighed. "I know. I guess...I was just scared."

"Of what?"

I shook my head. "My last relationship and its aftermath were really hard to move past. I'm scared of getting hurt again...scared of *you*..."

"Me?"

"Yeah. You make me nervous in a lot of ways. Even now, Hudson. Most things in my life have seemed really great from the outside—my parents' marriage, my engagement. I'm the type of woman who believes in a happily ever after, a fairytale. Sometimes that blinds me and keeps me from seeing things I don't want to see. I thought I was an idealist, but after my ex burned me, it made me wonder if I was just a fool. Plus, you're basically Prince Charming—a beautiful face, that body, successful, kind—when you want to be, mature, independent..." I shrugged. "You're almost too good to be true, and I guess I'm afraid to fall for a fairytale again. You know, Fisher and I used to refer to you that way."

Hudson's forehead wrinkled. "Refer to me what way?"

"As Prince Charming."

He looked away for a moment before his eyes met mine. "I'm no Prince Charming, sweetheart. But I do like you very much."

"Why?"

"Why do I like you?"

I nodded.

"A lot of reasons. I like that when I handed you that microphone at Olivia's wedding, you rose to the challenge and then called me an asshole with fire in your eyes. You don't back down. You're fearless, even though you somehow think you're a chickenshit. I love that even though you've been through some shitty situations, you refuse to let them get you down. Instead of letting all the negative crap in life eat at you, you made up some happiness system. I love that when you see a homeless woman, you give her a Hershey bar because you know it might make some chemical in her brain to help her feel a little better, even if for just a few minutes. I love that you're creative and invented your own product, and you're smart enough to write an algorithm I wouldn't have a clue how to formulate. And I love that you're stubborn and don't give up."

He looked down at my body and then took a second to examine my face before shaking his head. "All of that, plus what you look like. The better question is, what reason would I have *not* to like you?"

My eyes started to water. Hudson leaned in and pressed his lips to mine. "Do you feel scared right now?" he whispered.

My pulse raced. "More than ever."

He smiled. "Good."

"Good? As in you want me to be afraid?"

"No...but at least I'm not alone in this. We're only afraid of the things that mean the most to us."

I cupped his cheek. "I'm so glad you waited me out."

"I knew you'd be worth waiting for."

Hudson pressed his mouth to mine in a passionate kiss. We'd spent a large portion of the last twenty-four hours in this bed with our mouths intertwined, yet this kiss felt different—more filled with emotion than ever before. He held my face between his hands, and I wrapped my arms around his neck. But what started slow, quickly heated up. Our kiss became wild and fervent as we helped each other shed our remaining clothes.

There was a frenzied feeling in the air. Still, something about the way Hudson looked into my eyes told me he knew I was still fragile in many ways. Our gazes never broke as he lined himself up at my entrance and pushed inside of me. Hudson was thick, and it had been over a year since I'd had sex until last night. So he took his time, going slowly as he sank deeper with each measured thrust. Once he was fully seated, he circled his hips, and I could feel his pelvis press against my clit. It felt so good, so perfectly right. My heart was as full as my body, and my emotions became almost impossible to hold in. Tears prickled at my eyes, which I shut in an attempt to hold them back.

"Open, sweetheart." Hudson's voice was hoarse.

My eyes fluttered back open and met his. What I saw made it impossible to hold back the tears. Hudson's eyes were as brimming with emotion as mine. We stayed that way, connected in every way possible, as our orgasms built. Not wanting the moment to end, I tried to hold back as his thrusts grew harder and faster. But the sounds echoing through the room did me in. Our wet bodies slapped against each other as he fucked me with his body and soul.

"Hudson..."

His jaw strained as he kept going. "Let it go...let it all go."

And I did. With a voracious cry, my body took over for my mind, and waves and waves of ecstasy ran through me. Just as it started to ebb, Hudson's orgasm hit, and the heat of him spilling into me made my body continue to ripple with shock waves.

After, I had no idea how he could even hold his head up, much less still be semi-hard as he glided in and out of me.

"Wow...that was..."

Hudson smiled and kissed me softly. "Too good to be true," he whispered.

I smiled back, and a little bit of hope sparked inside me.

Maybe, just maybe, he'd be the one man who didn't let me down.

24

Stella

Sixteen months ago

"**D**o you know what Drummond Hospitality is?" I asked.

Aiden was sitting in the living room of his apartment grading papers while I sat at the kitchen table going through my emails. "Hmmm?"

"It's on your credit card statement for a hundred-and-ninety-two dollars. The other charge I recognize."

Aiden's eyes narrowed. "How did you get my credit card bill?"

"It comes to my email now. Remember a few months ago, I said I'd gotten a notice that Bank of America was going paperless, and you'd have to opt out if you wanted paper statements from now on? You asked me to have it sent to my email since everything goes to spam when you use your work email."

"I thought you were referring to our joint bank account statement."

I shook my head. "No, your credit card."

"How long has it been going to you?"

I shrugged. "Two months, I think? Half the time you don't have any activity. You rarely use your card. Last month it was a zero balance."

The look on Aiden's face troubled me. "Is it a problem?" I asked. "Do you not want me to see what you're charging or something?"

He tossed his pen on top of the pile of papers and looked away. "Of course not. I just wasn't aware that I wouldn't be receiving the paper bill anymore."

"Okay...well, do you know what that charge is? Drummond Hospitality?"

"No idea. The only thing I charged was dinner when we went to Alfredo's a few weeks ago. It must be a mistake. I'll go online and dispute it later."

"Do you want me to do it since I'm online anyway?"

"No, it's fine. I'll do it."

Something didn't sit right. But I let it go since Aiden and I had already had a few fights about my suspicions over the last few months. There'd been the time I saw an odd text on his phone, and then another time he'd said he was going to his office at the college on a Saturday to work on grades, which he normally did from home. I'd decided to surprise him with lunch since he'd been working a lot, and he hadn't been there. Then recently he'd come home smelling like perfume, and he'd gotten defensive when I'd asked him why—yelling that if I didn't have our entire apartment constantly smelling like perfume samples for a business that didn't exist, his clothes wouldn't smell like a cheap whorehouse.

Since I always gave him the summary of the diaries I read, he knew the woman in the diary I'd been reading was cheating on her husband, and he convinced me that I was seeing things that weren't there because of how ridiculously involved I got with the people I read about. Even now, I wondered if maybe he was right. Just last week, I'd read an entry where Alexandria had written about her husband questioning a charge on their credit card bill. She'd reserved a hotel suite for one of her rendezvous with Jasper, and then he'd paid cash when they checked in. But the hotel had accidentally done a duplicate charge.

So I chalked my paranoia up to what Aiden had warned me about. It wasn't any different than if I'd watched a horror movie and suddenly needed to check under my bed before I climbed in. The stress of what you're putting in your mind causes your brain to go places it wouldn't normally go.

"Okay," I said. "I think you can just pay the restaurant part of the bill, then. It's more than the minimum payment anyway."

"Fine." Aiden went back to grading papers. But a minute later, he said, "I'll probably remove the card from electronic billing and go back to having my statements come in the mail. I like to have paper copies for tax purposes since I sometimes buy things for work."

Again, why did that bother me? His reasoning made total sense. I really was looking for monsters under my bed and needed to stop. "Sounds good."

A month later, I'd forgotten all about the credit card bill. Aiden and I had just gotten back from meeting one of his colleagues for drinks, and I was staying over at his place. On our way upstairs, I grabbed the mail out of the mailbox. In the pile was his credit card statement from Bank of America.

I set the mail on the table, keeping that envelope in my hand. "How did that dispute go with Bank of America?"

Aiden's eyes dropped to the bill, and he plucked it from my hands. "Fine. They reversed it." He tucked the bill into his sports jacket's inside pocket.

Once again, I had no idea why him taking the bill bothered me. But it did.

Aiden walked toward his bedroom. "I'm going to take a quick shower."

"Okay."

While he was gone, I poured myself a glass of merlot and tried not to give it any more thought. Though this week I'd read an entire diary entry about how stupid and trusting Alexandria's husband was. She seemed to enjoy almost getting caught and being able to lie her way out of things...

I knew I was most likely being ridiculous. But last month I'd stayed awake half the night after the silly credit card thing had weighed on me. Aiden wouldn't need to know I'd gone online to take a peek at his bill. And once I did that, I'd be able to put everything to bed, once and for all.

Though...I'd still be violating his trust by double-checking, even if he had no idea about it. So while I tried to talk myself out of doing what I so badly wanted to do, I went to the bedroom to get changed instead. I opened Aiden's dresser to get one of his old T-shirts, and tossed my jeans and blouse on a chair in the corner. On my way out to the living room, Aiden's sports jacket caught my attention from the open closet door. I could hear the shower water still running in the adjoining bathroom, so I walked over and took it down. But instead of rummaging for the credit card bill, I brought the jacket to my nose and inhaled deeply. The unmistakable smell of jasmine filled my nose. Jasmine was *not* a scent I had at home for my Signature Scent samples. It wasn't even one I'd been working with lately.

The room grew still, and it took me a minute to realize it was because the shower water had stopped. *Shit.* I quickly hung the jacket back in the closet and left the bedroom. Panic overwhelmed me. There was no way I'd be able to sleep tonight with the way I was feeling, nor would I be able to lie next to Aiden and pretend everything was fine. It was no longer a question of whether I was going to violate his trust and sign into his credit card online. I had to in order to keep my sanity.

My fingers shook as I called up the website on my phone. The damn thing took forever to load, and every two seconds I glanced up at the half-closed door to our bedroom. When the data finally populated, I scrolled to this month's bill. Relief flooded me when I saw there were no charges at all. Overwhelmed with guilt, I went to sign off, but then I noticed the payments section had a payment of $261. I figured it was probably just the way they showed a credit given for that incorrect charge, but since it left a niggling feeling, I clicked to check.

And froze seeing it was an actual payment made weeks ago from a bank account ending in 588. I felt the blood draining from my face. That was Aiden's checking account.

It had to be a mistake. I clicked over to the disputes tab. No disputes in the last ninety days. Feeling freaked out and lost, I closed the website and did something I should have done a month ago. I Googled Drummond Hospitality.

The results sent my heart into my throat.

Drummond Hospitality is the owner of four New York City boutique hotels.

25

Stella

"This I could certainly get used to..." I'd woken up to find Hudson standing at my stove, wearing nothing but a pair of shorts and a backward baseball cap. His sculpted back was so muscular and tan. I wrapped my arms around his stomach and squeezed him from behind, placing a kiss on his shoulder.

"I just got back from a run and haven't showered yet. You're probably kissing dried sweat."

"Pretty sure my skin isn't much different after last night."

Hudson turned and wrapped his arms around my waist. The dirty smile on his face told me he was recalling just *how* sweaty we'd gotten.

He smirked. "You broke the bed."

I pulled back. "I didn't break the bed; *you* did."

"Pretty sure you were the one on top of me when the frame gave way."

"Maybe, but you weren't just lying there. You top from the bottom, you know."

Hudson chuckled. "What the hell does that mean?"

"You might appear to let me take control, but you never really give it up."

His face changed, and he looked a little concerned. "And you don't like that?"

I grinned. "No, I like it a lot. But that means you contributed to breaking the bed."

Hudson smiled and swatted my ass. "Go sit. Pancakes are almost done."

"Okay."

The week since we'd gotten home from California had been absolute bliss. Hudson and I were inseparable. We worked late every night getting things for Signature Scent ready, and we alternated between sleeping at his house in Brooklyn and my apartment here in the City. I probably should've been concerned that we were spending too much time together, but I was too happy to let anything spoil it.

Hudson set a plate in front of me.

I laughed. "This is adorable."

He'd made one big pancake and decorated it into a smiling sun with halved strawberries forming pointed sunrays and bananas and strawberries creating a face.

"That's how Charlie likes it. But don't be too impressed. It's the only dish I make other than macaroni and cheese. I don't want you to get your expectations up."

"Okay, I won't."

Hudson could've sucked at most everything else and I'd still be swooning over him based on how thoughtful he was—and how incredible in bed. To say I was falling for this man would be an understatement. A few times this week, I'd caught myself sitting at my desk randomly smiling. I hadn't even been thinking about anything in particular. I just felt...happy.

"In case that doesn't fill you enough..." Hudson set a banana next to my plate.

I was just about to say I'd never eat pancakes *and* a banana when I saw the ink on the yellow skin: *I'm bananas about you.*

When I looked up, Hudson winked and went back to the stove as if he hadn't just turned my insides into a pile of mush.

He looked back over his shoulder, pointing to my plate with a spatula. "Eat. Don't wait for me. It'll get cold."

Just as I put the first bite into my mouth, my front door swung open.

"Honey, I'm home!"

Shit. Fisher. I'd been single ever since he moved into the apartment next to me.

Hudson turned around, and Fisher caught sight of him and froze. "Crap. Sorry, man."

"It's fine. Come on in."

Fisher looked over at me and I nodded, so he walked into the kitchen.

Hudson extended his hand. "Hudson Rothschild. I don't think we've been formally introduced."

Fisher shook. "I guess the wedding doesn't count. Fisher Underwood."

Hudson pointed to the table with the spatula. "Have a seat. Stella already filled me in that feeding you is part of the package deal I get with her."

Fisher smiled. He swiped a handful of blueberries from the open container next to the stove and popped a few in his mouth. "You have my blessing to marry him."

Hudson and I both laughed.

He made Fisher a plate of pancakes with a side of fruit, but not the fancy smiling sun he'd made me. Surprisingly, breakfast wasn't awkward once the three of us were at the table.

Fisher shoved almost a half a pancake into his mouth. "So, what are you guys up to this weekend?"

"Hudson has his daughter. I have a few errands to run, but other than that, I'm open. You going to be around?"

"I was thinking about hitting the flea market," Fisher said. "It's my paralegal's birthday next week, and she loved the handmade ceramic mugs you picked out for her last year, so I figured I'd go back and see what else they have."

"Oh, awesome. Maybe I'll come."

Hudson's forehead creased. "I thought we were taking Charlie to the park. You said something about an ancient playground."

I thought back to the conversation we'd had earlier. "You said you were thinking of taking Charlie to Central Park, and I asked if you'd ever taken her to the Ancient Playground. I didn't realize you wanted me to come, too."

"I guess I just assumed you would..."

"Alright, well, I'd love to spend time with you and Charlie—if you don't think it's too soon."

Hudson shook his head. "I don't think she's ready to see you in my bed yet, but she needs to start spending time with us to lead up to that, right?"

Wow. It gave me a fuzzy feeling in my belly to know I wasn't alone in seeing a future for us. Reaching over, I squeezed his hand.

"That sounds great."

"I'll tell you what, I have to stop home before going to pick her up at two. Why don't you guys go to the flea market, and we can meet up at the park after?"

I looked over at Fisher, and he shrugged. "Sounds like a plan to me."

After we finished eating, Fisher left, and Hudson took a quick shower before putting the clothes he'd worn to work yesterday back on. I watched from the bedroom door as he tugged on one of his socks. He must have sensed me there because he spoke before even looking up.

"Think we could keep a few things at each other's places? So maybe I won't have to wear day-old socks and a suit for my Saturday morning walk of shame back home?"

I smiled, and a warm feeling ran through me. "I'd like that a lot."

A few minutes later, Hudson kissed me goodbye.

"Do you have any dinner plans for tonight with Charlie?" I asked.

"We usually just order in if we're out during the day."

"Do you think it would be too much if I made you guys dinner? I can pick up what I need on my way over."

"I'd love that. But I can pick up whatever you need. Just text me a list."

"Nope. I want it to be a surprise."

Hudson smiled and kissed my forehead. "Can't wait."

"So you and Hudson seem pretty tight."

Fisher and I strolled the aisles at the flea market side by side.

I sighed. "He's incredible."

He wiggled his brows. "I know. I got an eyeful of that chest at breakfast this morning."

I laughed. "That's not what I meant. But yeah, his body is pretty amazing, too."

"I'm probably not supposed to tell you this, but he didn't say not to, and you know I can't keep a secret, especially not from you..."

"What?"

"He knocked on my apartment door on his way out today."

"What for?"

"He asked if I was going to be home tomorrow morning. Apparently, he's going to try to have something delivered for you."

"Did he say what?"

Fisher shook his head. "No, but I gave him my number so he can text me. I hope I don't accidentally hit him up after a few drinks. His number is right above Hughes."

"The guy you hook up with sometimes?"

"Yeah, and we don't make small talk. I think last time I had a few drinks, I texted him *Wanna fuck*, and he responded with his location."

I laughed. "Okay, well, hopefully you won't do that. But you have no idea what he wants to have delivered?"

"Nope. Hopefully it's foam."

"Foam?"

Fisher nodded. "To put behind your headboard. I heard you guys going at it last night."

"Oh God, please tell me you're kidding."

"Your bed shares a wall with my television in the living room. I have that shelf that holds the cable box and some books underneath. You knocked Stephen King on the floor."

I covered my face with my hands. "God, I would *not* want to hear you having sex. We actually broke the bedframe last night. I'll move it away from the wall."

"Nice. I once broke a dentist's chair when I was sleeping with that orthodontist. But never a bed."

My nose wrinkled. "Thanks for sharing. Now every time I go to the dentist, I'm going to wonder whose naked ass has had sex where I'm sitting."

"You're welcome." Fisher winked. "But seriously, how dramatic would I sound if I said you looked radiant? Something about you has changed, but I can't put my finger on it."

"It's probably because I broke my year-long dry spell. Maybe you're just seeing the muscles in my face relax for the first time in a while."

"Mmmm..." He assessed me. "No, you had *that* going on this morning. The wild, just-fucked hair was a good look for you, by the way. But it's something more... You seem lighter or something."

There was no one on this Earth who could read me like Fisher—which really spoke volumes about my past relationship. Aiden had never paid enough attention to know if something was bothering me.

I reached over and took Fisher's hand. Lacing my fingers with his, I squeezed. "You're so good at being my friend. I wasn't going to say anything, because I don't want to make it more than it is, but I called my mom today, right before we left for the train, actually."

Fisher's eyebrows rose. "What made you do that?"

"I've been doing a lot of thinking about forgiveness... and trying to move on with my life." I shrugged. "I want to make Hudson something she always cooked for me that I loved, so I thought that might be a good place to start."

"She must've been happy to hear your voice."

I frowned. "She was. We didn't talk for very long, though. I asked her if I could have the recipe and then asked her if they were doing okay. She definitely seemed hesitant. I got the feeling she was afraid to say anything wrong. We were on the phone maybe five minutes. When we said goodbye, she asked if I'd call again soon, and I said I'd try."

This time it was Fisher who squeezed my hand. "Good for you. I think it's time, my Stella Bella."

After we finished shopping, Fisher and I took the subway back to the City. We were going two different directions, so we said goodbye at Grand Central Station.

He kissed the top of my head and gave me a big hug. "I'm happy for you," he said. "I have a really good feeling about things between you and the Adonis. I see a bright future."

Always afraid to jinx myself, I said *thank you*, rather than telling him I agreed. But deep down, I saw something bright in the future, too.

I just never expected that brightness to come from a giant explosion.

Hudson

"**W**hat are you two up to in there?"

Charlie held out her hand. "You're not allowed in here, Daddy."

"Why not?"

"Because we're making a surprise!"

"But I'm the only one going to be surprised since the two of you are in on it?"

My daughter giggled. "Surprises can be for one person, Daddy."

I caught Stella's eye and winked. "Why don't I put on some music while you guys work in the kitchen? Maybe some Katy Perry or Taylor Swift…"

As expected, Charlie jumped up and down. She pressed her palms together as if she needed to pray in order for me to do something she asked—as if I wouldn't jump off a cliff to make her happy. "Can you put on Dolly?"

I chuckled. "Sure."

303

I turned on the music, sat down in the living room, and put my feet up on the coffee table. Grabbing the TV remote, I flicked on ESPN with closed captioning and started to read the bottom of the screen. They were interviewing a new running back the Giants had drafted for the upcoming season. Big Blue was my team, so I was definitely interested, yet I couldn't stay focused. Every few minutes, my eyes wandered back to the kitchen. I could see Stella and Charlie working away on whatever they were cooking. Stella stood, while my daughter sat on the counter mixing something. I couldn't hear what they were saying, but I watched my daughter cover her mouth as she giggled. The smile on Stella's face was pretty fucking fantastic, too.

Not to sound like a pussy, but I got this fullness in my chest that gave me a warm feeling. Ah...fuck it, who was I kidding? I didn't give a shit if I sounded like a pussy. I was happy—*really* fucking happy. It had been years since I'd felt like I had a real family, and even though I'd only known Stella a few months, and this was the first time the three of us had hung out, my house felt like a home today.

I'd been looking toward the kitchen, but I must've zoned out while I was thinking, because when my eyes came into focus again, Stella was squinting at me. She smirked, as if to say, *What's going on in that head of yours?*

She probably assumed I was picturing her naked in my kitchen or remembering all the places I'd fucked her in my house over the last week, rather than daydreaming about spending nights with my two ladies, playing board games and making a fire for them this winter in the fireplace I never used.

A half hour later, the table was set, and I was finally allowed to see what the two of them had been concocting.

Stella set a towel-covered casserole dish on the table, and Charlie leaned across, looking at Stella, who gave her a nod.

"Ta-da!" My daughter ripped the towel off.

"Macaroni and cheese? You two find a new box to try out?"

Charlie shook her head. "We made it from itch!"

Stella smiled. "That's scratch, sweetie. We made it from *scratch*."

"It looks delicious." I looked around the table theatrically. "But where are yours? That one is just for me, right?"

Charlie giggled. "We have to *share* it, Daddy. There's enough for all of us."

I salivated as Stella dished each of us a heaping plate of my favorite food. I couldn't wait to dig in.

"This is really good," I said a few moments later.

"Thanks. I...called my mom for her recipe today."

I hadn't expected her to say *that,* and I didn't want to mention anything around Charlie, so I spoke cryptically. "How did that go?"

Stella shrugged. "It was pleasant, I guess."

I nodded. "Well, thank you. It really is delicious."

She smiled. "It was time."

Oblivious to my meaningful exchange with Stella, my daughter spoke with her mouth full. "Daddy, after dinner can we have ice cream and play secrets?"

I pointed to her dish with my fork. "You're not even halfway done with what's in front of you, and you're worried about dessert? Maybe you'll be too full for ice cream."

Charlie snickered as if I'd just told a joke. "There's always room for ice cream, Daddy. It melts once it's in your belly, so it's not even really food."

"What's the secrets game?" Stella asked. "I don't think I've ever played before."

"It's not really a game. We just eat ice cream and take turns telling each other secrets." I didn't want to explain in front of Charlie that it was something my dad had done with my sister and me after our mom first got diagnosed with cancer. It was his way of teaching us that we could always confide in him—trust him to keep our secrets and tell us his.

"Can it be any secret?" Stella asked.

"Whatever you want," I said.

She grinned. "I'm in."

The macaroni and cheese left us all full, so we retreated to the couch after dinner to watch a movie. Charlie laid her head on my lap with her body spread out to my left, and Stella sat on my right. Halfway through *Inside Out*, Charlie was snoring. I couldn't blame her. A nap sounded pretty good after that meal, and we'd watched this movie at least fifty times.

At one point, Stella got up to go to the bathroom, so I slipped out from under my daughter and carefully set her head down. Then I waited in the hall. When Stella opened the door, I grabbed her arm and yanked her into the adjoining guest bedroom.

She giggled, and I put my hand over her mouth. "Shhh...she has stealth hearing." Stella nodded, so I took my hand away.

She whispered, "What are you doing?"

"I wanted to say thank you for dinner."

"You already did."

"I meant properly."

Cupping the back of her neck, I sealed my lips over hers. "You always smell so damn good," I groaned.

She sucked on my tongue. "You always *taste* so good."

Fuck. This was probably a dumb idea. I could feel myself getting worked up already. But I hadn't had a minute alone with her since she got here, and I needed it. Pressing her against the door, I took her mouth in a rough kiss. When I was done, we were both breathing heavy.

I wiped her bottom lip as I spoke. "You called your mother."

Her face softened. "Yeah. I don't think I'll be going over there for dinner any time soon, but what you said really resonated with me. Life is short, and you never know what tomorrow is going to bring. I don't want to have regrets, and I'm ready to move on."

I looked back and forth between her eyes and cupped her cheek. "I'm glad."

She turned her head and kissed my palm. "Do you think Charlie's asleep for the night? Maybe I should get going."

"Definitely not. She's going to wake up and demand ice cream any minute now."

Stella smiled. "And then I'll get to hear one of your secrets. I was kind of looking forward to that."

"Oh yeah?"

She nodded.

"Well, let me tell you one now." I crooked my finger for her to come closer. When she did, I moved my mouth to her ear and whispered, "I'm fucking crazy about you, sweetheart."

She looked at me and smiled. "I'm crazy about you, too."

Sure enough, Charlie woke about ten minutes before the movie ended. She stretched her arms over her head. "Can we have ice cream now?"

I chuckled. "You're barely awake."

"I'm awake enough for ice cream."

"Alright. Why don't you two go sit at the table, and I'll make us bowls. You want the works?"

Charlie nodded fast with a toothy smile.

I lifted my chin to Stella. "How about you?"

"What's in the works?"

"Whipped cream, sprinkles, nuts, banana slices, and chocolate sauce."

She licked her lips. "Definitely."

In the kitchen, I whipped up three bowls. Setting them down at the table, I said, "Alright. Who wants to go first?"

Charlie pointed to Stella. "Stella! I want to know her secret."

"Oh boy..." Stella said. "You need to give me a minute then so I can think of one."

We shoveled ice cream into our mouths until eventually Stella raised her hand. "Thought of one!" She leaned over the table toward Charlie and lowered her voice. "No one knows this. Are you sure you can keep a secret?"

My daughter's eyes were wide with mirth, and she nodded rapidly.

"Okay. Well, when I was about eight or nine—not too much older than you—I found this turtle at the park. It was only about this big." Stella made a circle the size of a golf ball with her hands. "I brought it home and asked my parents if I could keep it, but they said no because they thought he belonged outside. So the next day, I went back to the park and tried to set him free. I put him back in the area of the grass where I'd found him, but he blended in so well that at least a half-dozen kids almost squished him while they were running around playing. I just knew if I left him there, he'd get hurt. So that night, I snuck him back into the house and kept him in a drawer in my room. A week later, my mom found him when she was in my room putting away laundry. She made me go put him back again. I did, but every chance I got, I'd go check on him. I tried putting him in a corner of the park that was safer, but he would find his way back to areas where kids ran around. I worried about him a lot. A few weeks later, my family was going to Florida for vacation—to Disney and SeaWorld. So I tucked the turtle into my backpack, snuck him into SeaWorld, and set him free inside the turtle exhibit. I figured he'd be safe there."

I raised a brow. "You smuggled an animal into SeaWorld?"

Stella nodded. "I like to think of it as helping him get asylum, but yes."

"Daddy, can we go to SeaWorld? Maybe we'll see the turtle Stella saved."

I didn't have the heart to tell her the thing was likely long dead. "Maybe someday."

Charlie shoveled a spoonful of ice cream into her mouth. "Your turn, Daddy."

I admitted that I'd never been to SeaWorld, and then gave the floor to my daughter.

She tapped her pointer to her lips as the wheels in her head turned. "Can mine just be a secret that Stella doesn't know? I can't think of anything you don't know, Daddy."

"Sure."

Charlie leaned toward Stella, mimicking what Stella had done earlier. She cupped both hands around her mouth and whispered, "My name isn't really Charlie."

"Wow. Okay. That is a pretty big secret. I had no idea." Stella's eyes flickered to mine, and I nodded confirmation before her attention returned to my daughter.

"Is Charlie short for something?" she asked.

My daughter shook her head. "I was named after my grandmas. My middle name is Charlotte, like Daddy's mom was."

"So Charlie is short for Charlotte, which is your middle name? But then what's your first name?"

"My mommy's mom's name—Laken."

"Laken?" Stella's brows drew together. "So your name is Laken Charlotte?"

Charlie nodded. "Daddy, can I have more whipped cream on my ice cream?" She tilted her bowl toward me and frowned. "Mine's all gone."

"That's because you ate it. But I guess so. Go grab the can from the fridge, okay?"

Charlie hopped off her chair, already done with the secrets game and moving on, but Stella looked confused.

"Her name is *Laken* Charlotte? That can't be a common name combination."

I shrugged. "Probably not. My ex-wife's mom passed away a few months before Charlie was born. She wanted to name her after her mom, so we combined our mother's names to honor them both. But after Charlie was born, Lexi had a little postpartum depression, and every time she called the baby Laken, it made her emotional and upset. So we started calling her by her middle name—Charlotte, but shortened it to Charlie. It stuck. By the time she was a month or two old, Charlie was Charlie, and calling her anything else didn't feel right."

"Laken Charlotte," Stella repeated. It seemed like it bothered her for some reason.

"It's not something I think about, because she's just Charlie to me. Are you upset I didn't mention that?"

Stella shook her head. "No...it's not that. I just..."

I waited for her to say more, but she just stared off, her head somewhere else. "Is Lexi short for something?"

My brows drew together. "Lexi as in my ex-wife?"

Stella nodded.

"Her full name is Alexandria, but everyone calls her Lexi. Why?"

Stella went pale and her eyes grew wide. She looked freaked out.

"Is something wrong?"

She shook her head. "No. No, I...I just have a headache."

"A headache?" I frowned. "When did it come on?"

"Uuuhhh...just now."

My gut told me she was full of shit, but Charlie came back to the table with the can of whipped cream and shoved her bowl in front of me. I sprayed more than I should've and slid it back to her before returning my attention to Stella.

"You want some Tylenol?"

"No. Actually...I think I'm just going to get going."

Something was definitely off. "You didn't even finish your ice cream."

"I know. I'm sorry." She stood and walked her bowl into the kitchen.

I followed, speaking quietly so Charlie wouldn't hear. "Is something else bothering you? Why do I feel like we just did something to upset you?"

Stella smiled, but it was clearly forced. "You didn't. I just...need to lie down, I think."

I looked back and forth between her eyes, then nodded. "Alright. Well, let me call you an Uber."

"I can take the train."

"No, I'll call you an Uber. You're not feeling well." I pulled the phone from my pocket and opened the app. Punching in Stella's address, the screen flashed that the driver would be arriving pretty damn fast. I turned the screen and showed it to her. "Four minutes."

"Okay. Thank you."

Stella spent a minute collecting her things and said goodnight to Charlie, who gave her a big hug.

"I'll be back in one second," I said to my daughter. "You finish up your ice cream while I walk Stella out."

"Okay, Daddy."

At the front door, I stepped outside with Stella and pulled it partially closed behind me. "You sure you're okay?"

"Yeah, I'm positive." She looked down. "Sometimes a headache can make me nauseous, so I just think it's better if I get home."

Again, I wasn't buying it, but I nodded anyway. "Okay."

A car that matched the description of the Uber pulled up at the curb, so I cupped Stella's face and kissed her lips softly. "Check the license plate before you get in. It should end in six-F-E. And text me when you get home."

She nodded. "Goodnight."

I watched as Stella walked around the car and read the back plate, then climbed into the backseat. She spoke to the driver, and I waited for her to look back and wave goodbye one last time. But she never did. The car simply pulled away from the curb.

Something was definitely off, and my gut told me it had nothing to do with a headache.

27

Hudson

Stella wasn't at work when I arrived on Monday morning. I walked by her office three times before my nine o'clock meeting. When she still hadn't shown up, I shot off a quick text.

Hudson: Everything okay?

The lack of my phone buzzing caused more of a distraction than if it had rung loudly during the presentation I was supposed to be watching. I couldn't seem to focus. The other night after Stella left, I'd managed to talk myself into thinking I'd overanalyzed shit—that it *was* just a headache, and everything would be back to normal by Sunday morning. But obviously that hadn't happened.

By the time my meeting ended, it was almost eleven, and I still hadn't heard from Stella. Her office door was locked, and the receptionist said she hadn't seen her today, so I headed down to talk to my sister.

"Hey. Have you talked to Stella today? She's not in yet."

My sister stopped writing and looked up. "Hi, Hudson. It's nice to see you this lovely morning, too. I'm doing well, thanks for asking."

"I'm not in the mood..."

She frowned. "What crawled up your butt?"

"Can you just tell me if you've spoken to Stella today?"

Olivia sighed. "Yeah, I spoke to her twice. She's working from home. Didn't she mention it to you?"

I shook my head. "Is she feeling okay?"

A look of concern registered on my sister's face. "She said she'd had a headache that kept her up the last two nights, but she was feeling better. Everything okay with you two?"

I raked my hand through my hair. "Yeah. I think so."

My sister gave me the once-over, and her lips formed a grim line. "You *think* so? But you're not sure. What did you do?"

"Me? Why do you think I did something?"

"Usually when a man isn't sure if he did something wrong, he did."

I shrugged. "Whatever."

When I got back to my office, my phone finally buzzed after more than two hours of waiting.

Stella: Everything is fine. Going to work from home today.

I felt a modicum of relief that she wasn't completely ignoring me, but not enough to make the uneasiness in the pit of my stomach go away. So I wrote back.

Hudson: Headache gone?

It seemed like a simple-enough question, yet I watched as the little dots started to move around, then stopped, then started again before completely stopping. Ten minutes later, a response finally came.

Stella: Yes, headache is gone. Thanks for checking in.

Thanks for checking in felt a hell of a lot like *Now leave me alone.*

Whatever. I had work to do. So rather than waste more hours than I already had overanalyzing shit, I tossed my phone on my desk. Maybe I just didn't understand women.

The next day, I was happy as shit to see light streaming from Stella's office when I arrived at seven o'clock.

"Hey. You're in..."

Stella had her nose buried in her laptop. She looked up and smiled, but it didn't quite reach her eyes. "Yeah. Sorry about not coming in yesterday."

"Nothing to be sorry about. You don't work for me. The space here is yours to use as you need. I was just worried maybe something more was going on than a headache..."

Stella shuffled some papers around on her desk and avoided eye contact. "No, nothing going on. Just a headache. I get them sometimes."

A few days ago, I would have walked into her office, shut the door behind me, and taken her mouth in a kiss that left me with a raging hard-on. Yet at the moment, the vibe I felt kept me at her door. In other words, it wasn't *just* a headache. But she was working, and I had a meeting I needed to prep for, so I wasn't going to push it right now.

Nodding toward my office, I said, "I have an early meeting that'll take up most of my morning. You want to get together this afternoon and go through the deliveries that haven't come in yet? We can talk about whatever else is a priority that you might want me to jump in on."

"I actually went through the deliveries yesterday. We're on track as of now. I think I have a handle on things. I'm going to sit with Olivia and go through the final marketing stuff in a little while."

"Oh...okay." I shrugged. "Maybe lunch later, then?"

"I'm going to work through lunch with Olivia. And I have a meeting later this afternoon uptown at Fisher's office."

"Fisher's office?"

"It's nothing to do with Signature Scent."

Clearly she was giving me the brush off, but I was thick...

"Dinner later?"

She frowned. "I'll probably just get a bite to eat with Fisher afterward."

I couldn't get my lips to turn upward to pretend everything was fine, no matter how hard I tried. The best I could muster was a nod to feign understanding. "Let me know if there's anything you need from me."

"Thanks, Hudson."

28

Stella

Three nights ago

It had to be a coincidence.

I knew that wasn't true, but I kept telling myself it was as the Uber pulled away from the curb. If I didn't, I was pretty sure I was going to vomit all over the poor guy's backseat. I was completely freaked out.

The minute we pulled up to my apartment, I flew out of the car and raced for the elevator. When it didn't come in two seconds, I decided I'd rather keep busy running up eight flights of stairs than stand waiting while the inside of my chest felt like a ticking time bomb.

In my apartment, I ran straight for my bedroom and dropped to the floor to pull out the plastic bins I kept stowed under my bed. In my panic, I couldn't remember what the outside of the diary I was searching for looked like, or even which storage bin had the most recent books. So I grabbed the first container and started to yank them out one by one.

The first bin had at least thirty different diaries packed into it that I'd collected over the years, but none that were recent. I didn't bother to put anything back before ripping the top off the next plastic container. Just a few books into that one, I lifted a red, leather-bound volume that sent a jolt of electricity through my body. Ten seconds ago, I couldn't have identified it in a lineup, but the minute I held it in my hand, I knew. *I just knew* it was the one.

Unlike every other book I picked up, I didn't immediately flip it open and rush to read. Instead, I took a deep breath and steadied myself as the seriousness of the situation hit me all over again. If what I suspected was right... *Oh God, I know I'm right.*

A wave of nausea rolled through me, and my hands shook as I cracked open the book and began to read.

Dear Diary,

This is the first page of a new book, which seems very fitting as I sit here and write today. I know it's been a while since I last wrote, but all the pages in my old book were filled, and I hadn't had anything good to write about to start a new one.

Happily, things have recently changed. Summer has been far from boring. In fact, I think this summer has been one of those that musicians write songs about. You see, I met the love of my life. He's sweet and kind, but also sort of broody and tough. Back in May, when I got home from college, my parents dragged me to some boring party that one of their friends was throwing. I hadn't wanted to go, but I'm damn glad I did because I met the man I'm going to marry someday!

More soon! ~A

I stopped to micro-analyze every word. Hudson hadn't mentioned how he and his ex-wife had met specifically, but he'd said their families were friends and they'd run in the same social circle. I'd assumed H stood for husband, but it could also be Hudson.

As I pieced the puzzle together, everything fell into place.

My ex-roommate Evelyn had given me this diary for my birthday. Evelyn and Hudson's ex-wife were friends. Maybe Alexandria had given her the diary for safekeeping, or who knows—maybe Evelyn had stolen it. Lord knows she had a penchant for taking things from friends.

Alexandria had gotten married at the New York Public Library—that I was certain of. I'd read every detail of her planning. *Hudson* had also gotten married there, just like his parents before him.

I was also 99.99-percent sure that the child Alexandria had written about was named *Laken Charlotte*. I remembered because it was the only time the writer had used anyone's name but her own. Everywhere else she'd referred to people with initials, but on the day her daughter was born, she'd written her name. *Laken Charlotte.*

It wasn't a common name, but I needed that extra hundredth of a percent of certainty, and I needed it now. No way I could keep reading from the beginning and wait until I got to that point. So I flipped frantically until I found the section I remembered.

Dear Diary,

Today I became a mother.

A mother.

I had to write that again because I still can't believe it. The birth was all the gruesome stories of pain I'd heard, and then some. But the moment they laid my little girl in my arms, I forgot all about the agony of delivery. She's perfect in absolutely every way.

At 2:42 today, my life changed. I took one look in my baby's eyes and knew in my heart of hearts that I needed to be a better person. A stronger person. A more selfless person. An honest person. I'm so proud to be my sweet girl's mother, and today I make the promise to become a person she can be proud of someday, too.

Welcome to the world, Laken Charlotte.

~A

I dropped the book to my lap and closed my eyes.

Hudson's ex-wife was Laken Charlotte's mother—*Charlie's* mother. But unfortunately, that was all I could say for sure. Because according to other entries in her diary, that was all *Alexandria* could say for sure. She'd kept a secret from her husband—*a big one.*

This time, I couldn't hold back my nausea. I ran to the bathroom and unloaded the contents of my stomach into the toilet.

29

Stella

Fifteen months ago

"You smell like perfume, Aiden." I took a step away from him after our hug.

He sighed. "Not this again. You have samples all over both of our apartments, of course some of it gets caught in my clothes."

He turned and walked to his bedroom. I followed.

"You smell like jasmine. I don't have that here or at your place."

"Well, then it's probably a combination of the shit you have laying around. You, of all people, know that when you combine a lot of smells, you make a new one. Whatever my wool coat picked up must be doing the combining."

"Where were you tonight?"

"Grading midterms in my office. Would you like me to get a note from the security guard I pass on my way out from now on? The better question is, where were *you*? You still have your shoes on, and your cheeks are red from the cold. So I take it you worked late yourself."

"I was at the lab working on the algorithm."

Aiden rolled his eyes. "The algorithm...right. I thought we'd put that to bed. We're buying a house with that money."

"Just because I agreed we could use our savings to buy a house doesn't mean I need to stop working on my product."

"No, but how do I know you were really there?"

"You don't. But I'm not the one who smells like perfume and has hotel charges on my credit card."

"I'm not doing this shit again, Stella." Aiden put his hands on his hips. "The hotel was a reservation for my parents who were coming to town. I made it a long time ago and forgot to cancel it after they canceled their trip to New York. It had completely slipped my mind when you asked me. A week later I remembered, so I paid the bill. I didn't think I needed to report back to you."

The story he'd told me did make sense, only he'd never mentioned that his parents were coming to town, and when they had in the past, they'd always stayed at a hotel near his apartment—not on the other side of town.

Lately it was always the same thing. He had an explanation for everything—the hotel charge, smelling like perfume, when my friend from work saw him at a restaurant with a brunette woman looking pretty cozy, a suspicious text. It wasn't one thing, but a bunch of small things that added up.

"Look." Aiden walked over and put his hands on my shoulders. "Those dumb diaries are planting shit in your head."

I wanted so badly to believe him. But I couldn't let go of all the similarities between the way Alexandria was treating her husband and things between Aiden and me lately. Alexandria would come home and go right to the shower to wash off her lover's smell—just like Aiden had started doing the last few months if I was at his apartment when he got home. Alexandria was super cautious with her phone. Aiden even took his into the bathroom when he showered now—except for that one time he was in the shower when I arrived at his place. I'd found his cell charging on his nightstand and tried to sneak a peek at his text messages while the water was still running, only to find he'd changed his password from the one he'd been using forever.

I looked into Aiden's eyes. "Do you promise me? Promise me there is nothing going on with anyone else. I just can't shake the feeling, Aiden."

He leaned closer and spoke directly into my eyes. "You need to trust me."

I nodded, though I didn't feel settled.

That night, we went to sleep like we had most nights lately—with a quick peck on the lips and no sex. That was yet another thing that had changed over the last six months and only added to my suspicions.

The following week everything had mostly returned to normal—until Fisher called one morning while I was making toast.

"Hey. You told me Aiden was going out of town tonight, right? That's one of the reasons you moved our monthly movie night from Sunday to Friday."

"Yeah. He's going to a conference upstate on incorporating new technology into college lectures. Why?"

"I ran into that weird guy Simon he works with— the one who parts his hair down the middle and brushes it straight down on the sides. I got stuck talking to him at your Christmas party a few years back, and he spent half an hour explaining how the helium balloons are bad for our marine environment."

"I remember Simon. What about him?"

"Well, we go to the same gym. I see him every once in a while and try to avoid him. But this morning, the only treadmill open was next to him. So I had to run beside the guy. He noticed my water bottle and started lecturing me about the effects of plastic on Mother Earth. I tried to change the subject, so I asked him if he was going to the conference."

"Okay..."

"He said it was last weekend."

"What?" I stopped with the butter knife mid-spread, my toast forgotten. "Maybe they have it over a few weekends?"

"That's what I figured. I know you've been having a hard time with trusting Aiden lately, so I wasn't going to mention it to you, but it was bugging me. So I Googled the conference. It was last weekend—*only* last weekend, Stell."

After I didn't say anything for a long time, I heard the worry in Fisher's voice.

"Are you okay?"

Oddly, I felt sort of numb, not frantic and freaked out like I'd been when I first started to suspect something. Maybe deep down I'd known the truth all along. But I was positive Aiden was never going to admit anything.

"Yeah, I'm okay."

"What are you going to do?"

"Do you think you can borrow your friend's car again?"

"Probably. Why?"

"Could you do that and be here at four?"

"I thought movie night was going to start at six?"

"It was. But change of plans. Aiden's leaving at four, and I want to follow him."

"There he is." I pointed to Aiden as he walked out the front entrance of his building, wheeling his luggage. Fisher and I were parked four cars away, waiting.

I slumped down in my seat even though Aiden had turned left, the opposite direction of where we were. He kept his Prius in a parking garage about two blocks away.

"Should I follow him?" Fisher said.

I shook my head. "It's going to take him a few minutes to get down to the garage, and then it's at least ten minutes for the valet to pull the car around. We should probably wait until he goes inside so he doesn't see us."

"Okay."

Tailing someone wasn't as easy as it looked on TV, especially in New York City. Since only a few cars at a time make any given traffic light, anxiety built inside me each time we got separated. But somehow we managed not to lose him. We trailed a few cars behind on the FDR Drive and then followed him onto I-87.

"It looks like he's heading upstate," Fisher said. "But I called the place that held the conference he told you he was going to. It was definitely only last weekend."

I shook my head. "I don't know what to think. Maybe he's meeting a woman up where the conference is anyway? So a new hotel charge makes sense?"

"Maybe. You've called him out on enough stuff that he knows you're suspicious."

We drove for a while, long enough that it seemed that was exactly what Aiden was doing, and we were going to be on the road for a while. But as we approached the exit near where Fisher and I grew up, Aiden put on his blinker and moved into the right lane.

"He knows the area, so he probably needs a bathroom break or gas and figured he'd stop here."

Fisher dropped back a bit, letting a few extra cars get between us so we weren't right behind him when we stopped at the exit ramp light.

"You're oddly good at this tailing thing, Fisher."

He smiled. "It's not my first rodeo, love. Gay men can't keep it in their pants for too long. Unfortunately, I've done this before."

"Without me?"

He shrugged. "I figured you'd lecture me for following someone."

He was probably right. A year ago I would've told him if he felt the need to follow someone, the person didn't have his trust, and the relationship was doomed. Yet here I was... It was a stark reminder not to judge others unless I'd walked in their shoes.

"Where the hell is he going?" Fisher asked.

Aiden had passed all the little stores and the gas station right off the parkway. He was actually heading toward the neighborhood Fisher and I had grown up in—where my parents and Fisher's dad still lived.

When Aiden made a right into the development where my parents lived, we had to drop back a lot since there were no cars between us. I again slumped down in my seat.

"Is he going to my parents' house? What the heck would he be going there for?"

Fisher wiggled his brows. "Maybe he's one of your mom's downstairs guests."

"Eww...don't be gross."

We'd been joking, but sure enough, Aiden made a left and drove down my parents' block.

"Don't turn," I said. "If he's going to my parents' house, we should be able to see from here. Can you just pull up to the corner enough for us to peek?"

Fisher parked right at the stop sign, and we leaned forward to peer down the block. The Prius slowed and pulled into my parents' driveway.

"What the hell is he doing? Why wouldn't he tell me he was coming here? I just spoke to my mom the other day and she didn't mention he was stopping by."

Fisher shrugged. "Maybe they're planning a surprise party for you or something?"

"My birthday isn't for nine months."

Once Aiden got out of the car and disappeared into the house, Fisher and I decided to pull down the block. We parked a few houses away and slid down in our seats.

For the next hour, I kept going over all the things that had made me suspicious. I finally sighed. "Maybe Aiden's right and the diary I'm reading has made me paranoid, making me see things that aren't there."

"You had suspicions before you started reading this one," Fisher reminded me.

"Yeah...but..." I shook my head. "I don't know. I've definitely become obsessive about the idea that Aiden might be cheating, and I think a lot of it might be because of the stuff I'm reading. I mean, it's my third time reading this damn diary, and I sit on the stairs at the library wondering if the people around me might be Alexandria or her husband. I just don't understand how she can cheat on him—and then not tell him the baby she gave birth to might not even be his."

"And the guy she's sleeping with, he's her husband's buddy, right?"

I nodded. "It's terrible. It's like the ultimate betrayal—your wife and your best friend."

"Yeah, that's pretty shitty," Fisher said. "Not much gets worse than that."

The door to my parents' house opened, and my heart jolted in my chest. "Someone's coming."

Fisher and I slouched down as far as we could while still being able to see out the window. My parents and my sister walked outside and stood on the top step, talking to Aiden for a few minutes. Eventually, my mom and dad said goodbye and went back inside, while my sister walked Aiden to his car. When they got to the Prius, they both walked around to the passenger side, and Aiden opened the door for Cecelia to get in. As she went to climb inside, he grabbed her hand. The rest seemed to play out in slow motion.

Aiden pulled her against him and backed her up against the car. A breeze blew her long, dark hair in front of her face, and he brushed it away...right before moving in for a kiss. Stunned and still in some sort of insane denial, I somehow expected my sister to push him off—like this was the first time it had happened. She'd smack him across the face and push him away.

But she didn't. My sister wrapped her arms around my fiancé's neck and kissed him back—two willing participants embroiled in a passionate kiss...in *my parents'* driveway.

I couldn't say a word. My mouth hung open in complete and utter shock. I'd forgotten Fisher was sitting next to me until he spoke.

"I stand corrected. There are worse things than your wife banging your buddy like in the diary you're reading." He shook his head in disbelief as he gawked with me. "*That's* the ultimate fucking betrayal."

30

Stella

"**A**re you shitting me?" Fisher shook his head. "Is that even possible?"

I hadn't planned on telling my friend anything—let alone the whole story—but that's exactly what I'd done. I'd told Fisher that Hudson might not be Charlie's father before I'd told Hudson, and I felt so guilty for violating his privacy. But Fisher had known something was off with me all week. Tonight when he'd walked in and found me in wrinkled pajamas with hair that hadn't been brushed in two days and swollen eyes...I didn't really have much choice.

I sighed. "I'm pretty sure I'm right. All the facts line up—plus, I got that diary from Evelyn."

"How did Evelyn get it?"

"I have no idea." I shrugged. "Olivia mentioned once that Evelyn and Hudson's ex had a falling out because Evelyn took something from her. Maybe what she stole was the diary."

"Alright." He put his hands on his hips and thought for a moment. "Here's what we're going to do. You're going to go brush your hair and wash your face, and I'm going to go next door and get a legal pad and two bottles of wine. When I come back, you're going to tell me all the facts, and we'll see if I come to the same conclusion. If I do, we'll figure out your game plan."

I slouched into the couch deeper. "I don't want a game plan."

Fisher grabbed both my hands and pulled me to standing. "Don't care. When you first started suspecting that Aiden was cheating, I blew it off. I should've sat you down right away and listened and come up with a game plan to get to the bottom of things. I didn't, and you spent months stressing and suffering. We're not going down that road again. We need resolution." Fisher eyed the top of my head. "Plus, I think there might be a rat or two nesting in here. So go brush. I'll be back in five minutes."

I sulked, so Fisher walked me to my bedroom. He kissed my forehead and pushed me toward the bathroom door. "Go."

Ten minutes later, we met on the couch. Fisher nodded to an empty wrapper. "You ate that entire thing of chocolate that was delivered?"

I frowned. The morning after I'd run out of Hudson's house, a beautiful bouquet of exotic flowers had been delivered, along with an enormous, five-pound Hershey bar. Hudson's note had read, *You make me feel better than any amount of chocolate.* I'd eaten the entire thing over the last few days while wondering if that statement would ever be true again. No amount of anandamide could get me out of my funk.

"Don't remind me," I said. "I feel awful. Hudson has to be freaking out about why I've disappeared and keep avoiding his calls and messages. But I can't look him in the eyes with what I know. *I can't, Fisher.* I'm crazy about him. I'm hurting him right now, but it's going to be so much worse when I tell him."

Fisher squeezed my hand. "Alright, honey. But you did the right thing. This isn't the type of thing you spring on someone if you're not absolutely certain. And once you're sure, you need to figure out how to break the news gently."

"Fisher..." I shook my head. "There is no *gently*. We're talking about his *daughter*."

"Okay. But you need to relax a little, so we can go through all the details. Let's have some wine, at least. You looked less nervous telling four-hundred guests how you met the bride at the wedding of a woman you'd never seen before." Fisher poured two large glasses of merlot and sat up straight, his pen ready. He looked very much in lawyer mode. "Let's get started. When did Evelyn give you this diary?"

"It was a birthday present—around eighteen months ago. I remember being surprised she had gotten me anything, because I didn't even think she knew it was my birthday." I thought back. "You'd sent me flowers. When Evelyn saw them, she asked what they were for. I said it was my birthday, and then she went into her room and came out with the diary. It wasn't wrapped or anything."

"Is there any indication of years in the diary—from television programs or anything?"

I shook my head. "I read it at least a dozen times from cover to cover over the last few days. I didn't find any."

"Okay." Fisher scribbled down *eighteen months* on his legal pad and underscored it with two bold slashes. "And when did Hudson and his ex get divorced?"

"He said Charlie was about two. So that would be four years ago."

"So the diary could've been written anywhere from a year and a half ago to a hundred years ago?"

I shrugged. "I guess. But the pages aren't yellowed or anything, so I don't think it's too old."

"Okay...so the timeline works, but it would probably work for a million other scenarios, too. Let's move on to names. Your woman's name was Alexandria. Do we know that's Hudson's ex-wife's name for sure?"

I nodded. "Hudson had only ever referred to her as Lexi, but the other night when Charlie mentioned her full name—I asked what her mom's name was. It's Alexandria—and, by the way, she also kept a diary. Hudson once mentioned that in passing."

"Okay. That's two names in common. What about Hudson? Does the diary ever say his name?"

I shook my head. "She only refers to him as H, which I assumed while reading stood for *husband*. But obviously that could stand for Hudson. And the guy she was having an affair with is her husband's best friend, and she calls him J. Hudson's best friend's name is Jack."

Fisher scribbled some more notes. "There're thousands of people named Jack. It's a common name. I bet Alexandria is, too. Again, all circumstantial."

"But she wrote down her daughter's name the day she was born—Laken Charlotte."

Fisher's brows pulled together. "And Hudson's kid's name is definitely Laken Charlotte?"

I nodded.

"Well, that's not such a common combination, obviously. I've never met anyone named Laken, but I'm sure there are quite a few in New York. We have more than eight-million people who live here."

"There are one-thousand-six-hundred-and-sixty-two people named Laken in the United States who are under the age of thirteen, according to the Census Bureau. I looked it up."

"Shit. Okay. Well, that's still more than sixteen-hundred people."

"But when I put in the first name and the last name—Laken Rothschild—they estimate that there is only one."

"Estimate? The Census Bureau isn't sure."

"They tell you based on old data. It's more of a statistical-type thing than an exact count. But basically, it's not a popular name combination."

"Alright, what else?"

"Alexandria was married at the New York Public Library. So were Hudson and Lexi."

"Ugh. This isn't looking so good."

"Alexandria and H also lived on the Upper West Side, same as Lexi and Hudson."

Fisher blew out a deep breath. "So there're definitely a lot of coincidences. But I once read about a set of twins separated at birth. Both were named James by their adoptive parents, and both grew up to be cops and marry women with the same name. They also had kids with the same name, then got divorced and married women with the same name for their second marriages. They didn't realize any of it until they met later in life. So strange shit can happen."

I sighed. "I guess. But what do I do? Say, 'Hey, by the way, I think there's a possibility your daughter isn't yours? Oh, and she might be your lifelong best friend Jack's because he was secretly banging your ex-wife'?"

Fisher shook his head. "Jesus." He knocked back the rest of his glass of wine. "I don't think you have any other choice."

"I could burn the diary and pretend I never saw it."

"And then what? Never tell the guy his kid might not be his? I know you, Stella. That would eat a hole in your stomach."

I looked into Fisher's eyes. "She's the light of his life. I think I'd rather it eat a hole in my stomach than break Hudson's heart."

"But you can't even function. You haven't had a real conversation with him since you figured all this out. You can't keep it in unless you're leaving his life entirely." Fisher frowned. "Christ, if it's true... Think of how many lives that one diary has ruined. You might never have found out what Aiden was doing had you not been reading it. And now this. It's really crazy." He paused, shaking his head. "But you need to tell him, honey. He has a right to know."

It felt like there was a golf ball stuck in my throat. I swallowed. "I know."

After our talk, Fisher and I proceeded to polish off both bottles of wine. I was trying to drown my brain, hoping maybe it would allow me to stop thinking about what I needed to do for just a few minutes. But all the alcohol seemed to do was make me feel sadder.

I felt tears threatening. "I don't want to lose him, Fisher. I miss him like crazy, and it's been less than a week since I saw him."

Fisher stroked my hair. "I saw the way Hudson looked at you. That man is crazy about you, too. You're not going to lose him, but you do need to talk to him. It can't be avoided anymore."

I sighed. "I know. I've just felt so paralyzed these last few days."

I walked Fisher to the door about ten. "I'll bring us breakfast in the morning when you're sober so we can talk about how you're going to tell him," he said.

I sighed. "Okay. Thank you."

He tilted my chin up. "You going to be okay?"

"Yeah. I'll be fine. I'll see you tomorrow."

After I shut the door, I cleaned up the wine glasses and tossed the empty bottles in the garbage. When I went to flip the kitchen light switch off, I saw Fisher had left his key to my apartment on the counter. I assumed he'd figure it out in the morning when he came with breakfast, so I flicked off the kitchen light and decided I couldn't put off a shower any longer.

In the bathroom, I got undressed while I let the water steam up the room. Just as I put one foot into the shower, my buzzer sounded.

I sighed. *Fisher realized he doesn't have his key.*

Wrapping a towel around me, I grabbed the key on my way to the front door. Maybe the alcohol had me acting carelessly, but it never even occurred to me that it might be someone other than Fisher. So without checking the peephole, I swung the door open.

"I know, I know. You forgot your ke—" I froze, finding a man who was definitely *not Fisher* on the other side of the door.

Hudson's brows pulled to a troubled V. "Expecting someone else?"

"I, uh, Fisher forgot his key, so I assumed it was him."

Hudson and I stood there looking at each other. I felt so rattled after we'd just spoken about him for hours that I didn't know what to say or do. Hell, I hadn't known what to say or do for a week now.

Eventually, he sighed. "Is it alright if I come in?"

"Oh...yeah, sure. Sorry."

I closed the door behind him and tried to regain my wits, but I was so nervous that I couldn't figure out how to function. Again we stared at each other awkwardly.

Hudson had to break our silence. "Sorry I didn't call first."

I tightened the corner of my towel. "It's okay."

"Is it? I didn't call because I figured you would say no if I did, and right about now it feels like it's not okay for me to be here."

I hated that I was making him feel unwelcome. "I'm

sorry. I just wasn't expecting you. Fisher was over and we drank wine, and I was about to take a quick shower and jump into bed."

He frowned. "I can go..."

"No, no..." I shook my head. "You don't have to go."

Hudson caught my eye. "I was hoping we could talk."

I nodded and thumbed toward my bedroom door. "Sure, yeah. Let me just go turn off the water and get dressed."

"Why don't you take your shower? I'll wait."

I did need a few minutes to gather my thoughts. I'd planned to deliberate for at least a few days on how to tell him what I knew. Now I had only the time it took to take a shower. "If you don't mind, that would be great. Thank you." I motioned toward the couch. "Make yourself at home."

In the shower, my head was a jumbled mess, and I felt a little lightheaded. But I didn't have time for a complete meltdown, so I stood under the water, closed my eyes, and took a few deep breaths until it felt like the world had stopped spinning so fast.

There was no easy way to begin the conversation I needed to have, and I could no longer hide behind any doubts I'd fabricated about the information. Everything lined up. Even Fisher was convinced. So I guessed I'd just have to start from the beginning. Hudson already knew I read diaries, and I was pretty sure I'd told him about the one where the woman got married at the New York Public Library. So I suppose something like, *I read this diary a while ago...* is how I would start. But then what? Did I say, *Hey, by the way, did you ever suspect your wife was having an affair?* That made me hyperventilate.

What if I'm wrong?

What if I'm right?

What if telling him takes the most sacred thing in his life away?

Am I ruining a little girl's life?

Would I want to know if my dad wasn't really my dad?

Oh, God. That thought made my head spin even more. The way my parents slept around, it was entirely possible that my father *wasn't* my father.

Oh, Lord. *Who cares about my family?* I wished it were *me* this was happening to, not Hudson and his beautiful little girl.

For the rest of my shower, random thoughts popped into my head, and I alternated between trying to keep up with them and trying to calm myself down with slow breathing. *Would I die if I climbed out my bedroom window to escape?* When my hands started to get pruney, I knew I had to pull my shit together.

So I turned off the water, dried off, brushed out my hair, and pulled on sweats and a T-shirt before wiping the steam from the mirror and giving myself a little internal pep talk.

Everything's going to be fine. No matter what the outcome, eventually things will fall into place the way they're supposed to be. It may be a bumpy road, but if a diary about a man I'm crazy about made its way into my hands before I met him—there's a reason for

342

it. Somehow God put this in my hands, and, in the end, everything will be right.

I took one last deep breath and whispered to myself, "It's all in fate's hands now." Then I opened the bedroom door.

Only to find it wasn't in fate's hands.

It was in Hudson's.

Because I'd left the diary on the coffee table, and he was currently reading it.

He looked up. "Why the hell do you have my ex-wife's diary?"

31

Hudson

"I don't understand. Why would Lexi sell her diary on eBay, and how the hell did you wind up with it?"

Stella shook her head. "I didn't buy that diary on eBay. Evelyn gave it to me for my birthday."

"Evelyn? Evelyn Whitley?"

"Yes."

"How did Evelyn get it?"

"I have absolutely no idea."

"When did she give it to you?"

"For my birthday last year—so about eighteen months ago."

I wasn't sure what the hell was going on, but I knew Evelyn and Lexi didn't speak anymore. I remembered a day a couple of years ago when I'd gone to pick up Charlie, and my ex-wife had been in a particularly bitchy mood. She'd asked me if I kept in touch with Evelyn. Of course, I didn't. Evelyn was my sister's friend, and not one I was too fond of to begin with.

"I just read the first page. It starts on the day we met."

Stella looked pale. "I know."

I rubbed the back of my neck, feeling something between bamboozled and angry, but I tried to stay calm. "You just *happened* to receive my ex-wife's diary? From the woman you were pretending to be the night we met?"

"It sounds far-fetched. I realize that. But, yes, that's what happened. I had no idea it belonged to your ex-wife until the other night."

"The other night? At my house when you said you had a headache and bolted?"

She nodded. "That's when it all clicked together."

I'd gone over that evening in my head a dozen times, trying to figure out what the hell had happened. One minute we were fine and laughing, and the next she was out the door. I shook my head. "I don't understand, Stella."

She sighed. "Do you think we can sit down to talk about this?"

I dragged a hand through my hair. "You sit. I need to stand."

Hesitantly, she walked over to the chair and sat down. I started to pace in the living room. "What happened the other night at my house?"

Stella looked down and spoke to her hands. "Charlie said her full name, and I remembered it from a diary I'd read a while ago. Do you recall I told you I'd read the diary of a woman who got married at the library? That I used to go sit on the stairs and look for the people I'd read about?"

I was so confused. "You were looking for me and Lexi?"

Stella nodded. "I didn't know it at the time, but yeah...I guess I was."

It seemed incredulous that my ex-wife's diary could fall into my new girlfriend's hands *by coincidence*. But even if that's exactly what had happened, I still didn't get why Stella got so freaked out the other day.

I held up the diary. "So this is why you've been avoiding me? Because you realized you'd read my ex-wife's diary?"

She continued to avoid my eyes. "Yes."

I paced a few times, trying to see the full puzzle, but I was missing a few pieces. "Why? If this was all some big coincidence, why not just tell me?"

Stella was quiet for a long time. That was freaking *me* out.

"Answer me, Stella."

She looked up for the first time. Her eyes were filled with tears, and she looked completely distraught. I felt torn between wanting to hold her and wanting to scream at her for whatever the fuck craziness she had going on.

Unfortunately, the latter won out, and I barked, "Goddammit, Stella. Answer me!"

She jumped in her seat and tears streamed down her cheeks. "Because...there are things...in the diary entries."

"What things?"

Lexi and I didn't have a great relationship, especially at the end. But I wasn't ever cruel to her. I hadn't given her anything to write about that would freak Stella out.

Stella started to cry harder. "I don't want to hurt you."

I couldn't take seeing her upset, so I walked over and kneeled in front of her. Pushing strands of wet hair from her face, I spoke quietly. "Relax. Stop crying. Nothing Lexi could have written in some diary is going to hurt me. *This* hurts me, seeing you so upset. What's going on, sweetheart?"

Trying to calm her only seemed to trouble her more. She sobbed, her shoulders heaving. So I pulled her in for a hug and held her until she calmed down a little. Once she did, I tilted her chin up so our eyes met. "Talk to me. What has you this upset?"

Her eyes jumped back and forth between mine, and it felt like I was watching her damn heart break.

"Lexi..." She sniffled. "She talks about having an affair."

I blinked a few times. "Alright... Well, I didn't know she had an affair. But I guess I can't say I'm shocked. I caught her in lies about meaningless things over the years, and at one point I had suspected she might be seeing someone, although she always denied it. Lexi's pretty selfish and did some shady shit, including hiding money and disappearing until late at night. Is that what's been eating at you? You thought I'd be upset to find that out? It's not pleasant to hear, but that part of my life is over."

Stella closed her eyes and shook her head. "There's more."

"Okay...what? What is it?"

"The man she was sleeping with, she wrote that he was your best friend."

My face wrinkled. "Jack?"

"She never says his name, but she refers to him with the letter J... And..." Stella swallowed once more and took a deep breath. "Lexi doesn't know who the father is."

I had to be in some serious denial, because I had no idea what the hell she was talking about. "Father of who? What do you mean?"

Stella's lip trembled. "Charlie. She doesn't know who Charlie's father is. She was sleeping with both of you at the time she was conceived."

Until a week ago, I'd felt like I had the world by the balls. I remember watching my little girl cook me dinner with the woman I was crazy about—the two of them laughing and smiling—and thinking how right everything finally felt after so long. And now...it felt like the world had *me* by the balls.

At first, I didn't believe it. Not that Lexi wasn't capable of doing that type of shit, but I couldn't believe my best friend was. At a very minimum, that part had to be wrong. J could stand for a thousand names; there was no way Jack would do that to me.

But when I was on my third scotch, sitting at a bar where I'd met my buddy countless times, I remembered a particular Valentine's Day years ago. I'd been up in Boston on business for a few days. My flight home had been scheduled for the evening. I'd told Lexi I'd take her out to dinner when I got home, but I'd finished up early and decided to take a midday flight and surprise her. When I walked in, Jack had been in our apartment. I remember having a fleeting uneasy feeling, but then Jack had said he'd asked Lexi to go shopping with him to buy his new girlfriend—now his wife—a gift for Valentine's Day. He'd said she loved emeralds and remembered Lexi had a necklace with one, so he'd figured she would be able to help him pick out a quality stone for a ring. I'd honestly thought nothing more about it—this was my wife and my best friend, for fuck's sake.

A few years later, I'd sat across from Lexi in my attorney's office. She had her hands folded on the conference room table, and I noticed an enormous emerald sparkling on her finger. Our negotiations had gotten contentious by that point, so I'd made a comment about her ridiculous spending and motioned to the ring. She'd flashed a wicked smile and said she'd had it for years—a gift from a man who actually appreciated her. I'd never seen the ring before, but Lexi had a shitload of jewelry, so again, I chalked it up to nothing and my ex just trying to get under my skin.

Rattling the ice cubes that had barely had a chance to melt in my glass, I decided to make a call. I didn't give a fuck if it was 2:30 in the morning.

A groggy woman's voice answered on the third ring. "Hello?"

"Do you have an emerald ring?"

"Hudson? Is that you?"

I heard a man's voice grumble in the background, but couldn't make out what he'd said.

"Yeah, it's Hudson, Alana."

"It's the middle of the night."

"Can you just tell me if you have an emerald ring?"

"I don't understand…"

My voice boomed. "Just fucking answer the question. *Do you* or *do you not* have an emerald ring from your husband?"

"No, I don't. But what's going on, Hudson? Is everything okay?"

Alana must've covered the phone, because I heard muffled voices, and then a few seconds later, my supposed best friend came on the line. "Hudson? What the hell is going on?"

"Your wife doesn't have a fucking emerald ring."

"Are you drunk?"

I ignored him. Whether I was drunk or not didn't change the facts. "You know who *does* have a fucking emerald ring?"

"What are you talking about?"

"My ex-wife. That's who has the fucking emerald ring. The one you told me you went shopping to get for your new girlfriend when I came home from Boston early."

The line went quiet for a moment. Eventually, Jack cleared his throat. "Where are you?"

"The bar down the block from your house. Get your scrawny ass down here, or I'll be at your apartment in ten minutes." Without waiting for a response, I hung up and tossed my phone on the bar. Then I held up my empty glass to the bartender. "I'll take another."

Jack said nothing as he settled himself on the stool next to me.

I couldn't even look at him. My voice was eerily calm as I stared down into my glass. "How could you?"

He didn't immediately respond. For a moment, I thought he was going to try to play dumb, or worse, deny it—but at least he gave me that much respect.

"I wish I had an answer to that question," he said, "other than I'm a fucking piece of shit."

I scoffed and brought my drink to my lips. "Probably the first honest thing I've heard out of your mouth in years."

Jack raised his hand for the bartender and ordered a double scotch. We waited until his glass was filled to continue.

"How long?" I asked.

He sucked back half of his glass and set it down on the bar. "About a year."

"Were you in love with her, at least?"

Jack shook his head. "No. It was just sex."

"Great," I sneered. "Twenty-five years of friendship for just sex. Lexi didn't even give a good blowjob. She was all fucking teeth."

Through my peripheral vision, I saw Jack hang his head. He shook it for a long time. "I think I wanted to win at something," he said. "You were always smarter, stronger, taller, more popular, and got all the girls you could handle. After we were dating for a few weeks, Alana admitted that the night we met her in that bar, she and her friend had walked over to talk to us after she'd called dibs on you. Even my wife would've picked you over me if she'd had the choice." He shook his head again. "We were drunk the first time it happened, if it's any consolation."

"It's not."

We sat side by side for a solid ten minutes without either of us saying another word. I finished off my fourth scotch while my loyal friend sucked back his double. I wasn't a big drinker, so the alcohol had really hit me. My vision was blurry, and I felt the room starting to spin.

Taking a deep breath, I turned to face Jack for the first time. He did the same, meeting my eyes as he blew out a jagged exhale.

"Is she yours?" Just asking the question caused a physical ache in my chest, and my voice cracked when I spoke again. "Is my daughter yours?"

Jack swallowed. "Lexi was never sure. As far as I know, she still isn't."

I pulled out my billfold. Tossing two hundreds on the bar, I raised my hand to call the bartender. "Hundred for the drinks. The other hundred is to not help him up."

The bartender looked confused, so as I stood and steadied myself, I pointed to the piece-of-shit man I'd called my best friend for more than two decades. "He was fucking my wife while I was married to her."

The bartender's brows shot up, and he looked between us.

"Turn around," I muttered at my oldest friend.

Jack turned in his seat to face me. I had to close one of my eyes to only see one of him, but he never raised his hands as I hauled back and landed a punch square in the center of his face. It was the least he could've done—taken it like a man.

"You don't tell my piece-of-shit ex-wife that I know," I warned before turning toward the door. I never bothered to look back to see if the bartender helped him off the floor.

32

Stella

Almost a week had passed, and I still hadn't seen Hudson. Though I supposed he was more entitled to disappear than I'd been when I was avoiding him.

I suspected he'd told his sister something, as Olivia had never once mentioned his name. The last of the Signature Scent samples came in, the artwork we'd shot in California for the boxes had been approved, and today, Thursday, the warehouse had started shipping the orders that had come in from the Home Shopping Channel. It was a monumental day; the dream I'd had for years had come true. Yet I wanted nothing more than to go home and climb into bed.

But Fisher wouldn't let the occasion go uncelebrated no matter how many times I told him I wasn't in the mood. So I wound up meeting him for dinner after I left the warehouse. He was already seated in a booth when I arrived, an ice bucket set up next to the table.

I slid into the seat across from him.

"Alright, now I know things are bad. I just watched you come in. The hostess has a giant vase of flowers on her podium, and you didn't even try to smell them."

I attempted to smile. "It doesn't feel like I should be smelling the flowers today."

"That's where you're wrong. Today is precisely the day you should be stopping to smell the flowers, my Stella Bella. You put your heart into this business, and today your first orders started shipping." He lifted the bottle out of the ice bucket and filled an empty glass in front of me before filling his own. "I even sprung for the good stuff."

While he of course meant well, seeing the gold label on the bottle of champagne—the label that had been on the bubbly we'd swiped from Olivia's wedding months ago—just felt like coming full circle. And the circle was now closed. Hudson and I had started and ended with these bottles. A heavy feeling settled in my chest.

Fisher lifted his glass in a toast. "To my smarty pants girl. You worked through the rain for years and finally got your rainbow."

I smiled. "Thank you, Fisher."

The waiter came and took our orders. I wasn't in the mood to eat, but I felt like I had to give it my best effort because Fisher was trying so hard.

"So I guess you haven't heard from Hudson?"

I sighed as my shoulders wilted. "He hasn't been in the office. I get business emails sometimes, but those always come really early in the morning—like four AM. He's still working, but from home, and he's not speaking to me on a personal level."

Fisher sipped his champagne. "So you don't even know if he's confronted his ex-wife? Told her he knows about the diary and everything in it?"

I shook my head. "He took the book when he left, but I have no idea what he's done with it or who he's spoken to."

"He can't hold this against you forever. None of it is your fault."

"I'm not even sure he believes me that it's a coincidence I had the book."

"How could it not be a coincidence?"

"Think about it. I just happened to show up at his sister's wedding—a woman I'd never met before—after reading his ex-wife's diary?"

"But you didn't know it was his ex-wife."

I shrugged. "I know...but it seems awfully convenient."

"So what does he think? You stalked him or something? You read his ex-wife's diary, somehow figured out who he is, and set out to make him fall in love with you? That's one boiling bunny short of a Glenn Close movie."

I shook my head. "I don't know what he thinks."

"Well, you want to know what I think?"

"Do I have a choice?"

"Of course not, silly girl." Fisher reached across the table, took my hand, and squeezed. "I don't think any of the things that happened are coincidence. I think life is a series of stepping stones that branch out in all different directions. We have no idea what path we're supposed to follow, so we tend to walk a straight line and follow the biggest stones, because that's the easiest thing to do. Coincidences are the smaller stones that lead you on a path that veers off. If you're brave enough, you follow those stones, and you wind up exactly where you're supposed to be."

I smiled sadly. "That's beautiful. When did you become so enlightened?"

"About ten minutes ago when I was seated at this table and the waiter walked over. The hostess had asked me if I wanted a high table or a booth. I said a high table, but she walked me over to this booth anyway. I could have told her it wasn't what I'd requested, but instead, I followed one of the little stones down a new path and look what it brought me."

My forehead wrinkled. "I'm lost. What did it bring you?"

Our waiter approached, carrying a tray with our appetizer. He set the dish in the middle of the table and flashed a dazzling smile at Fisher. "Can I get you anything else?"

"Not at the moment. But maybe later?"

The waiter's eyes sparkled. "You got it."

After he walked away, Fisher picked up a mozzarella stick and winked at me. "Him. That path brought me him, and I think that's exactly where I'm supposed to be in a few hours."

On Friday night, I left the office about seven. Signature Scent was shipping without a hitch, and next week the website would go live for orders from the public. Olivia had managed to get me time on some local morning news shows for various segments that featured women in business, and a few magazines had agreed to do interviews with me. Everything I'd dreamed about for so long was coming true, yet I couldn't find it in me to enjoy it.

This morning I'd broken down and texted Hudson *I miss you.* I could see he'd read it, but no return message ever came. I was heartbroken. Once, when I was a kid, I'd been jumping waves at the beach and one had hit me hard. It sucked me under, and I'd tumbled around like a ragdoll, losing sight of which way was up. *That*—that's how I'd felt this week without speaking to Hudson. I'd had to drag my ass out of bed to come to work.

Now it was the weekend, but for some reason, I wasn't ready to go home. On the train, I just sort of zoned out as it headed uptown. At one point I happened to look up as we were pulling into a station, and the name of the stop painted on the wall caught my attention as we slowed.

Bryant Park—42nd Street.

I stood. The train was packed, so I pushed my way through a dozen people to get to the doors and step off. The New York Public Library was right around the corner. The last thing I should be doing was sitting on the steps, reminiscing about the night Hudson and I had first danced, yet I couldn't have stopped myself from going if I'd tried.

It was fall, so the days were getting shorter, and not long after I sat down in the same spot I'd sat in a hundred times before, the sun started to set. The sky lit up in a purpley orange, and I took a deep breath and closed my eyes for a minute, trying to let nature's beauty lift my spirit. When I opened them, my gaze cast down the steps and snagged on a man stopped at the bottom, staring up at me.

I blinked a few times, assuming my imagination was playing tricks on me.

But it wasn't.

My heart seemed to skip every other beat as Hudson climbed the steps to where I sat.

"Mind if I sit with you?" His face was unreadable.

"No, of course not."

Hudson settled in next to me on the marble step. His legs spread wide, and he clasped his hands between his knees and stared down for the longest time. It gave me a chance to look at him. Only a week or so had passed since I'd last seen him, yet I could tell he'd lost some weight. His face looked drawn, he had dark circles ringing his eyes, and his skin—normally tan and bright—looked sallow and dull.

So many questions ran through my head. Had he come looking for me? Or had he come to do his own thinking? Was he okay? What had transpired over the last week? Based on Hudson's face, it looked like things had taken a turn for the worse. But it also seemed like he had something to say, and whatever it was, wasn't easy. So I fished inside my purse for the Hershey bar and offered it to him.

He smiled sadly. "You look like you could use it as much as I could. Wanna share?"

For the next ten minutes, we sat next to each other in silence on the steps of the New York Public Library—the place he'd gotten married, the place we'd met, the place his parents, whose relationship he revered so much, had also said their vows—and shared a chocolate bar while watching the sunset.

Eventually, he cleared his throat. "You okay?"

"I've been better. How about you?"

He smiled sadly. "Same."

Again we were quiet for long moments.

"I'm sorry I disappeared for a while," he finally said. "I needed some time to figure things out."

I shifted and turned to face him, though he continued to stare forward and not look at me while I spoke. "Did you?" I asked. "Figure things out, I mean?"

He shrugged. "As much as I can, I guess."

I nodded.

Hudson stared out at the sunset while tears pooled in his eyes. He swallowed before he spoke. "Jack admitted it."

My heart ached. I had no idea what we were to each other anymore, but that didn't stop me from offering compassion. I clasped my hand with his and held it tight. "I'm sorry, Hudson. I'm so, so sorry."

"I decided not to speak to Lexi about it."

Wow. I would've thought that was the first place he'd go. "Okay..."

"The only thing letting her know would accomplish is giving me the satisfaction of screaming at her. It wouldn't do me any good, nor Charlie. My head isn't screwed on straight enough to deal with things. As far as

I'm concerned, Lexi is the enemy, and it's never a good idea to let the enemy know your plans. I need to know exactly where I stand, and if need be, what my rights are, before dealing with her." Hudson swallowed again. His voice was hoarse when he continued. "Charlie is my daughter. That's not going to change if...if..." He couldn't even say the words.

Tears filled my eyes. "You're absolutely right. And you're an amazing father—an amazing man for putting Charlie's feelings first at a time when it would've been really easy to be irrational."

"I did get our DNA tested, though. I swabbed her cheek while she was sleeping and dropped it off at the lab yesterday, along with a sample of my own. I don't really want to know the results, but I feel like it would be irresponsible not to. God forbid something happens and she needs blood or something." He paused, and this time he failed at holding back his emotions. His voice broke. "I'll know in about a week."

He hadn't given me any indication that things between us were okay. But that didn't matter. Hudson was a broken man, and I couldn't just sit here and watch him fall apart. I wrapped my arms around him. "I'm sorry. I'm so sorry you're going through this, Hudson."

His shoulders shook as I held him. He made no sound, but I knew he was crying because I felt the wetness on my neck where his face was buried. I thought he might feel better if he got it out—crying is a physical release of pain. But I also knew the type of man Hudson was. He would keep some of it in to torture himself—because deep down, he probably felt like it was partly his fault. He would blame himself for working too much and not giving his wife enough attention, or not bringing home flowers for no reason. It was misplaced guilt, of course, but he was such an honorable man, I was certain he wouldn't see it that way.

Eventually, Hudson pulled back. He looked straight into my eyes for the first time. "I'm sorry I needed some time apart."

I shook my head. "There's no reason to be sorry. I understand. I hid from you for a while there as well. Just please know I never meant to keep any of it from you. I truly didn't make the connection until that night at your apartment. And then...I didn't know how to tell you. I didn't want to."

"I know that now. It was just a lot of coincidences to take in at once. I needed some time to absorb everything, and then to realize none of this was a coincidence at all."

I pulled back. "What do you mean?"

Hudson pushed a lock of hair from my face. "Why are you here right now?"

"You mean at the library?"

He nodded.

"I don't know." I shook my head. "I was on my way home from work on the train, and I looked up and saw this stop. Something just compelled me to get off."

"You know why I'm here?"

"Why?"

"I was also on the train, but heading uptown to your apartment. I glanced up for a half second, and through the sea of people packed into the subway car during rush hour, I saw you getting off at Bryant Park.

My train had stopped on the track directly across from yours. I tried to get off, but we started moving before I could make it. So I got off at the next stop and ran all the way back here."

My eyes widened. "You just *happened* to look up and see me getting off a train that I just *happened* to randomly get off when it wasn't even my stop?"

"If I wasn't sure what was going on before, I am now." He cupped my cheeks and met my gaze. "None of this is a coincidence, sweetheart. It's the universe conspiring for us to be together. It has been from the very start—before we even met."

Tears rushed to my eyes all over again. The hollowness I'd felt in my chest over the last week began to fill with hope. I thought about how much we'd both been hurt—Hudson, of course, far worse than me. That damn diary had been at the root of it all, but he was right. It was more than just a series of coincidences. There'd been a higher power working for us all along.

I smiled and leaned in to brush my nose against his. "You know, I think we should probably give in. We don't stand a chance if the whole world is conspiring."

"Sweetheart, I didn't stand a chance from the moment I looked at you."

33

Hudson

The last week had been grueling.

Though yesterday morning had been the worst. I was due to get my DNA results at 9AM, but the lab was running late. Stella had stuck around to be with me when I found out, but she'd had a lunch meeting with a vendor she couldn't miss. Which had turned out to be for the best, because I cried like a damn baby when they finally called around noon and confirmed that my little girl...wasn't actually mine.

By the time Stella came over in the evening, I was numb—and piss drunk. I'd passed out by nine o'clock, which was probably why I'd been awake since 3AM now, staring up at the ceiling.

How the hell was I going to look into Charlie's eyes knowing she wasn't mine? I'd feel like a fucking fraud lying to her. She was only six, but I was always honest with her. I wanted her to trust my word, like I had my father's. And now that was all ruined. I kept thinking about a conversation we'd had a few months ago. She'd told me she hadn't broken the handle off of a kitchen cabinet—one I'd often caught her using as a step stool to reach the counter.

Because of the way the screw was bent, I knew she'd been lying to me. So I sat her down and explained that no matter how bad a situation was, lying about it was always worse than whatever you were trying to cover up. That night, she'd come to me with the truth and told me her stomach hurt. I was pretty sure guilt had twisted her little belly into a knot. I was about to have a gaping ulcer from the lie I would be covering up.

About 6AM the sun started to stream in through the bedroom window. A ray of sunlight cut a thin line across Stella's beautiful face, and I turned on my side to watch her sleep. She looked so peaceful, which gave me some comfort since I knew the last few weeks had been as stressful for her as they had for me. I couldn't imagine how she'd felt the moment she put the crazy puzzle together. It must've been a lot like I felt right now, as if the bottom had dropped out of my world, and I no longer had footing to stand on.

As if she sensed me watching her, her eyes fluttered open.

"What are you doing?" she asked groggily.

"Enjoying the view. Go back to sleep."

Her lips curved in a sleepy smile. "How long have you been up?"

"Not too long."

She grinned. "Hours then, huh?"

I chuckled. The difficulty with soul mates was that when you shared a bond unlike anything you'd experienced with another human, they were pretty good at calling bullshit when you tried to hide your heartache.

I brushed a lock of hair from her face. "I don't know what I would've done without you this last week."

"Without me, you wouldn't have had the worst week of your life."

I shook my head. "It would've come out someday. You can run from lies, but the truth always catches up to you."

She sighed. "I guess."

"I think I've decided how I'm going to handle things with my ex-wife."

"You have?"

I nodded. "I think it's best that I continue not to say anything to Lexi."

"Oh...wow. Okay. How did you come to that decision?"

"The most important thing is that Charlie not be hurt. I'm the only father she's ever known, and right now she's too young to deal with finding out everything in her life is a lie. She needs stability, routine, and predictability—not for me to upend things just to ruin my ex-wife. Lexi wants child support and alimony from me. Jack does well these days, but he can't afford the cushy life I foot the bill for—trust me. So I think it's best she thinks she's keeping some big secret. If she knew I knew, she'd feel financially threatened, and I wouldn't put it past her to be spiteful and tell a six-year-old her father isn't really her father."

I rubbed Stella's arm. "I texted Jack earlier to let him know, because it felt like the right thing to do. He said biology doesn't make a family and she's mine. He doesn't sound interested in trying to push into Charlie's life. I despise the guy, but he's right. Charlie's my daughter, no matter what the biology says. Not having my DNA doesn't change that. Someday when she's older and ready..." I started to get choked up. "I'll tell her she's not mine."

Stella smiled sadly. "I think that makes a lot of sense. Though I can't imagine it will be easy for you to deal with your ex-wife, knowing what you know."

I shook my head. "Definitely not. But it's fine. I'll do whatever is best for my daughter...for Charlie."

Stella reached out and cupped my cheek. "Don't correct yourself when you say *my daughter*. You *are* Charlie's parent. Because a parent is someone who puts the child's needs before their own, and I'm pretty sure you're the only one of the three adults in this equation who has always done that."

I nodded.

Stella stroked my arm quietly for a few minutes. We laid on our sides facing each other, and my hand rested on the bed between us. Though when she attempted to weave her fingers with mine, I realized my hand hadn't actually been *resting* on the bed. It was balled into a fist.

She pried my fingers loose. "You're so tense."

"Yeah. I should probably go for a run to burn off some of the tension."

"Do you have to be anywhere today or do anything?"

I shook my head. "I'm not planning on going to the office for my usual half day on Saturday."

She lifted my hand and brought it to her lips. "You know, I can think of a much more pleasant way for you to burn off some steam than pounding the pavement."

Even with a sleepless night and the conversation we'd just had, the feel of Stella's lips on my hand and the mention of *pounding* already had my mood changing for the better. "Oh yeah? What did you have in mind?"

She gently nudged me to roll to my back and climbed on top of me. Straddling my hips, she lifted the T-shirt she'd worn to bed up and over her head. Her full breasts had the best natural lilt. When I sat up to reach for them, Stella held up her pointer finger and wagged it back and forth. "Nope. This is your stress relief. Just lie back and let me do all the work."

I folded my arms behind my head, assuming she meant she was going to be on top. But instead, she shimmied back and sat on my thighs. Her little hand pulled my cock out of my sweatpants, and her fingers wrapped tightly around it. She gave it a firm squeeze and licked her lips, then bent at the waist and slid her tongue across my crown.

Her eyes glinted devilishly as she licked the bit of precum from my tip and looked up at me. "Show me. Show me how you want me to suck you."

I groaned and slid my fingers into her hair. Stella's eyes closed. She lowered her jaw and took almost my full length into her mouth in one smooth motion.

Fuck.

So much better than running.

This was going to be embarrassingly fast, but so fucking needed. As if sensing exactly what it would take, Stella went to work. My entire shaft was soon soaked with her saliva—the kind of wet that every time she bobbed down and pulled back it made the sexiest gurgling sound. She took me in until I bumped the back of her throat and then slid back—over and over again. It was the most glorious feeling and yet also torture at the same time. I wanted so badly to lift my hips and push the rest of the way into her throat, but I didn't want to hurt her. After a few minutes, she released me and looked up. My hand still clutched her hair, and Stella covered it with hers and dug it in deeper. "Show me. *Show me.*"

Fuck.

She lowered her mouth again, and this time, after two slides down, I couldn't take it anymore. I did exactly what she asked for, and when she got to that point where it's sink or swim—that place at the back of her throat where she would start to pull back, I gently nudged her head down farther. And she opened her fucking throat—opened it wide and swallowed me all the way down.

"Fuuuuuuck."

She'd been able to do that all along and had waited for me to ask for it.

Jesus Christ.

She was already perfect. But now...

Stella pulled back, her cheeks hollowing as she sucked me to the tip. She made a sweet hum of approval when I wrapped her hair snugly in my fist and pushed her head back down again. I only lasted two more sucks before my release was suddenly barreling down on me.

"I'm going to come..." I groaned and loosened my grip on her hair.

But she didn't stop.

"Stella...sweetheart..." This time I used the hair still loosely in my hand to pull her back a little, unsure how loud my voice was. But that only caused her to take me in deeper.

Fuck. She wants me to come down her throat.

Stella didn't have to wait long. After one more suck I let out a pulsing stream that never seemed to end. I actually started to get a little concerned about how long it lasted, but my sweet girl swallowed every drop.

Even though she'd done all the hard work, my head lolled back on the pillow, and I was completely out of breath. Stella wiped her mouth and climbed up my body. She had the goofiest smile on her face.

"Jesus...that was...I feel like I might have to be taught to walk again."

She giggled. "Does that mean your stress has been relieved?"

"It does. Unless I think about how the hell you learned to do that."

"Actually, funny enough, a woman in one of my diaries had been struggling to try to do it, so she bought an instructional video. I bought it too because I was curious."

I shut my eyes and chuckled. "Those diaries. They're going to be the death of me, aren't they?"

EPILOGUE

Stella

8-1/2 months later

Dear Diary,

Tonight Stella fell asleep before me, and I watched her. Every once in a while there was a little twitch at the corner of her lip, and her mouth would curve upward. It didn't last long, a second or two, but I found it mesmerizing. I hope she was dreaming of me, because I want to make all of her dreams come true—just like she's made mine.

-Hudson

I clutched my new diary to my chest. Seriously? How did I get so lucky? Hudson and I had moved in together a few months after the public launch of Signature Scent—not that I needed a roommate anymore. For the first time in my life, I could afford my own place in New York City. I could have plunked down a nice deposit on a brownstone of my own, as my business had done better than I could've imagined in my wildest dreams. Oprah had even put my little invention on her list of favorite gifts to give this year. We now had a special-edition Valentine's Day Signature Scent box, and pretty soon a men's version would be ready to launch. I'd worked long days writing the new algorithms, but now the experienced staff at Rothschild Investments had taken over, and I finally felt like I'd found the work-life balance I'd always wanted.

Hudson Rothschild had made all my dreams come true, and then some. He'd even surprised me with a trip to Greece to celebrate shipping our first product internationally. We'd stayed at the most amazing hotel in Mykonos. When we pulled up, it had looked vaguely familiar. But it took until I walked into our suite to realize why. The hotel he'd booked for us was the one I'd picked out almost a year ago while dream vacation planning in the lobby of his office and waiting to speak to him. He'd remembered from just the quick look he'd had at my screen.

As for my diary-reading hobby...well, I stopped buying them. I was afraid having journals laying around might remind Hudson of difficult memories. A few months back, he'd noticed and asked why I'd stopped. I'd told him I didn't need to read about other people's lives anymore, because my love story topped anything anyone else could pen. I hadn't been lying, of course, but Hudson knew me well. He'd known I missed reading them and probably knew the reason I'd given them up. Which was why he'd surprised me with a diary last week—one he'd secretly kept for months. It was the sweetest, most romantic thing anyone had ever done for me. Well, most of the entries were sweet—some were just dirty.

Case in point... I flipped a dozen or so pages back and reread one of my favorites.

Dear Diary,

Today was a particularly hard day—pun unintentional, but damn if it isn't the truth. My girl has been out on the West Coast for almost a week now. This morning when I woke up, I'd been lying on her pillow. Inhaling her scent made my usual morning wood impossible to deflate on its own. Rather than fight it, I shut my eyes and pulled her pillow from beneath my head to cover my face. Taking deep breaths, I stroked my cock, imagining my tight fist was her beautiful pussy. There was no substitute for the real thing, but I imagined she was sitting on top of me, grinding down hard to take every last inch inside her. She'd throw her head back as she came close, her beautiful tits bouncing up and down and aching to have my mouth on them. I'd wait until after she came and then thrust so deep that some of my cum would still be inside her the next time she had to leave.

-Hudson

Another of my favorites was a few more pages back. It was a story he'd never told me, but it warmed my heart.

Dear Diary,

Today I took Charlie out to breakfast and told her Stella was moving in. After, we were walking home and passed a park. Inside were two little girls, maybe a year younger than her. They were jumping up and down with wide eyes and huge smiles plastered on their faces. I pointed to the girls and said, "What do you think they're so excited about?" Charlie's response was, "Maybe their daddy's girlfriend is moving in, too."

-Hudson

The man I was currently swooning over walked out to the backyard. I sat in a rocking chair on the deck next to the fire pit, with Hendricks at my feet.

Hudson shook his head. "My faithful friend there seems to forget who his master is."

I smiled. The sheepdog I'd bought Hudson for Christmas had become my shadow lately. I wasn't sure why, since all I seemed to do was yell at him for eating my shoes and furniture. He'd taken forever to housetrain, only to take up the lovely new habit of gnawing on thousand-dollar coffee table legs. To be honest, Hendricks was a pain in the ass, for the most part. But seeing the look on Hudson's face on Christmas morning—when he realized he'd finally gotten the dog he'd wished for as a little boy—made all the chaos worth it.

I now had a copy of the photo Olivia kept framed on her living room mantel on my own nightstand—the one with Hudson blowing out his birthday candles and making a wish for a sheepdog while covering her mouth. And yes, he'd named our dog after the gin that brought us together.

"It's only because I'm the one who usually feeds him," I said.

Hudson's eyes zoomed in on the book in my hands. "Remember our deal—you're only supposed to read one a day."

"I know. I was just rereading some of my favorites. I still have my one for today to read."

"Okay. I'm going to run to the store to pick up a bottle of wine for us to bring to Olivia's tonight. I'll take Hendricks to get his walk in. Anything else I should get while I'm out?"

Today was Mason and Olivia's one-year wedding anniversary, so we were going over to their place for dinner. They'd just moved out of Manhattan and into a house a few blocks away. I wondered if Hudson realized it wasn't just their anniversary, it was ours, too. One year ago today, I'd sniffed some gin and met the love of my life. Though *love* wasn't exactly the feeling I'd had when I'd hopped into the cab to flee the scene that night. I'd gotten him a little gift to commemorate the anniversary of our meeting and figured I'd give it to him later when we got home.

"No, I don't think we need anything but wine. I baked a cake for dessert already."

"Alright. I'll be back in twenty minutes."

"Okay. We can watch the sunset before we leave for Olivia's."

Hudson started to walk into the house, but he stopped and turned back with a warning finger. "Remember, one entry. No reading ahead."

"I won't."

Hearing his footsteps fall away, I sighed and opened my diary back up. I only had another twenty or so pages left. And the next entry was so damn short. I could probably read the entire book before he got back, and he wouldn't even know. But instead I'd savor the pages like he wanted me to.

At least...that's what I planned.

Until I actually read the next short entry...

Dear Diary,

Today I went shopping. I don't know much about jewelry, so I took my sister with me. She was a royal pain in the ass.

I smiled, imagining Hudson and Olivia shopping. His idea of shopping was walking into one store with the purpose of buying three suits and walking out within a half hour. Olivia, on the other hand, didn't as much shop as *graze*. She would set out to buy a pair of shoes to go with a dress and come home with a new dining room set, a coat for Mason, a toy for Charlie, and some electronic gadget for the office from The Sharper

Image. The shoes she set out to buy would no longer be necessary, because she'd also have a brand new dress.

I'd actually been with her once when she'd gone to shop for shoes for one outfit and come home with a completely different ensemble—only to realize she still needed shoes for the new item she'd brought home. Olivia was the woman who walked out of a mall with fourteen different shopping bags. Hudson was a man who requested they ship his suits to him when they were done being tailored, so he didn't have to return to the store.

But as I went back to reading, I realized Hudson hadn't mentioned he'd gone shopping with his sister. He also hadn't come home with any new jewelry recently... So I curiously returned to my diary.

We went to six stores. Anything I liked, Olivia hated. Anything she liked, I nixed. After a full day, I went home empty-handed and aggravated. My beautiful girl came home about ten minutes later—smelling like a forest. She'd been at the lab since early this morning working on her new Signature Scent for men. But she wrapped her arms around my neck, brushed those pouty lips with mine, and my shitty day evaporated. That's when I realized the problem with buying my love jewelry was that I hadn't found anything half as special as her. It took me thirty-one years to finally get it right, and I wasn't going to half-ass showing her what she meant to me.

-Hudson

Oh my God. There was no way I could stop reading here. Hudson was shopping for jewelry that's special for me? Could it be... Looking over my shoulder, I glanced into the house. Everything was still. It would take Hudson at least twenty minutes to walk to the liquor store and back with the dog. I had to read a little more—one more entry, at least.

Of course one entry led to two, and two led to three, and suddenly I was on the last page. Hudson had gone on a half-dozen shopping trips, written another vividly steamy entry about things he wanted to do to me, and penned a heartfelt few pages about the night my parents had come over for dinner. It had taken me a long time, but yes, my parents and I had finally seen each other in person. I'd had to work my way up to it, and I'd been a nervous wreck, but in the end, the evening had been pleasant. I hadn't yet rekindled my relationship with my sister, though I'd finally told Hudson the full story and admitted *who* Aiden had had an affair with. I remained hopeful that maybe someday I'd find a way to forgive Cecelia, too.

From what I'd heard, she and my ex had since broken up—after she'd found him cheating with one of her friends. I probably should have felt good learning that, but I didn't. I felt bad for Cecelia, which is why it gave me hope that there was a chance for us after all.

None of Hudson's entries specifically said what type of jewelry he was shopping for, but it was pretty obvious it was a ring. What other type of jewelry had to be so perfect and took so many shopping trips?

My pulse raced as I read the final pages.

Oh my God! He bought something.

And he hid it where he'd hidden my Christmas present in our room last year!

And he isn't planning on giving it to me until his birthday.

Hudson's birthday wasn't for two more months! No way could I wait that long to find out.

Hudson had no idea I'd stumbled upon his little hiding spot in the back of his closet last year. So I could—*no, I really shouldn't.*

Blood swished through my ears, and my hands started to sweat.

Maybe I could just go see if it was a ring box?

I didn't need to open it or anything.

Imagine the anticipation that would build over the next couple of months... Now imagine what would happen when the big day finally came, if he handed me a square box with...earrings?

There would be no way in the world I could hide my disappointment after waiting months. It almost felt like I *had* to go look now. Whatever he was shopping for had taken him a damn long time. He'd feel awful if I burst into tears, unable to hide how letdown I felt. So, in a sense, I would be doing it for him.

Sure you are.

I looked at my watch and glanced back over my shoulder into the house one more time. Maybe I should wait until a time when he was going to be gone longer...

No. I shook my head, even though I was answering my own thoughts.

I definitely couldn't wait.

So I rushed into the house and ran directly to the front door. Opening it, I looked right and then left to make sure Hudson wasn't already coming down the block. Finding the coast clear, I hurried to the bedroom. The door was closed, and I was such a nervous wreck that I had to take a moment to steady myself. My hand trembled as I took a deep breath before turning the doorknob.

But my heart stopped as I walked inside.

"Looking for something?" Hudson raised a brow. He was sitting on the edge of our bed with Charlie on his knee. Hendricks laid at his feet.

I blinked a few times. "What are you doing here? I thought you'd left."

He prompted his daughter to jump off his lap and stood. "What am I doing here? I could ask you the same question. What are you doing in the bedroom right now, Stella?"

"I, uh..."

He walked over to where I stood, frozen. With a grin, he took my hand. "You didn't *read ahead*, did you?"

My mind was so jumbled. When did he get back from the store? And where did Charlie come from? What the hell was going on?

Though I didn't need to wait very long for the answer. Hudson held out his hand to his daughter. Charlie took it with an ear-to-ear smile. If I'd thought I was nervous before, it was nothing compared to how I felt as I watched the man I loved get down on one knee.

He brought my trembling hand to his lips.

Seeing a bit of nervousness on his face as he looked up actually helped calm me.

"One year ago today, I met a beautiful, smart woman," he began. "When I've heard you tell the story of how we met, you say you crashed my sister's wedding. But the truth of the matter is, you crashed my heart. You're the kindest, warmest, strangest, most amazing person I've ever met."

I lifted my hands to cover my mouth, and happy tears filled my eyes as I laughed. "The strangest? You make that sound like a good thing."

Hudson smiled. "It is. And I love you *because* you're a little strange sometimes, not despite it. You've spent years reading everyone else's love stories, and tonight you read the last chapter of mine..." He winked. "...even though you weren't supposed to. But my last chapter is only the beginning, sweetheart." He looked over at Charlie, who pulled a little black box from behind her back and handed it to her father. "Stella Rose Bardot, let me give you your happily ever after. Be my wife, and I promise to try my hardest to make your life better than anything you've ever read in a book."

He opened the little black box, and inside was something I'd never seen before. The velvet-lined box contained two rings. On the right was a gorgeous, emerald-cut diamond set in white gold with tiny baguettes going all the way around the band. On the left side was a tiny replica of the engagement ring. He took the first one out of the box and held it out to me. "I'm not just asking you to marry me. I'm asking you to be my family with Charlie. So I had yours made, and then a mini replica in cubic zirconia for her—my two ladies. Whaddya say, sweetheart? Be ours?"

I looked over at Charlie. She had a giant smile on her face as she took something from behind her back and held it up.

A banana with writing on it.

Say yes, so we'll never split.

As silly as it was, the banana did me in. The happy tears now streamed down my face. Wiping them, I mouthed *I love you* to Charlie before pressing my forehead to Hudson's. "Yes. Yes! My heart already belongs to you both, so this is the icing on the cake."

After Hudson slipped the ring on my finger, we helped Charlie put on hers. The three of us held each other for a long time before my *fiancé* told her to go wash up to go to her aunt's house.

"Finally...a minute alone." Hudson cupped my cheeks and pulled my mouth to his. "Now kiss me properly."

As usual, he left me breathless. "You know, between your diary and that proposal, I think you might be a true romantic at heart, Mr. Rothschild."

"Oh yeah?" He smiled. "I'll deny it if anyone asks."

I laughed. "It's okay. I'll know the truth. Under that hard exterior is a big old softie."

Hudson took my hand and slid it down to his crotch. He cupped my fingers around a pretty damn steely erection. "I got more hard exterior for you later."

I smiled. "I can't wait."

He brushed his lips with mine. "Did you like the diary?"

"I loved it. It was the best love story I've ever read. But my favorite part was the ending."

Hudson shook his head. "That wasn't an ending, sweetheart. It was only our beginning. Because a true love story like ours never ends."

ACKNOWLEDGEMENTS

To you—The readers. Thank you for your support and excitement. Life has thrown us all some challenges lately, and I'm so grateful you allow me to provide you an escape for a short while. I hope you've enjoyed Hudson and Stella's love story, and you'll come back again to see who you might meet next!

To Penelope—The last few years have been a wild ride, and there is no one I'd rather be buckled in with.

To Cheri—Thank you for your friendship and support. Book friends are the best friends!

To Julie—Thank you for your friendship and wisdom.

To Luna—Life is like a book—it's never too late to write a new story, and I've enjoyed watching each of your exciting chapters unfold. Thank you for your friendship.

To my amazing Facebook reader group, Vi's Violets—20,000 smart women who love to talk books together in one place? I'm one lucky girl! Each and every one of you is a gift. Thank you for being part of this crazy journey.

To Sommer—Thank you for giving Hudson and Stella's story a face with your beautiful design.

To my agent and friend, Kimberly Brower—Thank you for being there always. Every year brings a unique opportunity from you. I can't wait to see what you dream up next!

To Jessica, Elaine, and Julia—Thank you for smoothing out the all the rough edges and making me shine!

To all of the bloggers—Thank you for inspiring others to take a chance on me. Without you, there would be no them.

Much love
Vi

OTHER BOOKS BY VI KEELAND

Inappropriate

All Grown Up

We Shouldn't

The Naked Truth

Sex, Not Love

Beautiful Mistake

Egomaniac

Bossman

The Baller

Left Behind (A Young Adult Novel)

Beat

Throb

Worth the Fight

Worth the Chance

Worth Forgiving

Belong to You

Made for You

First Thing I See

Cocky Bastard (Co-written with Penelope Ward) Playboy

Pilot (Co-written with Penelope Ward)

Mister Moneybags (Co-written with Penelope Ward)

British Bedmate (Co-written with Penelope Ward) Park

Avenue Player (Co-written with Penelope Ward)

Stuck-Up Suit (Co-written with Penelope Ward)

Rebel Heir (Co-written with Penelope Ward)

Rebel Heart (Co-written with Penelope Ward)

Hate Notes (Co-written with Penelope Ward) Dirty Letters

(Co-written with Penelope Ward)

My Favorite Souvenir (Co-written with Penelope Ward)

ABOUT VI KEELAND

Vi Keeland is a #1 *New York Times*, #1 *Wall Street Journal*, and *USA Today* Bestselling author. With millions of books sold, her titles have appeared in over a hundred Bestseller lists and are currently translated in twenty-five languages. She resides in New York with her husband and their three children where she is living out her own happily ever after with the boy she met at age six.

CPSIA information can be obtained
at www.ICGtesting.com
Printed in the USA
BVHW031649110121
597555BV00001B/4